EDUCATING
ANGLICANS

CW00433232

For Peg

EDUCATING ANGLICANS

Investigating Groupwork in the Church of England

ROGER GRAINGER

sussex
ACADEMIC
PRESS
Brighton • Portland • Toronto

The right of Roger Grainger to be identified as Author of this work has been asserted in accordance with the Copyright, Designs and Patents Act 1988.

2 4 6 8 10 9 7 5 3 1

First published 2013, in Great Britain by
SUSSEX ACADEMIC PRESS
PO Box 139
Eastbourne BN24 9BP

and in the United States of America by
SUSSEX ACADEMIC PRESS
920 NE 58th Ave   Suite 300
Portland, Oregon 97213-3786

and in Canada by
SUSSEX ACADEMIC PRESS (CANADA)
8000 Bathurst Street, Unit 1, PO Box 30010, Vaughan, Ontario L4J 0C6

All rights reserved. Except for the quotation of short passages for the purposes of criticism and review, no part of this publication may be reproduced, stored in a retrieval system or transmitted in any form or by any means, electronic, mechanical, photocopying, recording or otherwise, without the prior permission of the publisher.

British Library Cataloguing in Publication Data
A CIP catalogue record for this book is available from the British Library.

Library of Congress Cataloging-in-Publication Data
Grainger, Roger.
Educating Anglicans : investigating group work in the Church of England / Roger Grainger.
pages   cm
Includes bibliographical references and index.
ISBN 978-1-84519-578-6 (pbk. : alk. paper)
  1. Church group work—Church of England. 2. Church of England. I. Title.
BV652.2.G59 2013
268′.8342—dc23

                                                                    2012050210

Typeset & designed by Sussex Academic Press, Brighton & Eastbourne.
Printed by TJ International, Padstow, Cornwall.
This book is printed on acid-free paper.

Contents

Preface

Writers on groupwork distinguish several kinds of small group, each having a different structure and purpose, but all involving some kind of learning function associated with, or mediated by the experience of group membership

The Bible provides evidence in both Old and New Testaments of the awareness involved in group belonging, and Christian churches, among them the Church of England, have employed groups for pastoral and evangelising purposes. Within the UK, the Church of England concentrates its congregational training on one kind of directive group-based format: 'process evangelism.' This approach is examined here using examples taken from various dioceses in order to argue that, by concentrating on one kind of group, the Church of England (and perhaps other Church bodies) may be neglecting the possibility that other, more experiential and less directive, kinds of groups may more effectively educate church members in Christian belonging.

In order to discover how different groupwork structures affect learning, three group formats will be compared, one directive and two experiential. Questions will be asked as to their suitability for Christian learning and how they embody scriptural and ecclesiastical perspectives on learning. The same group of people, drawn from different congregations underwent a course of alternating group structures over a six month period. Each individual member was asked to keep a written record of her or his personal impressions of and feelings about each session, so that a comparison could be made of members' experiences of the three groups.

Using the qualitative research model of Interpretive Phenomenological Analysis, an investigation was carried out into the principal themes emerging from members' self-reports of their experiences of the three different group structures, revealing four value constructs — belonging/alienation, safety/danger, enrichment/impoverishment, and validation/rejection — which played a dominant role in all three kinds of group. As it turned out, no group format scored more highly than the others on all four axes of value. Taken all together, however, each of the three group structures gave a different degree of prominence to each of the four evaluative constructs, so that each of the three was shown to be particularly relevant for, and associated with, a particular area of experiential learning.

The book is addressed, in the first place, to churchgoers in England itself. It is the result of research into Christian groups undertaken for the degree of *Philosophiae Doctor* in pastoral studies, awarded in 2012 by North-West

University, South Africa. It has been adapted, with permission, from my PhD thesis 'Continuing congregational training: a comparison of group-work initiatives within the Church of England.'

When one of those who had participated in the research heard what the title of the book was to be, she commented:

> *Educating Anglicans* implies, to me, something done *to* people. But the group-work did not feel like being taught, nor, usually, being 'done to.' It felt more that we were given the chance to learn from each other and with each other. The essential elements to me were:
> - Inter-play — often quite literally, whether play-school activity or drama
> - Say hello to as many people as you can.Interaction between the different people. We learnt about them, and also about ourselves in relation to them, because of what we were doing, not just saying
> - Reaction — part of being in a group is discovering those with whom you gel; those who irritate you; those who really annoy you; those to whom you have no particular reaction
>
> Being in a group did not feel like being educated, it was learning together experience.

I hope the title will not obscure the fact that I see education as a shared experience and not something that is done *to* people.

Acknowledgements

My sincere thanks go to two groups of people who have helped bring this book to birth. On the one hand are the academics, notably Professor George Lotter and his colleagues at the Potchefstroom campus, without whose critical acumen the deep fascination which groupwork has held for me during the course of my own academic career would certainly have remained unaddressed. There is a world of difference between having an interest in a subject, however deep, and getting down to the business of writing a thesis about it. I would certainly not have reached the stage of writing these acknowledgements were it not for the support, hard work, and guidance of Greenwich School of Theology, Peg Evans in particular.

The other group, of course, consists of those who made up the group itself, and then went on to include me in what they had made. When you set out to examine what living Christians actually think and feel, you open yourself up to a life-changing experience; I would like to thank John Rowbottom and Robert Shaw for all their work in helping me make this experience available for others. Last but not least, I would like to thank my wife Doreen without whose patient encouragement and Christian faith the thesis could never have been written.

Introduction

Asking the question

During the last ten years, the Church of England in the UK has put an increasing amount of effort into the education of its churchgoing members in the nature and terms of their membership. This activity has concentrated on the use of learning groups. These are groups created for shared learning, as opposed to learning in classrooms or lecture theatres. In the past, these groups were usually left to individual parishes to arrange. Now, like so many other inter-personal events, they are often regulated by a central authority, usually the Diocesan Office, which has issued courses of study with accompanying 'guide-lines' as to how they should be conducted. The diocesan offices concerned usually assure churchgoers that these are not actual instructions, although in some cases they seem to be presented as such. On the contrary, they are to be seen as pastoral assistance, and should not be regarded in any way as compulsory (e.g. *Way Ahead* Diocese of St Edmundsbury and Ipswich, 2002; *Transforming Lives* Diocese of Wakefield, 2008; half of the 21 dioceses consulted had local versions of *Education for Discipleship* Archbishops' Council, 2005). The courses are usually extensive and detailed, and in the 22 examples that I have studied the emphasis has been on cognitive understanding rather than experiential learning; the emotional components within the groupwork process are not taken into account. Almost without exception, these are directive in intention.

In view of the range of different kinds of groupwork available, there is reason to believe that the current scope of groupwork within the Church of England may not be wide enough. There is little evidence in the material cited of awareness of the value to congregations of involvement in the group process itself as a medium for personal development (Ottaway, 1966; Corey and Corey, 1997; Yalom, 1995). Similarly, the important advances in understanding group experience, spearheaded by the arts therapies, are completely ignored (Pitruzzella, 2004; Jennings, 1990; Pitruzzella, 2009; Jones, 2004). Certainly, there has been no attempt to compare these latter approaches with the Church of England's directive one.

It would be natural to assume that this kind of structured approach to reinforcing, and hopefully extending, congregational membership achieves the required result; why, otherwise, would church leaders so enthusiastically adopt it? There are, however, other factors in the equation, one of which is the need to combat decreasing church membership figures (Brown, 1992,

1

passim; Davie, 1994, *passim*; Abrams et al., 2004, *passim*) by a process of congregational re-education aimed at increasing group awareness and corporate solidarity. To a certain extent all 'out of hours' groups (i.e. those held in people's homes or on church premises outside the usual service times) may be expected to have this effect, the mixture of formality and spontaneity being a potent one for fostering a sense of belonging, so that it would seem natural to try to regularise what was already happening, and always had been done in the past. Urgent times, however, require a more sustained and goal-directed approach. A more involved membership would provide a united front, able to promote the Church's mission more effectively.

That, at least, is the argument. It is a familiar one from a psychological point of view, as both individuals and groups react to situations which they perceive to be threatening by tightening their hold on whatever it may be that they feel able to control (Abrams et al., 2004). It can be argued that this is a counter-productive process if aimed at increasing group membership, as an expanding group tends to be more welcoming than one engaged in protective self-definition. This, at least, is the verdict of some who have studied group psychology during the last half century (Rogers, 1969, 1970; Yalom, 1995; Brown, 1992; Jacobs et al., 2002; Bion, 1961; Foulkes and Anthony, 1957; Douglas, 1993). From this point of view, the study of groups overlaps with that of social inclusion/exclusion (Corey and Corey, 1997; Abrams et al., 2004).

There are, of course, several kinds of group, some more goal-directed than others: a group aimed at teaching effective management skills will differ in important respects from one which has been formed in order to give its members an opportunity to enjoy one another's company; both will function differently from groups whose purpose is directly psychotherapeutic. There will also be groups that set out to combine these and other specialisms, as in the user groups associated with current community-based mental health provision. In the informal survey of the church groups mentioned above, I came across some that were more flexibly organised than others, adaptations being sometimes encouraged in order to fit the stated purpose of a particular group. However, both those who organise groups and those who take part in them tend to agree that group experience is different from other ways of relating to one's fellow human beings (Ottaway, 1966; Corey and Corey, 1997; Yalom, 1995).

Carl Rogers (1973) claimed that groups themselves possess a particular kind of spirituality: 'in the group we're wiser than we know' — and this itself provides a valid reason for churches to pay special attention to the groups that they run. In his work on group process, Rogers expresses his faith in the capacity of a group to move on its own initiative, thus in a manner of speaking assuming its own corporate 'life' (Grainger, 2003). Human beings who meet together in the understanding that they form an identifiable group 'move towards wholeness and self-actualisation' (Corey and Corey, 1997, 146–149). In other words, they discover what Tillich (1962: IV) identified as 'the courage to be as a part.' This notion of a group process that is essentially creative goes back to the origins of group psychology; in our own day it has been most forcibly and eloquently expressed in the work of Yalom and his associates (1995).

According to this theory of group creativity, in which individual members inspire one another to become more lively, more themselves (as existential psychology would put it), a group progresses from being a collection of individuals to 'an entity capable of diagnosing and solving problems and making decisions.' Mutual support and shared feelings work together to foster a sense of belonging. There is evidence in the introductory material supplied for use with church groups that this is part of their intention. The mere fact that they are groups of any kind makes this kind of belonging potentially achievable. This being the case, the question of whether or not groups intended for the 'training' of congregation-members are the best kind of group for such a purpose is obviously important.

Having been involved for a considerable part of my professional life as a dramatherapist in a particular kind of groupwork, one which aims to 'facilitate change through drama processes' (Jones, 2004, 41; Andersen-Warren and Grainger, 2000; Grainger, 2002, 1988, 1999, 2003, 1990), I am particularly interested in the ways churches set about their evangelistic task of deepening the personal involvement of their members. There are several fundamentally different types of human group, but, by concentrating on a directive approach to educational groupwork, one which depends on instruction rather than discovery, it appears that the Church of England (and perhaps other Christian bodies as well) may be neglecting the possibility that other, more experiential, less directly cognitive, kinds of groupwork may more effectively educate its members in Christian belonging. Process-oriented training groups and art therapies approaches — that is, groups in which members learn from observing their relations with one another, and those that use art as a medium for personal encounter — are two examples of different educational paradigms that are less cognitively directed. Among process-oriented theorist-practitioners, Yalom (1995), Ottaway (1966) and Corey and Corey (1997) direct special attention to the beneficial effects of groupwork for personality development and Grainger (1990), Jennings (1990), Jones (2004) and Pitruzzella (2009) to the liberating effect of the arts therapies upon personal relationships. A comparison among these three kinds of groupwork (directive, process-oriented and art-based, the first leader-directed, the other two group-led) would possibly be able to open up new avenues for congregational groupwork in educating its members in Christian belonging.

The question to be answered was a quite straightforward one: how may directive and experiential groupwork affect group members and be used successfully in educating members of the Church of England? In conjunction with this, the individual problems to be investigated were:

- What varieties of group structures can be identified in educational groups, and what are their purposes? Do they conform to particular structural types?
- What scriptural perspectives may be brought to bear on group experience?
- What is the strategy of the Church of England (and other Christian churches) regarding educational groupwork in an ecclesiastical context?
- What would a comparison between instructional, process orientated and art-based groups reveal about the differences in their over-all effect upon group members?
- How could such a comparison be made?
- What model may be proposed regarding educational groupwork in the Church of England and other church settings?

As to the aim of the research, this was to discover how directive and experiential approaches affected group members during educational groupwork/group training. Thus the objectives could be set out as follows:

- To examine the ways in which different kinds of group-structure and group purpose relate to one another in the context of an educational group.
- To consider the scriptural evidence concerning groups.
- To review current practice within church congregations (Church of England, UK), identifying the types of groups involved and the purpose for which they are intended.
- To arrive at an operational basis for distinguishing between directive — learning and experiential — learning groupwork approaches.
- To design a research instrument to compare these two categories, and organise the necessary groups for doing this.
- To carry out the investigation in an appropriate way, examining and comparing members' protocols regarding the exercise.
- To make recommendations for a revised approach to groupwork in church settings.

All of this obviously called for a particular kind of research methodology, one which was designed to register, and report on, the experiences and values of real human beings.

Searching for the answer

During the preparation of this book I spent time searching for ways of looking at groupwork from the inside, which meant taking account of it as a human phenomenon, which includes investigation as a participant, not as a detached observer — a status which is theoretical rather than real and distracts from

4

the reality of the actual experience. The phenomenological approach has been described as 'a means for getting at the directness of experience through the reconstruction of language possible to the experience' (Natanson, 1978, 195). This is language produced by experience itself, emerging from it as a direct response to it. The phenomenological approach to research works recursively within the parameters of such language, in other words, by going more deeply into it instead of extending it by association with a string of other ideas or feelings. This is the process which phenomenologists refer to as 'reduction,' which is a way of discovering what something is really like by isolating ('bracketing') it from other considerations, specifically, so far as possible, from material which does not characterise this particular experience. In order to do this, the process of phenomenological analysis is one of narrowing down the original evidence regarding an experience in order to disclose what it was really like, apart from the meanings which have become attached to it. The phenomenological attitude, says Natanson,

> is in search of a language adequate to the comprehension of the phenomenon, and not the phenomena yielded in a secondary manner, through what is said . . . Without actually engaging in phenomenological analysis through reduction, there are no results, only reports about 'results'. (Natanson, 1978, 188, 192)

In the investigation carried out in Chapters 4 and 5, I describe a process of analysis carried out in a series of stages designed to allow the reactions of a group of individuals to the experience of being involved together as members of a groupwork research project. At each successive stage of the process the material which they wrote down in order to describe the process was re-examined with a view to moving closer to identifying the areas of experience which they had discovered to be most personally involved in, and relevant to, the groupwork which they had shared. The procedure is 'recursive' because reduction to the actual reaction to an experience depends on successive re-examination of the data.

This way of carrying out research would not satisfy those for whom quantitative assessment is the *sine qua non* of any investigation which claims to be scientific. Phenomenologists, however, have strong misgivings about the relevance of mathematics to situations of an interpersonal nature. Edmund Husserl (1859–1938), the founder of phenomenology as a philosophical approach to human reality, spoke of 'approximation,' rather than measurement. Group experience, such as that analysed here, belongs firmly to the *Lebenswelt*, the realm of life as it is actually lived rather than simply thought about; consequently, the attempt to achieve 'scientific objectivity' is actually counter-productive for an investigation into what people are actually investigating. Phenomenology stresses the fact that the firmness of our conclusions obscures the truth of experience in accordance with the psychological reflex which homologises them with what is already known and understood, cancelling out the 'strangeness,' i.e. uniqueness, of their original impact. Those who aim to work phenomenologically must attend directly to the phenomena given them by way of a 'reduction' which establishes the original strangeness of their experience, seeing whatever it is as an example of *this* and not automatically as an example of *that*. In phenomenology, the experienced world is bracketed for focused contact instead of detached from itself in the name of scientific rigour, a lived inter-subjectivity replacing an objectivity which can never be more than theoretical.

With regard to the present investigation, the data itself, in the form of ideas and feelings, opinions and judgements expressed by participants, becomes progressively more concentrated in a way which preserves its meaning while clarifying the underlying structure. Analysis is directed throughout the reduction process towards discovery of areas of experience which are responsible for the actual things said so that, all the time, the investigator's attention is directed towards understanding what subjects themselves feel to be most important, most in need of expression, rather than interpreting the material according to their own preconceived ideas.

listening

In its approach to understanding the reality of ordinary human experience, phenomenology shuns clinical (pathology based, rigorously scientific) techniques and turns its attention to everyday examples of the lived world, Husserl's *Lebenswelt*, to which life as a member of a group belongs.[1] In this way it aims to make explicit the meanings which we attach to the world we live in and the things we do, think, feel and intuit within it. Phenomenologists concentrate on how things feel to people because this is a principal — even the principal — ground of their attitude towards them, which in turn governs the way they understand and act towards them.

'The job of phenomenological analysis,' says Davina Allen, 'is to show how the everyday world, which is ordinarily taken for granted, is made up' (1993, 555). If such be the purpose of this tradition of human enquiry — and I myself am reasonably convinced that such is the case — then it is from this standpoint that I carried out my own investigation. The limitations of scientific methodology with regard to the study of human beings who are participating in the social nexus on which they must depend in order to be fully human — in other words, the context to which they must belong in order to be anything like themselves — have frequently attracted attention. Thomas Luckmann states the difficulty in straightforward terms:

> What is required is a science that analyses man as that peculiar part of nature that is not only capable of understanding nature but also of understanding itself as part of it. (1978, 217)

To summarise: phenomenology ascribes value to the acquisition of knowledge through the direct experience of the world as we ourselves are personally involved in it. 'Interpretative Phenomenological Analysis' (IPA) is a methodology scientifically designed with this aim in view. It is particularly appropriate for the study of relationships existing between and among human beings because it is able to take into account the specific parameters within which relationship takes place, the setting as well as the people involved in it. The method of reduction leaves room for a reflexiveness with regard to the presuppositions which underlie an experience because of the particular circumstances in which it takes place. It is not enough to 'control' for these 'variables' by refusing to allow them to figure in any enquiry. In the present investigation into the groupwork experience of church members, these 'background' effects become progressively more noticeable and consequently much more important.

Note

1   Alfred Schutz describes the *Lebenswelt* ('life world') as the sphere in which 'in the natural attitude we, as human beings among fellow human beings, experience culture and society, take a stand with regard to their objects, are influenced by them and act upon them' (1966, 118).

1

Types of Group-Based Learning

The nature of group learning

If it were possible for the overworked hypothetical man from Mars to take a fresh view of the people of Earth, he would probably be impressed by the amount of time they spend doing things together in groups. (Cartwright and Zander, 1968, 3)

This chapter looks at some of the main categories of learning through involvement in groups, with a view to opening out the subject of group learning and attempting to show that to see it in only one way would be seriously to limit its availability as a way of expanding human experience. The chapter begins by examining the concept of the learning group itself. Next, the claim that group membership bestows its own kind of identity on those taking part is considered. After this, various kinds of groups are reviewed from the point of view of the purpose served: cognitive learning, discussion of the understanding of the group process itself, groups aimed at self-understanding and psychoanalysis, growth groups and ones that are art-based.

Some group formats are more didactic than others; in other words, the group is led by an expert, whose job is to communicate facts, ideas and attitudes on behalf of the authority responsible for the group's existence. In this case the group's function is to learn whatever its leader is qualified to teach. These are what might be called 'directive groups.' Other kinds of group are intended to provide the individuals taking part with the experience of being a member of a small group brought together to share thoughts and feelings related to who they are and what has happened to them in their lives. These are 'experiential groups,' whose leadership is shared in a democratic way. These groups also require organisation; here, however, the job of the person is to enable rather than to direct. This important distinction between directive and experiential groupwork is taken as axiomatic, as evidenced by recent studies.

In the following chapter a good deal of reliance is placed on contributions to the study of groupwork made in the latter part of the last century, when the modality first came into prominence, giving rise to much in depth research (Ottaway, 1966; Corey and Corey, 1997; Cartwright and Zander, 1968; Yalom, 1995; Whitacker and Lieberman, 1964; Bion, 1961). Later research, including that carried out in the present investigation, has substantiated the relevance, fortunately, of principles laid down by the fathers of groupwork study, which have been the main inspiration for this investigation.

At the most fundamental level, groups constitute an essential component of human experience. We are characteristically unable, as human beings, to understand ourselves without taking some account of other people; their presence or absence is always part of our picture of the world. To be human, then, is to be related to others, which means always to perceive them as similar to ourselves, even when, by reason of personality or circumstances we may be particularly conscious of the difference between us. Our relation to others is always a dialectical one, according to the *Concise Oxford Dictionary*'s definition of this word, which is 'Testing the truth by discussion' (Soanes and Stevenson, 2004). Discussion is not the same as agreement, although of course it may lead to it; for a relationship to be dialectical both these things must be present. There is a sense, therefore, that when we come into contact with another person we cannot be totally in agreement with them if agreement means congruence.

For human beings, however, agreement involves the willing exchange of person-hood rather than the unilateral surrender of individuality (Bakhtin, 1981; Buber, 1961). We may seem to be going along with whatever it is that is happening while at the same time keeping our real thoughts and feelings to ourselves. Human beings are always capable of deceiving themselves about this even when it is not actually their intention to do so. Sometimes they do this because they are frightened — as with Jesus's disciples (Jn 18:27) — sometimes, more often in fact, because the truth is too painful for them to bear and they have the ability to ignore it by putting it out of their minds and managing to keep it there, in psychoanalytic language, repressing it (Freud, 1940, 51–55; Pargament, 2007, 182, 183; Marshall Cavendish Corporation, 2010).

The aim of those investigating human groups is to explore the ways in which human beings interact with one another when they are encouraged to see themselves not only as individuals but also as members of a group. How does this experience of group membership affect our sense of who we ourselves are? Stress is laid upon the focused interaction of individuals, who benefit from the opportunity to discover more about themselves, their sense of identity both confirmed and expanded by the fact of group-membership and the cognitive and emotional support which this provides:

> Groupwork provides a context in which individuals help each other — it is a method of helping groups as well as helping individuals, and it can help individuals and groups to influence and change personal, group organisational and community problems. (Brown, 1992, 8)

Groupwork, says Brown, is 'an umbrella term for a wide range of activities, actions and therapies' (1992, 5). Its action is psychological and

9

psychotherapeutic (Corey and Corey, 1997; Yalom, 1995; Corey et al., 2010; Bion, 1961), sociological (Goffman, 1963; Gergen and Gergen, 2003) or spiritual (Grainger, 2003). Palmer points out that 'there is at present little consensus as to which theories are the most useful and the most accurate for describing and interpreting group behaviour' (1972). Although made forty years ago, Palmer's comment is perhaps even more relevant today, when the scope of groupwork is vastly enlarged by the facilities afforded it in an age of cybernetic communication. Groups nowadays may contain members who are in contact with one another across distances unheard of and unimagined by groupworkers in the 20th century. The groups we are dealing with in this book met face-to-face, their thoughts, feelings and behaviour influenced by one anothers' physical presence, a fact that cannot avoid influencing the nature of the experience involved (Lotter, 2010). It is this kind of 'traditional' approach that is in question here, and there is no reason to expect that the difficulties in arriving at an overall theory regarding group dynamics that would apply to every kind of group would be any less pronounced now than they were then. Indeed, the existence of 'twitter' and 'Facebook' adds even greater force to Palmer's remarks about what groupwork, in itself, actually is: it can be any one of a number of things!

At the same time, current ways of looking at inter-personal communication that take account of postmodernism's distrust of what Lyotard identifies as 'meta-narrative' (1984, 60), along with the post-modern stress on diversity within human modes of thought and action, mean that groupwork theory is now open to a considerably wider range of ideas, attitudes and philosophical positions than was the case in the 1970s (Lamb and Cohn-Sherbok, 1999).

Jacobs et al. list seven categories of groups: those aimed at education, discussion, task completion, growth experience, counselling and therapy, support, and self-help, dividing them into two main types, those concerned with 'support, growth, counselling and therapy' and those created for 'discussion, education and task completion' (2002, 185). The distinguishing feature, they say, is the degree of clarity with which the purpose of the group is understood by its members and reinforced by the group teacher. In practical terms, this means that the question to be asked at the outset is always the same: 'Should the group be task-oriented or more relaxed?' (2002, 126).

This matter is dealt with in various ways by other groupwork specialists. Douglas distinguishes between 'contextual groups', whose purpose is to benefit from the special context provided by group membership, and 'instrumental groups', which are overtly task-orientated and set out to change a particular situation in a particular way. Even so, the fundamental process is the same: the basis of all groupwork is

- to create or adapt human groups in either contextual or instrumental forms, or in some combination of both;
- to generate actual and/or potential resource systems to meet the actual and/or potential assessed needs of group members; and

10

- to remove, diminish, change or circumnavigate obstacles to the discovery, recognition, accessibility and use of these resources (1993, 108).

Douglas sees groupwork as a practical and effective way of releasing human potential by working towards overcoming those factors or elements in personal and social experience that get in the way of human relationship (1993, 108). Thus his definition is both task-orientated and supportive, as it is directed towards the removal of barriers to adaptive functioning which exist both 'within' and 'between' (i.e. 'among') human beings. This he says is 'the basic consideration of group design' (1993, 112). This being so, the best kind of group for effective groupwork will be the one most suited to work on hindrances that are known to exist within human relationships and to reveal the presence of those as yet unacknowledged. All the same, the basic distinction still exists between the two ways in which the process is to be carried out: directly by confrontation, in task-orientated groups, or indirectly, via the investigation of human personal experience in action within the group itself — Douglas's 'contextual' approach.

Douglas also makes a second distinction, this time within the nature of actual group leadership: 'The manner in which support is obtained and from whom, shapes and influences our central behaviour patterns' (1993, 20). In line with this, he draws attention to two different kinds of leadership, 'directive' and 'facilitative'. The second type he sees as more closely in line with his underlying purpose for groupwork, which, he says 'has arisen as a way of helping and supporting, of teaching and ameliorating the condition of those who, for whatever reason, find difficulty in coping both with themselves and parts of society' (1993, 39).

The fact that man is a social animal means that we are likely to learn more about him from observing groups than we are from any ideas we may have about how groups of people should, or ought to, behave; hence Douglas's preference for 'facilitation' rather than 'direction' as the most important mode of leadership (1993, 30).

Groupwork as a way of understanding human behaviour concentrates on the idea of letting the group be itself rather than using any 'natural' characteristics it possesses as a particular kind of human interactive behaviour for a pre-conceived purpose. People in groups are encouraged to find out things about themselves and their relationships with others rather than receiving instruction from a source of information perceived to be authoritative as to how this can be achieved. Both approaches are to do with learning, but only the first is authentically group-centred. Kenneth Ottaway, a firm supporter of groups aimed at self — and other — discovery sees the central question to be answered by the individual member of a group as 'What sort of a person am I?' The answer, he says, comes from the group itself rather than from its leader, for 'in the end it is always the group solution that counts and the leader is there to facilitate it' (1966, 51; see also Park, 2010, 1).

This attitude to groupwork is usually associated with therapeutic groups, which are designed to teach members about what Yalom describes as 'maladaptive interpersonal behaviour' (1995, 460; see also Foulkes and Anthony, 1957; Bion, 1961). It is not only confined to the treatment of specific psychological problems affecting individuals' social behaviour, however. Ottaway lays great stress on the universal applicability of groupwork to all human situations:

> The group has to be weaned from dependence on the leader. As soon as the members begin to realise that they have common problems, the group becomes more cohesive and the members tend to be identified with each other and identified with the tasks of the group . . . (through) understanding what it means to be a human being. (1966, 14)

The leader's task in such a group is to supervise 'a social laboratory' (Yalom, 1995, 283). The laboratory however is not for sick people but healthy ones exercising their human ability to observe themselves and other people and to change through their own emotional involvement with the group and its individual members. The leadership involved is 'of a democratic or integrative kind' (Ottaway, 1966, 7). Ottaway comments on the health-creating action of group involvement and its universal relevance for the exercise of humanness:

> In my experience all groups tend to become therapy groups under certain conditions . . . the more the group becomes a genuine 'permissive' group, in which a 'free-floating' discussion can go on, the more it has a potential therapeutic function. (1966, 92)

Other authorities on the subject of group therapy make the same point (Corey and Corey, 1997; Yalom, 1995; Jacobs et al., 2002; Corey et al., 2010). Nevertheless, this is not the only way of regarding groupwork or the role of the leader within it. Douglas recognises

> a dichotomy between those who believe that all group outcomes result in the growth, development and change of the individual to a greater or lesser extent, and those who regard the outcome as essentially the binding of the individual into membership of a unit. (1993, 105)

Thus, although Ottaway claims that every group may be categorised as a 'training group,' there can be a high degree of difference with regard to the way in which 'training' is understood, and consequently put into practice. Douglas draws attention to the importance of group structure in determining the nature and purpose of groupwork:

> If the resources [of a group] are to be exploited for the mutual benefit of the group members, the way that the group is designed, its *modus operandi*, must be of paramount concern. (1993, 113)

12

Groups intended for purposes of imparting information regarding a particular situation, which exists outside the group but which affects the members
of the group in some well-defined way or ones designed for the transmission
of specific skills, call for directive leadership and strict rules of procedure, as
do groups whose aim is to reinforce membership of an organisation. Certainly,
as Jacobs et al. point out, 'Being clear about the purpose of the group is
perhaps the most important group-leadership concept to be learned' (2002,
49).

In practice, function and structure are perceived as a co-dependent: our
view of what constitutes groupwork determines the way in which we estimate
the success or failure of any particular group with which we may be concerned.

Group identity

If there are various kinds of group, each of them made up of members identifying themselves as belonging to that particular group, can we say that
'belonging to a group' is a recognisable human experience, distinguishable
from other experiences? Douglas regards group awareness as a biological
'given' for all human beings:

> Human beings are indeed creatures born and bred to group behaviour
> patterns — the similarity of all groups is a much more striking fact than the
> differences of the manners in which they arise or of the uses to which they
> may be put. (1993, 100)

He goes on to claim that, however much the effective conditioning has been
suppressed or superseded as a matter of habit or conscious choice in favour
of independence and individuation, it must still exist (1993, 100). The social
behaviour of human groups bears powerful witness to the stubbornness with
which we persist in attempts to exclude strangers (i.e. members of other
groups) from any group to which we ourselves belong (Goffman, 1963;
Becker, 1963; Gergen and Gergen, 2003). Groupwork focuses the intensity of
social relationship as a human experiential phenomenon. The intensity of individuals' awareness of one another in a group situation is evidence of the
significance of a drive towards relationship characteristic of human beings,
for which I intend to provide evidence during the course of this study. In my
own work with groups I have been aware of a personal presence which is
recognisably more intense than any multiplication of the contributions made
by individual group members, myself included. This 'group personality' lifts
groupwork beyond a strictly scientific enterprise and makes it impossible to
analyse its nature and effects with any degree of precision (Grainger, 2003).

The same is true, of course, of personal encounters of any kind whatsoever.
Indeed, as Gunzburg reminds us, it is evident in the reaching out to the other
person which takes place in ordinary human conversation when individuals

encounter each other 'as existential equals meeting within the conversational space between them' (1997, 6). In the group situation this holism is the factor (if it can be called that) which characterises the group as a living organism in itself. Group solidarity, the feeling that 'united we stand, divided we fall,' needs no explanation, founded as it is in the concept of cumulative abilities. Group holism, the synergy of groups, depends on a willing exchange of separateness, what Buber (1961) calls 'between-ness.'

It is this contact-in-separation that makes groups safe enough to join, so that we consciously choose to participate socially with others in a particular way to form an identifiable whole. As I myself have written elsewhere:

> The action of identifying a number of people as a social unit bestowing on them a new corporate identity as a group, or even the group, does a great deal to defuse the defensively heightened self-consciousness that people of all ages tend to feel when thrown amongst strangers. (Grainger, 2003, 138)

This differentiated solidarity of the group has been described in terms of a spiritual presence which is able to counter individual feelings of self-consciousness and encourage self-expression — a positive force promoting a sense of shared identity (Grainger, 2003, 242). Spirituality, however, has never been a phenomenon which commends itself to the scientific approach or to those who subscribe to it. This being so, the precise way in which group holism functions — and why it functions at all — remains something of a mystery to psychologists and students of social practice. All the same, the subject is obviously an important one: Cartwright and Zander's 'man from Mars' would still find himself having to conclude that 'if he wanted to understand much of what is happening on Earth he would have to examine rather carefully the ways in which groups form, function and dissolve' (1968, 3). He would also have to work out how a whole group can be so much greater than the sum of its parts.

Groups directed towards cognitive learning

(i) Groupwork and cognitive learning

The *Concise Oxford Dictionary* (Soanes and Stevenson, 2004) defines 'learn' as 'get knowledge of (subject) or skill in (art, etc.) by study, experience or being taught.' 'Teach' is defined as 'enable or cause (person etc.) to do by instruction and training.' There is obviously a sense in which every group of people who have gathered together to perform a particular task is a learning group, and the difference between particular kinds of groups concerns ways in which they set about answering the basic question regarding who will assume the role of teacher within a group, fulfilling her or his specific task of enabling the rest of the group to obtain the knowledge and/or skills seen by all concerned as the main purpose of the group's existence, the reason why it has been formed. It need not be one person's task to do this, of course, as groups may be intended and organised to enable the roles of 'teacher' and 'learner' to be shared and interchangeable. However, for such a group to stay together within a recognisable group format, it is necessary for the members to be aware that each of them is committed to playing both roles, as both are essential for the identity of the group as a group (Bieling et al., 2006; Free, 2007).

The groups identified here as learning groups then are about teaching *and* learning; using the self-contained group format as a way of holding together two mutually dependent human functions and the various individual human beings involved in carrying them out in this focused and purposeful way. From this point of view all learning groups are instrumental and the group itself represents the most effective way of distributing information, precisely because it allows its members to combine two functions which in other learning experiences are often kept separate. The group occupies both roles, as teacher as well as learner; it is an event in itself, not simply a contributory factor, requiring input from elsewhere to make it functional within some wider and more comprehensive system. Certainly groups exist in relation to the rest of society, and the understanding to which they give rise bears witness to wider and more comprehensive networks of meaning; but what each group contributes to these networks remains its own. How can it be otherwise, when, to use Brown's words, 'each individual's role and behaviour is in varying degrees a function of the group-as-a-whole and of group process as well as an individual characteristic?' (1992, 123).

Group process affects group learning because it combines processes of teaching-as-learning and learning-as-teaching, an interaction uniquely able to reinforce learning-as-understanding. Nowadays educationalists are becoming increasingly interested in the group as a medium for academically-based learning, groups as educational events of one kind or another (Cartwright and Zander, 1968). Douglas (1993, 33f.; see also Beebe and Masterson, 2003) describes how group organisation (or organisation into a group) has the effect of 'unfreezing' the resources of those constituting it, making it a more efficient instrument for the encouragement of learning in general, as well as a way of teaching the group itself how to stand on its own feet, with a consequent increase in the members' confidence in themselves as learners. Yalom, writing thirty years earlier, describes how therapeutic groups depend on cognition as well as affect to produce their effect. In such groups, he says:

> The high learners characteristically showed a profile of catharsis *plus* some form of cognitive learning . . . (our desire for knowledge and exploration for its own sake). (1995, 83)

Working things *out* is equally important as working them through. Indeed the two activities are interdependent. Both involve guidance, whether it be in the form of direct instruction or the modelling of appropriate behaviour.

Therapeutic groups depend largely on the latter, as 'it is the group therapist's task to create a group culture maximally conducive to effective group interaction' (Yalom, 1995, 110). He goes on to say:

> To observe others' response to a situation in a manner markedly different from one's own is an arresting experience which can provide considerable insight into one's behaviour . . . (1995, 325)

Groups, he says, provide 'the therapy setting *sans pareil* for individuals to learn about maladaptive interpersonal behaviour' (1995, 460). Ottaway's seminal treatment of the subject refers to groups set up to investigate a group process apart from any ostensible therapeutic (i.e. psychiatric) purpose as 'training groups':

> The main objective . . . is the understanding of human behaviour. The members come together to gain more insight into interpersonal relations and human motivation. (1966, 4)

Ottaway claims that 'what might be called "therapy for normal people" undoubtedly occurs in educational groups' (1966, 21). His approach may be described as education 'in' rather than 'about.' In other words, it is *implicit* rather than *explicit* education. The agenda of those responsible for training others is not directed towards the transmission of specific information and the inculcation of ways of thinking and acting considered appropriate to them, but with creating the kind of interpersonal situation in which individuals may explore the ways in which they find themselves relating to the presence of other people whose claim for personal consideration is equally as valid as theirs.

Ottaway (1966) points out that during the 1960s a great deal was written about group dynamics, the study of the inner life of groups which sets out to examine the parts played by specific factors whose interaction affected the group as an identifiable whole. See, for example, Lewin's classical analysis of group formation (1948). Group organisation, it was realised, represents a nexus of human activity possessing its own unique synergy, something which was worth studying for its own sake in all its various manifestations. Hence, Ottaway reminds us that

> groups have been studied from the point of view of decisions and goals, cohesiveness, communication, efficiency, size, social climate, leadership, norms and values and psychotherapy in settings which have been experimental, educational, industrial and clinical. (1966, 1; see Corey et al., 2010)

In the field of education, this 'group explosion' had a powerful effect on the way formal education was structured, particularly in the USA, where it was associated with a hands-on approach to learning as opposed to the age-old academic tradition which relied on blackboards and exercise books, and rows of desks facing in the same direction.

Cartwright and Zander describe how:

> Teachers became interested in instilling skills of leadership, co-operation, re-sponsible membership and human relations . . . There began to emerge the con-ception of the teacher as the group leader, who affects his students' learning not merely by his subject-matter competence but also by his ability to heighten motivation, stimulate participation and generate morale. (1968, 9)

All these things made it easier for students to become involved in the learning process for its own sake, so that the group could become a setting for self-teaching rather than simple instruction. Kolb (1984) provides an in-depth analysis of learning through actual group involvement. His pioneering work in this direction continues to influence educational theorists (Miettinen, 2000). Formal education then was becoming conscious of the power of groups to create vitality out of individual uncertainty, and to use it in order to arrive at a balanced responsiveness in which the input made by the more self-assured would no longer have the effect of making their less confident class-mates feel more inhibited than ever. 'Group dynamics,' say Cartwright and Zander, 'drew upon this experience in formulating hypotheses for research' (1968, 9). As empirically-orientated psychologists, they offer an operational definition, founded on the work of Brodbeck (1958) and Lewin:

> A group is a collection of individuals who have relation to one another that makes them interdependent to some significant degree. (1948, 46)

They do not say how this significance is to be evaluated — whether intu-itively or by some kind of objective measurement — but they are quick to point out that, as an observable class, they 'differ greatly in the nature and magni-tude of inter-dependence among their members' (Cartwright and Zander, 1968, 9). For instance, an audience at a theatre is a group because their reac-tions to the play trigger, and are triggered by, one another's reactions. This would be an example of loose association within a group. A tighter degree of group membership would be that subsisting among 'a collection of people who are striving to attain a common good' (Lewin, 1948, 46).

Learning groups united by an intention to achieve a well-defined purpose are likely to concentrate on gaining information in the form of clear cut propo-sitions and ideas which are characterised by being logically consistent. More traditional approaches tend to be associated with fixed teacher–student conformations and text-based learning procedures. Compared with models of group-based learning they present a profile of human communication which is lacking in any real flexibility, being role-rigid as well as text-bound — role rigid *because* it is text-bound. Learning groups in this tradition run the risk of

17

conforming to an expectation, substantive in many educational settings, submerged in others, that the group leader (i.e. the teacher) knows the answers to specific questions, and that it is her or his task to transmit them as clearly as possible to group members, whose job it is to take instruction regarding the correct understanding of specific kinds of information and the learning of appropriate skills for applying it to particular situations. Group members learn together at different rates, according to individual ability, so that they will be in a position to train others in the same way as they themselves have received training — i.e. one which, although it takes place in a group setting, still manages to be strictly determined by a rigid structure of authority imposed by the information itself and those authorised to communicate this to others.

The way furniture is arranged cannot help being a reflection on the kind of meeting envisaged. The disposition of classroom furniture, in which rows of seats face a raised podium, illustrates an attitude towards education which is fixed and lacking in flexibility, whatever may be the actual content or subject matter of what is being taught. These things reflect the purpose for which they were designed: the straightforward communication of information with the least chance of distraction, so that individual differences among those whose role it is to be instructed may, as far as is humanly possible, be discounted by the focused attention of the class as a whole — focused, that is, away from themselves and towards their teacher. All this is communicated by the setting in which learning is to take place.

The fact remains, however, that groups transmit a different message via the context in which they take place. The arrangement of chairs in a circle suggests shared learning just as vividly as rows of chairs imply instruction at the hands of an outside authority. Groups are known to be ways in which people get together for mutual support — all groups, not simply therapeutic ones. The idea of being a group member offers the possibility of being accepted on a personal level by a manageable number of other people, or being in a position to negotiate acceptance with them. This is true of cognitively based learning groups, formed for the exchange of information and expertise, just as much as for investigating the way we relate to one another. The contrast obtaining between the sense of individual isolation characteristic of examination rooms, with their rows of preoccupied students at work in an atmosphere of competitiveness, and the experience of undertaking problems which require to be solved in close co-operation with other people highlights the difference between group learning and other forms of education.

The shape of the space in which learning takes place is important for the communication of human understanding. Classrooms are suitable for *ex cathedra* pronouncement, open spaces for the action of drawing people together and the experience of learning from one another. Space itself is important, as semioticians point out, semiotics being the study of ways in which the juxtaposition of people and objects within the physical environment transmits messages about human personal reality even more clearly than words. This is cognitive understanding, and used as such, even though it applies to the right hemisphere of the brain, where understanding by-passes translation into language:

> what the 'right brain' receives, the 'left brain' can usually find words to describe; but the cognition takes place before it ever gets spoken about. (Springer & Deutsch, 1997)

Elam cites Osmond, an American psychiatrist on the subject of *sociopetal* space, used to describe areas like theatres, cafés and Italian piazzas, in which people are brought together, 'as distinguished from *sociofugal* spaces, like waiting rooms and the offices of company chairmen' (Elam, 1980, 64). The groupwork approach depends for its effectiveness in encouraging learning upon its group format. The action of forming a ring of chairs facing inwards to the centre is markedly sociopetal (Grainger, 2003, 32, 33). To take one's place in the group is to receive a clear message about sharing information by passing it from hand to hand around the circle. The fact that space is provided for this kind of group communication actively transmits the same message about being given permission to exchange ideas and feelings (Brown, 1986). Just as 'nature abhors a vacuum,' so a space which has been left empty but not separated from other spaces invites people in, in order to 'make their own space,' claiming this particular one as theirs and no-one else's. If chairs or cushions are to hand, they can be arranged to suit people's purposes and rearranged when these purposes change, when *the message to be got across* changes, as in the incident described below:

> At first, people just stood around in clumps, either talking or keeping silent. Then a couple who were already friends and obviously knew each other well, moved into the clear space in the centre of the room. They stood for a moment, and then one of them went over to fetch a chair and brought it back into the centre, so she could be more comfortable. Gradually others decided to do the same . . . (Anon, 2001)

This is an extract from the description of a discussion group, taken from a number of such accounts submitted by group members as part of a series of sessions devoted to learning about social inclusion. The member concerned went on to describe how, once the ice had been broken in the way she describes above, the various dyads, triads and quartets formed wider alliances 'and the whole room became everybody's space' (Anon, 2001).

The role played by spatial disposition in the communication of ideas and attitudes, and consequently behaviour, is graphically presented by the group situation. This subject will be taken up later in this chapter. For the time being it is worth establishing as a fundamental property of group behaviour that it uses actual bodies in order to give its propositions greater cogency than any achieved by abstract ideas.

(ii) Discussion groups

The action of talking about attitudes and experience is also, of course, a form of human behaviour, although generally distinguished from the kinetic communication described above. Groups formed specifically to discuss various subjects depend on cognition just as much as teaching groups. If it is important to understand what the teacher or group leader is saying, it is equally fundamental for those discussing to be clear about what they are saying to and hearing from one another. Groups categorised as 'discussion' groups concentrate on the exchange of ideas. As Jacobs et al. say, 'the focus is usually on topics or issues rather than any member's personal concerns . . . the purpose is to share ideas and exchange information' (2002, 8).

Instrumentally focused discussion groups aim at reducing the degree of difference among conflicting ways of dealing with a particular problem. When it is a case of choosing the appropriate action to be taken in interpersonal situations, the aim of the group is to move from a position of polarised dissonance to one of greater harmony among the group members. Sometimes it may be a matter of thrashing out differences of opinion, as in the group described by Cartwright and Zander which consisted of members of a youth club in the 1960s:

> In a typical meeting, after preliminary introductions each member read a short version of the 'Johnny Rocco' case, the life history of a juvenile delinquent . . . The case was presented as that of a real person. The leader asked the members to discuss and decide the question 'What should be done with this kid?' . . . At the end of the discussion a final census [of opinions] was taken. Then the discussion turned to the future of the club [i.e. the one to which the members all belonged]. (1968, 167, 168)

The aim here was to achieve a higher measure of consensus regarding members' attitudes towards young offenders, and so to instruct people as to how the exchange of views could actually reduce intra-group tensions and increase group cohesiveness. Obviously not all discussion groups will discuss such potentially explosive issues, but discussion groups in general are often directed groups aimed at achieving a shared understanding of a particular issue of procedure: 'The presence of other people with similar problems which they wish to tackle is a powerful motivating factor' (Priestley et al., 1978).

Priestley et al. (1978) and Beebe and Masterson (2003) recommend the discussion group format for fostering individual motivation, the sharing of experience (and the insight into personal problems and attitudes of mind to which this gives rise) and the presence of mutual supportiveness (cited by Brown, 1986, 117). The combination of assorted backgrounds with a single unifying circumstance is an advantage:

A short-life 'closed' discussion group was composed of widowed, separated and divorced fathers, bringing up children on their own. There was a mixed social class and cultural background and male/female co-workers . . . The combination of basic descriptive similarity [i.e. single fathers] . . . plus behavioural variations in personality and life-style . . . seemed to provide a dynamic group composition and a more effective group (as rated by consumer feedback). (Brown, 1986, 53)

As we shall see in the next section, this kind of learning by shared experience and example is the basic characteristic of groups formed in order to study group processes as well as those whose purpose is to solve problems located within the world 'outside' the group. Such groups are more experientially than cognitively based, their members concerned to discover more about themselves by allowing themselves to become involved in other people's experience and relating it to their own, rather than exchanging advice and instruction. To be involved in any kind of group, however, is to communicate, explicitly or implicitly, an openness to giving and receiving, whether it be thoughts, feelings or both, either openly or at a remove. The group itself is a paradigm of human sharing.

Discussion groups provide a clear example of the problem described by Ottaway (1966) regarding the difficulty of dividing groups into watertight compartments for the purpose of analysis. At first sight there may appear to be an obvious difference between a group of people organised for the purpose of teaching and a discussion group. Both kinds of group are ways of using a group format for increasing understanding; both will be experienced by its members as a way of learning involving the focused communication of information; thus, both are recognisably learning groups. The distinction between them concerns the role of the teacher. In discussion groups, ideas are passed backwards and forwards among the group members themselves, so that all combine the two roles of learner and teacher. Learning thus becomes an experience of communal assimilation and accommodation in accordance with the way in which, according to Piaget, intelligence itself develops and functions, as it responds to situations by adapting them:

It extends this creation by constructing mental structures which can be applied to those of the environment. (1953, 4)

The environment in this case is the human group regarded as a form of co-operative learning; although one which is strikingly different from the traditional class-room where attendance is compulsory and information restricted to data considered by the organising authority to be in line with its own specific purposes.

Process-orientated groups

(i) Self-teaching groups

Groups are often put together as a convenient, and effective, way of fulfilling a predetermined educational task. What happens when the teaching given to the group takes the form of one specific instruction: that it should find its own way of learning *about itself*? In self-teaching groups, the group is its own agenda.

We have already suggested that the study of what happens in groups is its own specific subject, apart from any consideration of groupwork as an effective means of transmitting information originating outside the group experience. To put this in another way, the 'focused information' referred to in the last section is not only communicated in a cognitive way. It also proceeds from, and is addressed to, other kinds of human awareness. Emotions and intuitions, sensory experience itself all carry powerful messages within, between and among individual participants in the action of allowing oneself to become involved in a group, or even of resisting any impulse to do so.

The notion of focusing of attention, which is purposefully directed rather than random, is important in groupwork. Certainly, groups only attain awareness of themselves as groups, only achieve what might be called group-consciousness, when they discover some kind of shared territory. The process of group formation depends on feelings of interpersonal involvement that cannot be imposed, yet must be allowed to develop. In fact, as Douglas (1993) says, this may be more a matter of providing opportunity for it to emerge than attempting to factor it within the situation in any directly purposive way. Once group members have discovered for themselves whatever it may be that they have in common, an assembly of individuals whom others have brought together for one purpose or another becomes the group which has now decided, for its own purposes, to bring itself.

As Whitaker and Lieberman pointed out, the concerns of the group originate within its own shared awareness, and this is illustrated clearly in group therapy:

> Whatever is said in the group is seen as being elicited not only by the strictly internal concerns of the individual, but by the interpersonal situation in which he finds himself. (1964, 16)

This, they say, is because 'of all the personal issues, worries, impulses, and concerns which the patient might express during a group session, what he actually expresses is elicited by the character of the situation'. In other words the group is conscious, first and foremost, of its identity as a group and this awareness has a polarising effect on the sense an individual has of being herself or himself as opposed to everyone else present. Their presence focuses his or her own presence on herself or himself and renders the human need to belong, to be part of a supportive alliance of selves, more powerful than it would be in other circumstances. Research into therapeutically orientated groupwork

22

(Foulkes and Anthony, 1957; Yalom, 1995; Bion, 1961) has provided information about the way human groups function as revealed by intra-group dynamics, as the group focuses on what is happening to relationships within itself, and individuals learn from the way they find themselves reacting to one another, their similarity of response as well as the perceived varieties in personality which exist among them.

Other investigators have pointed out that this interactive, synergistic process is not restricted to therapy groups as such (Ottaway, 1966; Whitacker and Lieberman, 1964). In process-orientated groups, by which is meant those which exist for the study of inter-personal process occurring with the group itself, the focus is inwards towards individual reactions and interpersonal behaviour and attitudes rather than outwards towards achievement of a set purpose or specific task which has been set by an authority regarded as higher than that of the group members. However, this narrower focus may be experienced as a source of confidence owing to the feelings of belonging to which it gives rise. Members feel themselves to be protected against the outside world; there is a sense of 'united we stand, divided we fall.' This increased security has therapeutic importance in that it works against feelings of isolation which may go back a long way in the life-experience of individual group members (Bowlby, 1980), leaving even those who do not actually suffer from depressive illness with a pervasive sense of sadness and loss. Douglas reminds us of the long-term effects of this sense of helplessness, which he says, according to Koestler, 'may be partly responsible for man's ready submission to authority wielded by individuals or groups, his suggestibility by doctrines and commandments, his overwhelming urge to identify himself with tribe or nation . . . ' (Douglas, 1993, 28). In this way 'group-as-context' may become 'group-as-instrument', with powerful effects.

On the other hand the notion that group experience in itself is a threat to individuality has been strongly denied by Whitaker and Lieberman. On the contrary, they say, groups encourage individuality rather than inhibiting it. Group and individual are in no way necessarily antithetical. They point out that such a view 'may prevail because of the powerful and mysterious quality of the group forces' (1964, 283). This seems to have been the opinion of many people in the early years of group therapy, perhaps because of the view taken by Freudian psychotherapists that groups undermine an individual's sense of personal identity and give free reign to 'primitive' impulses. Those investigating group process found themselves subjected to criticism from opposing directions, as the discipline involved in groupwork was considered either too strict or not strict enough.

Many psychotherapists, however, continued to believe enthusiastically in the advantages of group experience for personal well-being. Writing almost thirty years after Whitaker and Lieberman, Douglas describes how

groupwork . . . has given us a way of helping and supporting, of teaching and ameliorating the condition of those who, for whatever reasons, find difficulty

23

in coping both with themselves and those parts of society with which they are in immediate contact'. (1993, 33)

Groups, he says, offer vital experience with regard to the way in which we learn to regulate our self-presentation in our dealings with other people, obviously a matter of the greatest personal significance for every human being: the human being, he points out, 'has always been a social animal, but the question has always been not one of whether or not to join, but how much to offer' (1993, 77).

This, specifically, is the area in which the identity of the group as a focus of human learning is most clearly defined. Groups focus on the business of learning how to be human — something which no human being can possibly learn alone, but can only be successfully learnt within a particular kind of inter-personal environment — one in which there is a carefully regulated balance between safety and danger, exposure and protection (Suttie, 1988).

Writers on group therapy draw attention to the small group as 'the opportunity for corrective emotional experience' (Walton, 1971, 101). Group membership can provide vulnerable people with an opportunity for self-expression which ordinary social life may deny them. 'Heightened emotionality,' says Walton, 'is a crucial element in social learning;' at the same time, however,

this is not ordinarily acceptable in Western culture. Politeness, good taste, morality etc., may be offended by the free expression of feeling . . . In any group situation a strong trend occurs towards conformity to the norms and expectations of society'. (1971, 101)

The result of this heightened awareness, coupled with the presence of others in the same situation, has a releasing effect on our hold over emotions we normally manage to keep well under control. The result is a release of tension which group therapists regard as an emotionally healing experience (Yalom, 1995).

All the same, showing emotion increases our feelings of vulnerability whether we are receiving psychotherapy or not. It is as a counter to human vulnerability in the face of a choice between loneliness and exploitation — now usually referred to as bullying — that groupwork has proved its usefulness in the most striking way. Yalom points to 'a corrective emotional experience in group therapy' (1995, 26) intrinsic to its nature as a group:

Goals may change, from wanting relief from anxiety or depression, to wanting to learn to communicate with others, to be more trusting and honest with others, to learn to love. (1995, 21)

For Yalom, the group is a channel of restoration through inter-personal love. This is its therapeutic importance, and it is available to all, even the so-called healthy:

24

It is not the sheer process of ventilation that is important; it is not only the discovery of others' problems similar to one's own, and the ensuing discon-firmation of one's own wretched uniqueness, that is important: it is the effective sharing of one's own inner world and then the acceptance by others that seems of paramount importance. (1995, 49)

listening into sp.

A group which has learned to be a group — that is to belong together in this particular way — acts as a symbol of forgiveness and hence of personal renewal, for 'to be accepted by others brings into question one's belief that one is basically repugnant' (1995, 49).   → *confidence*

The division into teaching groups and therapy groups obscures the fact that this teaching is a form of healing. All the same, a clear distinction is drawn between groups which are directed 'from outside,' whether they are aimed at imparting knowledge or passing on expertise, and those which are self-regu-lating, in which understanding is brought about by sharing, and leadership moves round the group. These latter are the ones described by Ottaway, which are therapeutic to the extent that they are self-regulating, and the influence of the group-leader is directed towards their remaining so. Any teaching done in such circumstances can be described as being primarily about the experience of learning itself:

> We learn from the group process, from the method of its working, from the way people behave in it, from personal involvement and from gaining insight into other people's problems and our own. (1966, 153)

In groupwork concerned with promoting this kind of understanding, the group learns about what is involved in being a group. In other words, it learns about itself, developing the awareness that comes from having made a conscious choice to belong together. 'Groups,' says Mathers, 'adopt a sense of identity larger than themselves, co-extensive with the group' (1972, 106). Thus, process-orientated groups are not just supportive, they are expansive. Their origins, however, are to be found in the attempt to provide assistance for beleaguered individuals.

(ii) Psychoanalytic groups

This is a notion of group therapy which has moved some distance from the pragmatic origins of groupwork during the 1939–1945 war, when sheer weight of numbers led to 'shell-shocked' service personnel receiving psychi-atric treatment in groups rather than individually (Foulkes and Anthony, 1957). In the early days of group psychoanalysis attention was firmly concen-trated upon the analyst's relationship with individuals comprising the group. He or she was the doctor, and each of them a patient. This polarising effect of pre-existing role determination may be observed in Bion's ground-breaking investigation (see also Kapur, 2009), where the group analyst records feelings of antagonism originating within the group which are now focused painfully upon him as 'The doctor in charge', whose job it obviously was to make each one of them feel 'better.' The effect of bringing unhappy people together in a group was to turn the product of their corporate unhappiness upon the one person who was trying to relieve their distress. No wonder then that Bion corroborates Freud's conclusion that 'the individual is a group animal at war' (Bion, 1961, 131).

Even at this comparatively early stage in groupwork development, before the logistics had really begun to shift in the direction of a group learning which was consciously interactive, commentators drew attention to the unconscious activity in which members shared one another's experience, learning from one another and not simply receiving instruction from the individual who was officially in charge of operations. Writing in 1957, Foulkes and Anthony state that

> Within the group-analytic situation we have, instead of the individual transference relationship between patient and therapist, a whole spectrum of relationships in active operation before our eyes. (1957, 75)

In their opinion, it is the group interaction which is the principal component in any therapeutic effect a group may have:

> The material produced in a group and the actions and interactions of its members are analysed — they are voiced, interpreted and studied by the group. (1957, 58)

The result of such study, carried out not by the analyst but by the group itself, is to produce material regarding the underlying significance of our behaviour in groups giving rise to 'theoretical formulations which throw light on the unconscious processes operating in other groups' (1957, 58); ones, that is, where the intention is not actually clinical, or even consciously therapeutic.

Bion points out that the intentional purpose-driven activity of a group is obstructed, diverted and occasionally assisted by certain other mental activities that have in common the attribute of powerful emotional drives. These unconscious forces which, says Bion, characterise all human activity may, through expression in a group setting, actually contribute to its achieving its conscious aims, as

> These activities, at first sight chaotic, are given a certain cohesion if it is assumed that they spring from basic assumptions common to all the group. (1961, 146)

It would seem that even psychoanalysis may further learning which is genuinely corporate. Although Bion himself does not make the connection, the phenomenon[1] of religious belonging provides a striking example of this (cf. Fordham, 1995).

Bion's ground-breaking work with groups shows psychoanalysis moving away from its preoccupation with the psychological economy of individuals in the direction of a more relational stance, in which members 'show evidence of acting "as one" in the harmonious and efficient pursuit of a conscientious and explicit goal' (Mathers, 1972).

Thus, Mathers, writing in the psychoanalytic tradition, finds himself 'reluctant to accept the suggestion that a group is "nothing but" a collection of interacting individuals' (1972, 103). Even for analysis, then, group experience is an irreducible phenomenon.

(iii) Growth groups

The idea of a group holism functioning at an unconscious level, born of psychoanalysis, spread into areas outside psychiatry, emerging over the last fifty years in the study and practice of groupwork as a separate and distinct discipline; albeit one with wide ramifications. Brown characterises it as

> an umbrella term for a whole range of activities, actions and therapies . . . Groupwork provides a context in which individuals help each other as well as helping individuals, and it can help individuals and groups to influence and change personal group organisational and community problems. (1992, 5, 8)

Brown's characterisation of group process as 'a dynamic interacting system', in which 'individual behaviours may often have group purpose' (1992, 123) gave rise to the concept of the 'growth group'. Jacobs et al. use this term to cover a range of groupwork intended to actualise this inherent ability of the group to exert an influence greater than the sum of its parts:

> Sensitivity groups, awareness groups and encounter groups would all be considered growth groups. (2002, 8)

These are groups which Douglas described as having been brought together for

> alleviating isolation, promoting social learning and maturation, preparing for an approaching crisis, solving or clarifying problems at the personal or social level, solving or clarifying problems in the members' environment, and achieving insight. (1993, 83)

The main point being made here, of course, is the one about insight. A group able to encourage this, says Douglas, may authentically be recognised as 'transformational' (1993, 94) in character and purpose. It is never an easy thing to do. The original psychoanalytic investigators into the dynamics of group belonging were correct in their assumption that a degree of systematic work would need to be done in order to free thought and feelings which had been kept under wraps for some considerable time and through the exercise of a good deal of effort. Foulkes and Anthony (1957, 8) stress that people reared in the western civilized world appear to have a good deal to hide.

Psychoanalytic groupwork aimed to disturb a psychological equilibrium which could only be maintained by a persistent refusal to acknowledge the presence of emotional tensions. Groups aimed at encouraging personal growth concentrate on bringing us into contact with ourselves in conditions that encourage us to take the risk of revealing our vulnerability in the face of the need for self-disclosure. Within an atmosphere of shared acceptance, these groups act as the microscopic representation of some of life's most crucial and painful issues (Yalom, 1995, 365).

The result of belonging in one is a measure of self-acceptance almost impossible to achieve in any other circumstances, as it is entirely dependent on the reality of other people's acceptance of the individual's own self, which is the liberation in human beings of their personhood. For Yalom, as for later groupwork theorists (e.g. Corey and Corey, 1997; Jacobs et al., 2002; Brown, 1992; Corey et al., 2010), the essential liberating factor remains the group itself:

What groups do best of all is to help people understand about their relationships with others. (1995, 474)

Thus Corey and Corey claim that:

The group is a context for Thou-ness — a focus of human development [. . .] Before we can have any solid relationship with another we must have a relationship with ourselves. (1997, 178, 181)

And Ottaway reminds us that:

Because it is the function of groups to evoke and to focus this relationship, the learning involved in process-orientated groupwork is learning about relatedness, in which the group explores the relations of the members to each other and to reality in the present [by] recognising the meaning of one's own behaviour. (1966, 100, 101)

For, as Ottaway points out, 'one's personal relationships are the most satisfying part of life' (1966, 114). To discover how and why this is so, however, we must penetrate below the surface of psychological accounts of human learning and consider personal relationship as participation in a reality which is irreducibly spiritual (Grainger, 2003).

The group holism described by Yalom (1995) and Rogers (1969) in which individuals become aware of an ability to transcend their limitations by taking on a source of life and strength indistinguishable from experiences undergone within the group context — so that the group itself is observed to add its own

28

presence to the individual presences within it — suggests the spiritual more noticeably than any category open to scientific analysis. Groupwork lends itself to psychological approaches of a transcendental nature (Boyd, 1991), whereas approaches such as Cognitive Behavioural Therapy, Cognitive Analytical Therapy and Process Psychology, which are mainly directed towards individual psychotherapy, make use of a group format for reasons of convenience as it allows a single therapist to give treatment to more than one person at a time.

Art-based groups

(i) Art and personal change

It is a cliché that art 'carries a message' — not always one which may be spelled out, but definitely one which is able to register itself subliminally. To say that an object, form of words or idea 'means nothing to me,' whatever it may actually say about it, certainly denies it any kind of artistic value or significance. All the same, as we are all of us familiar with messages capable of striking home although we remain incapable of describing why or how, we may be inclined to suspend any final judgement as to whether or not it may, in the long run, turn out to have some significance for us.

A lot of course will depend on our willingness to use our imagination to transform the value and significance of what lies within our grasp, as children make use of toys in dramas which mediate emotional realities able to give life and meaning to their personal worlds (Winnicott, 1971). This imaginative transformation of loneliness into fellowship, isolation into engagement, separation into relatedness is the mainspring of every kind of art (Grainger, 2010). The relational nature of art, its function in building bridges between separate individuals is most graphically expressed in drama, the imaginative enactment of human relationship.

Drama presents ideas about relationship in embodied form; in fact it presents them not as ideas, but as people. As in process-orientated groups, this is learning about human relatedness in which those involved learn by living through the things the group experience is teaching them. The only difference here is the element of imaginative participation, the 'as if' factor on which drama depends. These people are not actually the people whose actions and reactions they are witnessing and whose joys and sorrows, success and failures, anger, jealousy and fortitude they are being invited to share; if they are actually playing themselves, and not pretending to be anybody different, then these particular circumstances have undergone changes brought about by shared imagination — a transformation which is literally fictional but emotionally real.

The use of an art-form, in this case drama, might be described as an emotional journey which the medium itself manages to make safe, or at least safe enough for the purpose of exploration. This, of course, is an ancient idea, dating back at least as far as Aristotle (Butcher, 1951) and re-stated by Coleridge (1817) in terms originally meant for poetry although they actually refer to any use of an artistic medium. Art, says Coleridge, 'reveals itself in the balance or reconcilement of opposite or discordant qualities . . . a more than usual state of emotion with a more than usual order' (1817, quoted in Grainger, 2010, 10).

This ability to balance harmony and discord, beauty and ugliness, joy and pain, proceeds from the fact that although art distances it also unites: the distancing effect of our awareness of an artificial reality is balanced here by our discovery that whatever it is we encounter has the power to draw us to itself and involve us in this 'third world' of shared imagination. In drama, this world subsists in the presence of people like ourselves who in fact might *be* ourselves if we were in the circumstances they are engaged in presenting, the world which they bring to life in our presence. This, of course, is Aristotle's *catharsis*, the purging of our preoccupation with self through the gift of pain on behalf of others, whose humanity we find ourselves sharing and whose suffering we imagine as our own (Grainger, 1995, 2010, 1990).

Drama demonstrates this in a striking way, but the reconciliation with things we find unacceptable characterises art itself. Art is perhaps the only place where we systematically look for trouble in this way; and we do so because we believe ourselves to be safe. In drama we do not do it alone; in fact we need the real (or imagined) presence of others to do it at all, so that drama based learning may also be seen as a type of groupwork. As in a process-orientated group the learning involved is about relatedness to one another and oneself; and as pointed out in the last section, this involves the risk of emotional pain. As Corey points out,

> Just as many shrink from accepting freedom and responsibility out of fear of the risks involved, some may attempt to avoid accepting their loneliness and isolation. (1991, 192)

He comments that those involved in encounter groups 'are encouraged to look within themselves to recognise their own contribution to their plight' (1991, 197). The pain of this kind of self-disclosure, which is disclosure both to other people and to oneself, is focused by the expectation which is implicit in such groups that members will be willing to 'go public' in those special circumstances for, as Yalom says, 'Self-acceptance must be preceded by acceptance of others' (1995, 354), however difficult this may be.

Well-being and relatedness go together. Nowhere is this more clearly shown than in groupwork. Drama-based groups use art to promote involvement, countering anxiety, the human fear of isolation and rejection, with shared imagination. In other words they provide the kind of support which process-orientated groupwork aims for (and may take some time to achieve) through an approach to human vulnerability which is itself a corporate commitment to sharing under the token of *catharsis* (Scheff, 1979). Corey and

Corey include this as a crucial factor in process-orientated groupwork, characterising the central transitional stage around which the entire process revolves, and on which its action may be said to pivot:

> As participants came to more fully trust one another and the leader, they became increasingly able to share their concerns. (1997, 177)

Such sharing does not come easily, owing to participants' resistance to abandoning their defences against threatening material that has previously been repressed or denied. Resistance, however is 'a normal process and should not be thought of as something that needs to be 'gotten around quickly' or by-passed' (1997, 178).

Catharsis is achieved when unacceptable feelings are acknowledged by being encountered head-on and not avoided. In art-based approaches, involvement in an imagined world renders emotional pain less private, easing the pressure upon minds and hearts which have been sealed-off by suffering and turned in on themselves. 'Pity and fear,' aroused by sufferings which, however familiar they may be to us, are nevertheless not actually ours intervene to allow us to relinquish the grasp we have over our own feelings, and with this change of focus comes a sense of freedom and release from emotional bondage.

This is the artistic definition of *catharsis*, which is a term used to explain the action of drama long before it was taken over by psychotherapy (Grainger, 2008, 2010; Scheff, 1979). It is a very positive and life-enhancing way of regarding imagination, a faculty we tend to undervalue, or even sometimes disparage. We feel that if something is imaginary we have no need to take it seriously. This, however, is imaginative involvement in others' pain, which is able to transform the quality of our own. It does this by transforming the actual nature of that pain, turning it from a burden into a gift. *Catharsis* operates as a release mechanism, setting us free from the psychological chains with which we bind ourselves, which lose their weight when we exchange them with someone else. By taking on their burden, ours is somehow made easier to bear. Perhaps the same kind of disinhibition releases our laughter once we find a way to share it with others. *Catharsis* belongs to comedy as well as tragedy; it is an emblem of psycho-spiritual transformation.

Ever since Aristotle's *Art of Poetry*, the form of art most intimately associated with human transformation has been drama. Drama cannot exist without the presence of opposing forces of one kind or another, in the same way that the opposition of old and new, former and latter, provides the fulcrum for changes both in individuals and societies. Human groups demonstrate and explore the terms upon which persons belong together in the form of works of art whose subject matter consists of people like themselves, and whose argument traces the arrangements they make for living and dying. The result may be theatre or corporate ritual of one kind or another, religious or secular. On the other hand, it may be a less formal, more spontaneous kind

31

of playmaking, as in dramatherapy (Jenkyns, 1996; Jennings, 1992,1987; Jones, 2007), whose content, as with all drama, is actual people, present to us as we are to them 'in the flesh.'

The experience of sharing imagination in this way is the combination of reassurance and challenge, safety and danger, which makes it possible to quieten fears of becoming involved with situations we feel we will not be able to handle, giving rise to feelings we will not be able control. Scheff describes a cathartic exchange of feelings according to which the nature of drama as fabrication reduces the pressure on those involved to 'take things personally' in a way that, most of the time, they manage to avoid doing. Thus aesthetic distance and cathartic release function together; the former being defined as 'the simultaneous and equal experience of being both participant and observer' (1979, 60).

The phenomenon Scheff describes does not characterise drama only, however, although it is most strikingly apparent in enactment. The balance between distance and involvement takes place wherever a medium is interposed between emotional experience and aesthetic discernment, in which one of them unlocks whatever may be increasing the restraint placed upon the other. It is art itself which has this liberating effect, which is why all forms of artistic experience have been used therapeutically. From this point of view, each of the arts therapies may be seen as 'dramatic.' As we saw in the last section, process-orientated groupwork is concerned with learning about relatedness. What such groups have to teach is mirrored and expanded for us in the work of those who have written about the arts therapies in general, and particularly those who have concentrated on dramatherapy (Jennings and Minde, 1993; Mitchell, 1996; Duggan and Grainger, 1997; Pitruzzella, 2004; Jennings, 1990; Jones, 2007; Grainger, 1990; Schattner and Courtney, 1981).

(ii) Creative therapy

Specialists in groupwork have laid stress on the generalisability of the group process (Ottaway, 1966; Douglas, 1993; Yalom, 1995; Jacobs et al., 2002). In a similar way, arts therapists have been at pains to point out that, although their approaches may be used clinically for the treatment of medically diagnosed psychopathology, they have a wider applicability than this, one centred upon the action of focusing individual awareness through an experience of willing involvement in shared creativity (Liebmann, 2004; Gersie and King, 1990; Grainger, 2010; Jones, 2007).

Creative Therapy is an extension of groupwork aiming at disarming the distress which people feel when they are put under pressure to reveal to others those aspects of their own experience which make them feel nervous or ashamed. The discovery that other people feel the same way about themselves is always a relief, and may even be a revelation (Corey and Corey, 1997; Corey et al., 2010). It has the effect of loosening the grip exerted by unthinkable thoughts and emotions which cannot be acknowledged, so that attention may be properly directed to the feelings themselves and away from the individuals feeling them, and the group set free to address what turns out to be a shared problem. In this way personal reaction may become subsumed into corporate action, emerging in symbolic transpersonal form as an image, a scenario, a sequence of expressive movements, a story unfolded among the group in which each member may see him or herself to the extent that she or he is able to do so by making use of art's ability to conceal and reveal, and reveal by concealing.

The learning which takes place in the creative therapies proceeds by means of discovery, not direct instruction. This is an ancient and venerable way in which human beings — and of course other animals and birds — learn about life in co-operation with others of their own species. Confronted at an early age with a whole range of alternative courses of action, they make social sense of their world by a process of corporate trial and error, setting out to explore their options in company with others of their kind (Lorenz, 1952; Tinbergen, 1965). For us imagination expands the choices available, creating a range of solutions of greater or lesser feasibility. As in all human ways of knowing, including scientific ones, imagination leads the way for more solid conclusions. In groupwork settings, under conditions which call for individual experience to be shared, learning requires agreement among the people involved as to what it might be that has to be learned. This must happen before any plans are made as to *how* it should be learned. Is it facts which the group is after, or an expanded knowledge of what it is to be human? Creative therapy aims at a shared understanding of the latter kind of understanding, and improvises its own conditional scenarios for doing this. In the same way, it judges success or failure retrospectively, using the conditions of shared experience — the 'real' world, that is — to do so. The outcome is learning via the exchange of uncertainty and involves setting forth as a group into unknown territory making conscious use of imagination to achieve a practical purpose, in this case, a shared understanding about being human.

In his seminal work on the arts therapies, Jones describes how they 'have emerged from an explosion of experimentation and exploration by opening up the therapy space to work creatively, to develop and to change' (2004, 11). They have done this by bringing into awareness the understanding that things previously consigned to the realm of 'scientific medicine' — i.e. actual psychiatric conditions — relate to problems of living which are only communicable by artistic means (McNiff, 1998) — in other words through our willingness to trust to creative imagination, in which, according to Jung, 'all the works of man have their origin:'

> What right then have we to disparage fantasy? The creative activity of imagination frees man from his bondage to the 'nothing but' and raises him to the status of one who plays. As Schiller says, man is completely human only when he is at play. (1997, 91; quoted by Jones, 2004, 103)

33

During the last two decades, art-based groups have begun to be used educationally and within the area of spirituality (Grainger, 1995; Gersie and King, 1990; Jennings et al., 1994;Grainger, 2003). Chesner and Hahn (2002) have collected evidence of the sustainability of working from traditional group theory within a range of flexible and imaginative frameworks.

To summarise then, in this chapter we have been looking at several alternative approaches to group learning. Three of these have been identified for closer scrutiny in the following pages. The approaches under consideration were chosen from many different group structures, each of them associated with its own specific purpose, but all of them ways of affecting the lives of those taking part (Corey and Corey, 1997; Jacobs et al., 2002; Brown, 1992; Corey et al., 2010). These approaches share a particular intention, however, because they are all three aimed at exploring basic issues regarding what it means to be a human being, so that they are likely to commend themselves to theologically aware people.

The conclusion to be drawn is that the three types of groupwork are based on three major kinds of learning:

- Text-based learning, in which instruction regarding people's relationship to God and one another is based upon teaching material prepared beforehand.
- Process-orientated learning, in which the group itself is both the content of, and the context for, learning about personal relationships.
- Art-based learning, using shared imagination to provide a medium for interpersonal encounter able to overcome some of the barriers to relationship.

All three approaches may be used as ways of sharing understanding about individuals' relationship with God and one another. In the first kind of group, a specific religious message is communicated, whereas the other two approaches may remain silent on the subject of explicitly religious belief. Where such belief already exists, however, its presence may be experienced implicitly in the quality of relatedness which constitutes the nature and purpose of the group itself. Under such circumstances it simply waits for the opportunity to express itself in the form of personal testimony and corporate celebration.

Each of these three types of group represents one of the ways in which learning may be communicated by means of group experience. All constitute one of the avenues through which we may discover more about what it is that is involved in the ongoing process by which we learn to understand ourselves, other people, and also our faith.

Note

1 Perhaps it should be noted that the British National Health Service's espousal of Cognitive Behavioural Therapy (CBT), an avowedly individualistic approach, has

brought about a current revival of interest in groups on the part of psychotherapists of other traditions than the psychoanalytic. Douglas, for example, reminds us that 'it is in group therapy that individuals can explore the impact of stigma, social isolation and social exclusion upon their psychological identity and well-being, and through this empower themselves as individuals in society as a whole' (2008, 9).

Judg. 12:1-7
Lk. 17:11-19

2

Groupwork among Believers

Groups in Scripture

In this chapter we will be looking at the specifically Christian use of group-work, beginning with a brief overview of evidence of group awareness within the Bible itself, which forms the background to the research carried out, as well as the context for any conclusions which may be drawn in the book as a whole. The chapter moves from the Old Testament into the New Testament, before looking at groupwork in churches, concentrating on the Church of England within England itself. Consequently, the groupwork focus in the following chapters is that current within the Anglican Church in England. (For groupwork within a wider context, see http://www.smallgroups.net/.)

(i) The Old Testament

At first sight the notion of groupwork does not appear to fit in well with the Old Testament, unless of course one takes the family as a form of small group. Certainly one would search for a long time for an example of the kind of group described by Ottaway (1966), Yalom (1995) or Corey and Corey (1997), although the growth of self-understanding which develops from the experience of belonging together in a close relationship, in which an individual's sense of who and what they are — indeed, of being anyone at all, is closely bound up with and dependent upon the group of people with whom they are associated, and consequently associate themselves.

From this point of view, the Old Testament immediately springs to mind as the *locus classicus* of relationships of mutual commitment and the assumption of a corporate identity by all those bound together in this way: 'I will be your God and you shall be my people' (Jr 7:23).

God shows himself to his people within a covenant relationship, and the divine action is taken as the revelation of his own identity as the One who makes covenants and is to be encountered within the covenants he makes. His covenants are established as the template for human behaviour: men and women are to regard one another in the way he regards them (Jn 13:34) — with trust, commitment and the sharing which is love. Johnson reminds us that 'Salvation in the Old Testament isn't discussed primarily in terms of "going to heaven" — but in terms of belonging to God as his people' (2010, 1). This approach has been explored in some depth by Woodall:

> The standing of the concept of covenant is not only validated by Scripture; I believe it is absolutely indispensable to our growth into maturity as believers. (2011, 192, 193)

In the Old Testament it is God who lays down the rules. The agreements made in groupwork between a group's leader and members are a pale shadow of this, but these too constitute a pledge of loyalty and commitment that is founded in mutuality: from now on group and leader 'belong together.' Corey and Corey see the group leader's responsibility for establishing the terms of membership as rooted in her or his own attitude towards members:

> Through your behaviour and the attitudes conveyed by it, you can create group norms such as openness, seriousness of purpose, acceptance of others and the desirability of taking risks . . . (Corey and Corey, 1997)

Corey and Corey regard the taking of risks as evidence of a leader's involvement in the dangerous business of exposing oneself to the possibility, often amounting to the probability, of rejection by the people to whom you are reaching out. The leader describes a shared journey which will involve risk for all involved and almost certainly lead through territory which will be painful — which will not arrive at its destination at all if the purpose of those making the journey is simply to avoid pain.

Certainly, the notion of journeying relates directly to the Old Testament. Like the Children of Israel, group members are bound by a common purpose, each of them aiming for the same destination and striving to follow the same route in order to attain it. The psalmist tells the history of God's people by listing events on a journey, praising God for his loving care as a refrain at every step on the way, as in Psalm 136 where God is praised for rescuing Israel from captivity in Egypt:

> with a strong hand and an outstretched arm,
> for his steadfast love endures for ever;
> who divided the Red Sea in two,
> for his steadfast love endures for ever
> (Ps 136:12, 13; cf. Pss 78, 81, 106, 107)

The authorities on groupwork cited in Chapter 1 describe group process as taking place in distinct stages, according to which it achieves its underlying purpose of enabling its members to learn, through their relationship with one another, how to be fully themselves. It is the presence of others that brings this about, as the group format is capable of developing the ability to share oneself with others. In non-religious language, Douglas speaks of [generating] actual and/or potential resource systems to meet the actual and/or assessed needs of group members, and to remove, diminish, change or circumnavigate obstacles to the discovery, recognition, accessibility and use of these resources. (1993, 108)

In other words, groups of any kind require structures (i.e. 'systems') in order to function as groups rather than collections of individuals. Free expression is never just enough, any more than uncontrolled action would be. What we want to say or do, and what the situation calls for, are obviously not the same thing at all, even in groupwork!

The agreements made in groupwork between a group's leader and its members are a reflection of the longing for mutuality expressed and fulfilled in scripture. They, too, constitute a pledge of loyalty and commitment, participating in the demonstration of these values in corporate action, which in its own way corresponds to the symbolism belonging to organised religion — while not, of course, claiming to be, in any explicit sense, religious. In the Old Testament, the ongoing journey of the people of God through time into a deeper and more real relationship with the Creator is enacted within the present as a 'rite of passage' (Van Gennep, 1960) in the temple rituals in which cultic procedures spell timelessness out in the language of symbolic gestures performed in time. The rules are laid down by God himself. They are rules which concern both practical action in the world and symbolic action within the sanctuary (Douglas, 1966; Bouyer, 1963; Pfeiffer, 1961; Santrac, 2012).

The rules of groupwork are not expressed in so clear and explicit a symbolism. However the shared intention to abide by rules concerning our relationship with others needs to be publicly recognised and signified in symbolic actions which express our intention to change from an old way of being towards one another into a close relationship, from hostility into love. The rite of passage, which Van Gennep and others have claimed to be the pattern for rules of spiritual transformation everywhere (Grainger, 1998; Gorman, 1972; Eliade, 1958; Van Gennep, 1960; Grainger, 1988, 1987), involves a succession of stages which are structurally distinct but belong together as an identifiable unity of meaning and intention, which is to communicate change as an experience rather than simply an idea:

> For groups as well as individuals, life itself means to be separate and to be reunited, to change form and condition, to die and be reborn. It is to act and to cease, to wait and then to begin acting again, but in a different way. (Van Gennep, 1960, 189)

According to Van Gennep,

> a complete scheme of rites of passage includes pre-liminal rites (rites of separation), liminal rites (rites of transition) and post-liminal rites (rites of incorporation). (1960, 10)

In terms of an actual journey through time, post-liminal rites constitute arrival, just as pre-liminal ones are a setting out into the unknown. Liminality, 'thresholdness,' is precisely what it says: at best a time of uncertainty and confusion, at worst a place of chaos where, in the words of W.B.Yeats's 'The Second Coming:'

Things fall apart; the centre cannot hold;
Mere anarchy is loosed upon the world.
(1950, 210)

Thus, the unwillingness to change, grow and be transformed causes conflict when it is no longer possible to stay the same, resting within the well tried and familiar, the place in which we feel safe, with the problems we know how to solve. This pain is dramatically presented in the rite, at the point where a new state of affairs has not yet emerged and the old one has been left behind. In fact, it has been 'done to death.'

Group process, although it does not take on a ritualised identity, reproduces this movement from a condition of 'separation,' when the group decides to undertake the experiment of working together as a group, to one of 'incorporation,' when this aim is actually achieved in practice. In between are stages of the process which, Brown says, involve 'jockeying for position . . . issues of control and power' (1992, 101). He is describing the stage in group process which Tuckman characterised as 'storming,' which takes place halfway through a sequence beginning with 'forming' and ending in 'norming' and 'performing' (1965). For Corey and Corey, the middle stage in the group process is identified as the 'working stage' precisely because of the open oppositions and identifiable conflicts it exposes:

Control issues, power struggles and interpersonal conflicts within the group are frequently the basis for discussion and *tend to be explored at a deeper level*. (Corey and Corey, 1997, 230. My italics)

Yalom, too, discusses how discordant elements in group interaction come to the surface as 'members gradually engage more deeply in the group and discover and share their problems in living' (1995, 326). People find themselves brought face to face with emotions that existed all the time in a submerged state, but now require to be openly acknowledged; in particular, a chronic defensiveness in the presence of whatever is perceived as a threat to one's way of being and behaving. Groupworkers find themselves the object of hostility that originated elsewhere and is now projected onto them. Relationships within the group at this critical stage are reminiscent of the hostility shown towards leadership which plays such a part in Exodus, when 'the whole congregation of the children of Israel murmured against Moses and Aaron in the wilderness' (Ex 16:2).

Certainly, leaders of groupwork exercises are not encouraged to see themselves as either prophet or priest. On the other hand, the issue of loyalty, both to the group leader her or himself and also to the overall project in which members have elected to be enlisted, is the same in both cases. Also, the question of responsibility for what, in the long run, may happen to the group is a recurrent theme in groupwork, which sets out to conduct those taking part through a process aimed at intensifying the emotional conflict caused by self-protectiveness in order to achieve the emotional release which the acceptance of one's fellow human beings is capable of bringing about. In this, the role of the healer is undertaken by someone 'whose job is to harness conflict and use it in the service of the group' (Yalom, 1995, 350). In this way, the group leader moves within his or her group as advocate and intercessor, putting people's points of view on their behalf and drawing attention to the need for members to be aware of one another's areas of sensitivity and everyone's need for acceptance and forgiveness. Leaders guide and direct, but always participate. Groupwork commentators, such as Ottaway, agree on this point: 'The basic feeling is one of personal involvement in a common task' (1966, 161). Yalom spells out the quality of this involvement: 'The leader wishes to guide the group through anxiety, through the impasse or difficult stages, rather than around them' (1995, 445).

This catalytic action undertaken by a leader-participant, conducting his followers onto higher ground through participation in their experience, 'going with them on the journey,' is a central theme of the entire Bible and, according to historians of religion, of religious thought throughout the world (Eliade, 1958 *vide* also Pss 23, 105, 106, 144). In the New Testament, of course, it comes into even clearer focus.

In both Testaments, however, we have a vision of the peace which is to be found in fellowship with others, particularly those with whom we have endured hardship, and on whose support we have come to depend. As the Psalmist puts it: 'How very good and pleasant it is when kindred live together in unity' (Ps 133:1). In fact, according to Corey and Corey, the aim of the group process is to create

> a climate of support, bonding, attractiveness, sharing of experiences, mutuality within a group, the togetherness that unites members, a sense of belonging, warmth and closeness, and caring and acceptance. (1997, 254)

The concept of the 'support group' is well known in groupwork literature (Douglas, 1993, 126–130; Jacobs et al., 2002, 15–18). These are groups set up as refuge-points, places of shelter, providing sanctuary for people sharing the same kinds of problem, or suffering as a result of social or political circumstances which affect them all in the same way. A good example would be the self-help support groups set up to give a measure of relief to individuals suffering from stigma (*cf.* Grainger, 2009). The Book of Joshua describes how Moses was instructed by God to care for those who found themselves held responsible for crimes they had not intended to commit by setting up six cities

40

of refuge in which individuals, who 'without intent or by mistake' had killed another person, might take refuge:

> The slayer shall flee to one of these cities, and shall stand at the entering of the gate of the city and explain the case to the elders of that city: then the fugitive shall be taken into the city and given a place and shall remain with them. (Jos 20:4)

cf. David's outlaws

Certainly, the Old Testament is no stranger to suffering, nor to the human need for acceptance and support on the part of one's fellow men and women, particularly those described by the Psalmist: 'As they go through the valley of Baca they make it a place of springs' (Ps 84:6). In this way those making the pilgrimage through life share the waters with those whose need is great, thus fulfilling the Levitical commandment (Lv 19:18).

(ii) The New Testament

The scriptural perspective on groupwork becomes clearer when we turn to the New Testament. Certainly Jesus's disciples, with their Master, constituted a recognisable learning group. Jesus teaches his followers to have love for one another: 'Just as I have loved you, you also should love one another' (Jn 13:34 cf. 15:12, 17). The lesson is so important, so fundamental to human fulfilment, that it is given in the form of a commandment. This section explores some of the ways it was to be brought home in terms of group awareness and shared identity. Thus the factors to which we have been drawing attention find fulfilment within the *Weltanschauung* of the New Testament, in a way which is focused and exemplified by concentrating upon the experience and behaviour of a small group of people, whose bonding was to be taken as a template for the shared belonging of an expanding group, the membership of which would be identical with the human race itself:

> And he said to them, 'Go into all the world and proclaim the good news to the whole creation.' (Mk 16:15 cf. also 13:10; Mt 24:14)

This New Testament gospel is, in a literal sense, the apotheosis of the instruction give in the Old Testament — literal in the sense that, here, God is the message, not only the messenger, as was the case with Moses and the prophets (Mt 5:17).

> The days are surely coming, says the Lord, when I will make a new covenant with the house of Israel and the house of Judah. (Jr 31:31)

Jeremiah foretells supercession of Yahweh's covenants with Adam, Noah, Abraham, Moses, Phinehas and David by a new and infinitely far-reaching agreement according to which, 'I will put my law within them, and will write it on their hearts' (Jr 31:33). This is to be a contract of a kind which will be qualitatively different from any preceding one, a life-and-death involvement from which neither party will be able to withdraw, in which the nature of the relationship between the parties concerned is drastically altered, even revolutionised, for this is to be a covenant made not between but actually on behalf of, the pledge of God's self-giving love for his creation. This time the sacrificial victim is God Himself, the Second Person of the Trinity, offering his own life for the salvation of mankind:

> He said to them, 'This is my blood of the covenant, which is poured out for many'. (Mk 14:24; see also Mt 26:27; Lk 22:17)

Christian doctrine teaches that this constitutes a covenant between and among persons. The manner of its making reveals it to be the exchange of love and self-giving, 'bearing with one another in love' (Eph 4:2). From now on group and leader will belong together more closely and intimately than ever with the result that the world will have no difficulty recognising Christians as those bound together in a commonality of love and trust: 'The warmth of mutual love was the mark of their credibility' (Suenens, 1977, 138).

This closeness of belonging together is what Yalom means when he describes 'the richness and complexity of the group' (1995, 333). Such is the ideal state of affairs presented by the New Testament to any kind of joint enterprise that aims to maximise the potential inherent within groupwork. It is certainly a high standard to aim for, and Christians believe that it is impossible to achieve it without divine assistance, freely given to all who admit that they stand in need of it.

In St Matthew's Gospel Jesus comforts his disciples by telling them that, in fact, they have no need for anxiety on this point: 'For where two or three are gathered in my name, I am there among them' (Mt 18:20). This, surely, is the foundation upon which Christian groupwork rests. It is also the main justification for Christian interest in work carried out within the setting of small groups of people who share the same or similar intentions regarding the purpose of their pulling together in this way; the sharing involved is guaranteed by Christ and inspired by Holy Spirit (Ac 13:1–3; cf. Grainger, 2011).

Obviously the quality of mutual love and acceptance, if it is to come anywhere near the standard required by the 'new commandment' (Jn 13:34), must call for the presence of Holy Spirit. Human loving, by itself, is not enough (although Jesus's words imply a human involvement, albeit that of a humanity restored and remade in the Image of the Creator). For one thing caring for others goes beyond simple love of neighbour, asking more from us than we would otherwise consider reasonable to ask of ourselves (Mt 5:44; Lk 6:27, 35). This is particularly relevant to the kind of work carried out in small groups, where human insecurity gives rise to personal rivalries and resentments, and individuals are called to work at close quarters with people towards whom they are conscious of feeling a degree of fear or resentment that is nonetheless intense for being short-lived. Such enmities are regarded by groupworkers as belonging to a process of 'working through' the difficulties which stand in the way of any group determined to achieve its aim of arriving together at a state of affairs in which it will be able to function effectively as a group (*cf.* Tuckman, 1965; Yalom, 1995, 293ff; Corey and Corey, 1997, 177ff). Members who share the belief that they, as a group, are engaged in this journey in the company of their Lord and Saviour are obviously in a very privileged position; but the advantage bestowed must be used in the service of love towards all with whom they are associated, with special concern for any non-believers in the group.

In this movement towards a deeper, more personal concern for others, the group format itself plays an important part. Yalom describes the often painful progress towards understanding of self-and-other which characterises group formation:

> Goals may change, from wanting relief from anxiety or depression, to wanting to learn to communicate with others, to be more trusting and honest with others, to learn to love . . . (1995, 21)

The history of the Christian Church itself is the story of a process which is almost always beset by pain and failure yet continues to provide the deepest fulfilment for those willing — or called irresistibly — to immerse themselves in it and give themselves to it.

(iii) The twelve disciples as a learning group

If we look at the twelve original disciples as a group formation with Jesus as its leader, and ask what kind of group this was in terms of the various options described in Chapter 1, we arrive at several answers. Each one of these has its own degree of relevance to the picture presented by the Gospel accounts, and possessing recognisable significance for pastoral theology.

- The disciples as an action group
    You did not choose me, but I chose you. And I appointed you
    to go and bear fruit, fruit that will last (Jn 15:16).

The learning involved here is instrumental. The disciples are to perform a specific function, aimed at producing a recognisable effect on the state of affairs in the world. This is seen by writers about groupwork as a 'task group' (Jacobs et al., 2002, 6, 126). Douglas describes 'instrumental associative patterns, or more properly, group-as-instrument patterns' which 'appear in a group when the group members are able to work as a unit to explore and exploit the resources which the group contains, or to which it has access' (1993, 31). This, certainly, has more relevance to the disciples' post-Pentecost behaviour than to the way this particular collection of individuals sometimes functioned during Jesus's lifetime (*cf.* Mk 9:33–35). The Acts of the Apostles, however, bears powerful and convincing testimony to the fact that the earliest followers of Jesus 'learned by doing.'

- The disciples as members of an *educational* group
  I have called you friends because I have made known to you everything I have learned from my Father (Jn 15:15).

Jesus taught his disciples by example, not only through the things he did and said, but in the drama he was to live out for the redemption of the world. He not oly did so propositionally — 'speaking plainly, not in any figure of speech' (Jn 16:29), but by calling on his hearers' capacity for imaginative involvement, using fiction in the service of truth in his choice of illustration for the lessons he had to teach, so that abstract ideas which had to be firmly grasped could be shown to be of immediate relevance to the actual business of living in the world, and the fundamental behavioural truth brought home without the possibility of intellectual confusion. For the disciples, however, it was necessary to spell out things which could not be so directly perceived. In Luke 8:10 the disciples receive assurance that they are indeed called in order to be taught things which others are still not ready to receive, or indeed, capable of understanding. They are identified as a particular kind of learning group, one brought together in order to acquire a particular skill, for the performance of which a special kind of information is needed.

It is worth noting that authorities on group dynamics lay considerable stress on the connection existing between task-performance and interpersonal communication — which, of course, depends on the quality of relationship within a group, notably its willingness to share information:

> When the nature of a task is such that it must be performed by a group rather than by a single individual, the problem of working relationships arises. One of the most important of these relationships is communication. (Bavelas, 1950)

With regard to the disciples' ability to carry out their task of evangelism by proclaiming abroad what they themselves now possessed of the knowledge of God in and through his Son, our immediate human tendency to get the facts out of perspective by filtering them through the lens of our own personality and prejudices receives its answer at Pentecost. Seen from this perspective, what took place on that occasion must be considered the educational event of all time, as 'all of them were filled with the Holy Spirit and began to speak in other languages as the Spirit gave them ability' (Ac 2:4).

The experience of being alive is registered for human beings through speaking, if not to others then to oneself, either as literal description or metaphor, in symbols which may make use of any of the senses, but are usually verbal. In the words of Peirce:

> 'Perfect accuracy of thought is unattainable, *literally unattainable.*'
> (1958, 381; author's italics)

Actual human experience, however, and the conclusions we draw from it is communicated by means of language. It certainly appears to be possible to learn in other ways, but not consciously. What is certain, however, is that for learning which will strike home and be translated into action, some kind of shared language is necessary.

- The disciples as members of a support group
  Foxes have holes and birds of the air have nests; but the Son of
  Man has nowhere to lay his head (Mt 8:20).

From the point of view of this groupwork model, Jesus is regarded not as a teacher but as the travelling companion of his disciples, and therefore of the rest of humanity. To see things from this point of view calls for a robust appreciation of the doctrine of Incarnation and a willingness to recognise the ordinary business of living as our 'common life in the Body of Christ' (Thornton, 1942), thus embracing our human as well as our divine fellowship with Christ, and moulding our own attitude and behaviour to his:

> You call me Teacher and Lord — and you are right, for that is what I am. So
> if I, your Lord and Teacher, have washed your feet, you also ought to wash
> one another's feet. (Jn 13:13, 14)

Jesus Christ supports his followers by demonstrating that he is actually their companion as well as their teacher. Ottaway describes the leadership of groups which are aimed at helping their members learn about growing in relationship with one another as being 'of a democratic or integrative kind, rather than an authoritarian or dominant kind' (1966, 7). In Philippians, St Paul describes the action of Christ, 'who, though he was in the form of God, did not regard equality with God as something to be exploited' (Php 2:6).

In support groups, the leadership passes from hand to hand among the group members, so that individuals may have practice in the skills of living with others and sometimes taking the initiative with regard to the direction taken by the learning process. The learning is about human behaviour towards others whose difficulties turn out to be very like one's own. This is essentially something which is carried out from within the group itself rather than being imposed from outside. Members learn how to obey St Paul's instruction that they should 'Bear one another's burdens, and in this way you will fulfil the law of Christ' (Ga 6:2), as they gain enhanced insight into their own motives and attitudes regarding their lives together. This is learning-as-sharing, aimed at learning to share. According to Yalom, it is 'what groups do best of all' (1995, 474).

- The disciples as members of a process-orientated group
  When he was at the table with them, he took bread, blessed and broke it, and gave it to them. Then their eyes were opened, and they recognised him: and he vanished from their sight (Lk 24:30, 31).

As leader of a group concerned with members' awareness of themselves as a group, the Incarnate Lord guides his disciples on the road from pre-occupation with the conflicting goals of individual members to a shared purpose and sense of corporate identity. It is a painful process, as all real change must be, for the old state of affairs must give way to something authentically new, and this always requires a kind of dying so far as the human spirit is concerned (*cf.* Eliade, 1958; Grainger, 1988). For the disciples it meant being caught up in Jesus's own agony and brought face to face with their own total inability to sustain the collapse of all their hopes and the spectacle of a shattered universe. Jesus said, 'I tell you, Peter, the cock will not crow this day until you have denied three times that you know me' (Lk 22:34). The result was that at the crisis point in the process of testing, when the disciples' identity as followers of Jesus was under an intolerable strain, as St Matthew records, 'all the disciples deserted him and fled' (Mt 26:56).

Of course, the story does not end here. As with Christ himself, the disciples' fellowship was reborn, its identity reasserted, not as a mere continuation of the old state of affairs, characterised by struggles for precedence and a state of mind governed wholly by the world's expectations concerning social organisation (*cf.* Mt 20:20; Mk 10:37). The situation described in Acts stands out in contrast to this: 'Now the whole group of those who believed were of one heart and soul . . . ' (Ac 4:32. The story of Ananias and Sapphira in the following chapter, alarming as it is, bears witness to the place of sincerity in the self-giving required, and expected by the first Christians).

All the same, God's purposes made use of human weakness and betrayal, as the part played in the divine drama of the New Creation by the figure of Judas Iscariot reveals. Peter's three-fold denial, Judas's betrayal, the self-righteousness of the religious leaders, the crowd's blood-lust all contributed to the death of the old human universe and the emergence of a new way of being human. All contribute to Christ's agony and consequently to the redemption of the world, nailed to the cross for our deliverance (Col 2:14).

The dissonance which is an inevitable part of the group process — the jealousies and resentments, the stubborn refusal to take account of the feelings of other people or to admit one's own vulnerability, the anger frequently turned against the leader simply because he or she is the leader — may not seem to bear comparison to the emotional conflict in which the disciples were involved. All the same, it is the fact of dissonance occurring during the course of the group which allows it to grow towards unity. Our experience of group-mediated change is not one involving the destiny of the entire human race; but all the same, there is a crucial moment in the experience of every member of a process group when truth about oneself which has up to now been kept safely hidden requires exposure. This is a 'moment of truth' which, somehow or other, has to be faced by each individual if he or she is to benefit from the group process. Yalom described self-disclosure as 'the microscopic representation of some of life's most crucial and painful issues' (1995, 365). It is a personal gesture of self-opening to a totally different kind of relationship towards other people, and constitutes the pain upon which all real transformations depend.

- The disciples as members of a *'self-help'* group
  When it was evening on that day, the first day of the week, and the doors of the house where the disciples had met were locked for fear of the Jews, Jesus came and stood among them and said: 'Peace be with you' (Jn 20:19).

Like their forefathers (*cf.* Ezr 3:3, 4:3), the followers of Jesus suffered persecution both on account of the message they were delivering and for the fact that, by delivering it at all, they were considered to be acting anti-socially or even blasphemously. Jesus himself had warned his disciples that such would be the case (Jn 15:18, 30), reminding them such was the worldly destiny of all who deliver the word of God to mankind (Mt 5:10, 12). The Acts of the Apostles certainly provides ample evidence of persecution of those who followed 'the way' (Jn 14:6), as, of course, does the entire history of the Christian Church from St Paul onwards:

We are afflicted in every way, but not crushed; perplexed but not driven to despair; persecuted but not forsaken, struck down but not destroyed; always carrying in the body the death of Jesus . . . (2 Cor 4:8–10)

Such is the origin of the term 'stigmatisation,' referring to the wounds suffered by Jesus on the cross (Mt 27:35; Mk 15:2; Lk 23:33; Jn 19:18). The fact that Jesus was crucified between two criminals identifies stigma itself as the badge of deviance, whether this be religious, social or both. Stigmatised individuals and groups regard themselves as the victims of an unjust social categorisation. To some degree or other they are persecuted 'for righteousness's sake,' in that they are suffering exclusion which they do not deserve (Abrams et al., 2004; see also Goffman, 1963).

For those whose faith is not as strong as St Paul's, or who have no religious belief to sustain them, social exclusion constitutes a major problem in living, not least because it leads to the formation of groups of people organised for aggressive-defensive purposes. This has the effect of increasing social alienation rather than decreasing it, by provoking 'responses which tend to establish a self-fulfilling prophecy and a downward spiral of self-pity' (Douglas, 1993, 130).

With regard to groups formed to give support to victims of stigma, Brown draws attention to a circular effect, which can take place:

> Certain kinds of groups can attract labelling and stigma, e.g. single-parents group, school-refusers group, sexual abuse perpetrator group, schizophrenics group, control or violence group. Some people's primary need is 'normalisation' and the last thing they want is group identity, reinforcing their stigmatised label. (1992, 16)

Thus, groups conceived as an escape from stigma have the effect of reinforcing it. They also draw attention to its presence so that the subject is drawn out into the open, away from secrecy and closed doors. For those whose mission is to reduce stigmatisation the presence of its victims, and of the measures they take to relieve their condition, has the benefit of bringing the problem before the attention of those who can do most to relieve it, the non-stigmatised majority. The result is a dialectical relationship between secrecy and exposure, courage and defensiveness, in which the fact that people may need the security of secrecy in order to be in a position to support one another may actually make them more effective instruments of social change than they would otherwise have been.

The emergence of 'self-help' groups created by ex-psychiatric patients (now referred to in Great Britain as 'service users') on strictly non-authoritarian and democratic lines has had a recognisable effect on the attitude of the general public to mental illness itself and more specifically, towards individual people diagnosed as suffering from it (Galbraith and Galbraith, 2008; Grainger, 1993,2009; see also Scull, 1977). Psychiatric 'service users', members of groups for those guilty of sexual abuse, asylum seekers, victims of alcohol or drug misuse, single parents, ex-prisoners — all are very different from many important points of view from Jesus's disciples. What they share is the need to take refuge in time of peril, whatever direction it may come from. As with the other groupwork approaches we have been considering, the relevance of this to pastoral theology is evident.

Groupwork is seen as a re-integrating experience. Groupwork analysts (Corey and Corey, 1997; Jacobs et al., 2002; Tuckman, 1965) describe the groupwork process as taking place in three identifiable phases, representing stages on the journey undertaken by the group. This is a familiar model of human change described in terms of corporate ritual practices by Van Gennep (1960), and reminiscent of the symbolism of the Hebrew *cultus* and its function as a marker on the journey to the 'land of promise' (Dt 10:11). The median phase of ritual symbolism is characterised by the iconography of chaos and disruption, as the old is cleared away in order to give place to the new (Grainger, 2010; Van Gennep, 1960). This stage, as it occurs in groupwork, is examined by Brown (1992) and also, in detail, by Corey and Corey (1997,

174ff). With regard to human behaviour outside the conscious symbolism of the *cultus*, the Old Testament account of the progress towards Jordan provides very convincing evidence of the fact that no real progress in the sphere of personal relations can be made without some degree of emotional and cognitive disruption. Old ideas and assumptions never give up that easily, but growth into maturity requires the ability to free oneself from the chains of the past which impede our progress (Erikson, 1985). The achievement of harmony and fellowship is as central to groupwork theory as it is to scripture. So, of course, is the need to have places of refuge (Jos 20).

Thus, although specific information regarding the characteristics of group experience is limited in scripture, the principles underlying groupwork find vivid expression in both Testaments. The covenant relationship between God and humankind provides the template for the mutual trust and acceptance which remains the ideal for any kind of groupwork. This is outstandingly the case with regard to groups within the Judao-Christian tradition, but the principle extends to groupwork practice everywhere. No group can function without it, for human groups require a covenant in order to realise their potential for being a genuine group of inter-relating persons, as distinct from a collection of individuals (Ottaway, 1966; Douglas, 1993).

The covenant relationship is associated with the idea of a shared existence within time, and hence with a view of human life which sees it as a journey to be undertaken in accordance with particular principles laid down by Yahweh himself and communicated by whoever occupies the pivotal position of Yahweh's officer to all his or her travelling companions along the way. This is still the underlying model of groupwork which is explicitly religious; but it remains in the background of all groups led, or organised by, those whose authority to direct operations has been officially recognised by constituent members of any group of individuals, even if such authority derives from within the group itself rather than any outside source. Groups of the kinds which we are concerned with in this book not only have leaders — people authorised by the group to be in charge of what is actually taking place at any stage of the process — they also have an itinerary, as indeed is bound to be the case with companions setting out on a journey.

The principles governing our relationship with God and one another which are established in the Old Testament find full realisation within the New, where they become presences rather than precepts and God shows himself to be incarnate within human community (Thornton, 1942, see also Mt 18:20). Here the seminal grouping is that of the twelve disciples, expanding both quantitatively and qualitatively in order to become the *koinonia*, the fellowship of the Christian Church, with a more comprehensive ethic than simply that of caring for 'those who love you' (Mt 5:46; Lk 6:32, 35). This is something which all groups must work together to achieve, and groupworkers have written extensively about it (Ottaway, 1966; Corey and Corey, 1997; Yalom, 1995; Douglas, 1993; Jacobs et al., 2002; Brown, 1992). The group format itself provides a structure for containing the discord, which always accompanies real human change (Grainger, 2003).

In short, the common life of the disciples who accompanied Jesus reveals some of the characteristics of groupwork considered in Chapter 1. We have looked at them here as:

- an action group, where learning is instrumental and goal-directed;
- an educational group, where the teaching is authoritative and task-orientated;
- a support group, the members of which depend on one another and the group as a whole;
- a process-orientated group, where learning is disclosed through members' interaction; and
- a self-help group, organised by its members for mutual defence.

Looking at the disciples from the point of view of group theory and practice underlines the pastoral importance of working with groups as well as individuals. Group awareness, the experience of sharing faith with friends, lies at the heart of religious belonging. At the same time, it is worth pointing out that students of social behaviour draw attention to a 'secular' spirituality which is implicit within groups which are not explicitly religious, yet are characterised by commitment to the group as something able to focus their experience of life and give a spiritual dimension to everything with which it comes into contact (Lord, 2006; Bailey, 2002).

Groupwork in Churches

(i) Bible study groups

The subject of groupwork in the Christian Church immediately suggests meetings organised for studying the Bible. At some time during the church year, frequently during the seasons of Lent (leading up to Easter) or Advent (in preparation for Christmas), many Christian congregations organise series of group meetings for the express purpose of studying the Bible together. Much of the mission activity of the churches of Great Britain during the last twenty five years has been focused upon promoting Bible study as widely and comprehensively as possible through the medium of campaigns aimed at those 'interested in learning about the Christian faith' (Alpha, 1993) — or indeed anyone who can be persuaded about the possibility of becoming so interested. These 'mission-initiatives' are inter-denominationally organised and, according to their own publicity, have been strikingly successful.

Two examples, *Alpha* (1993) and *Emmaus* (Cottrell et al., 1996),[1] are groupwork based, as so come within the area covered by this book under the heading of 'Groups directed towards cognitive learning.' They are to be included within this category because each of them, to some extent, involves the study of Biblical texts and the assimilation of information contained there, with the aim of persuading people to become Christians. The aim of traditional Bible study, whether undertaken at home or carried out under the auspices of the local church, is to refresh the human spirit and enable the student to 'grow in the Lord' by meditating on the work of God. This, however, is 'mission-directed' Bible study, aimed at conversion rather than growth, although it would certainly be wrong to suggest that the two things can really be separated and very many long-standing church members have found their faith strengthened and their commitment increased as a result of their church's decision to 'do *Alpha*.'

This is what *Alpha* aims to do. Operating on a much wider scale than any individual parish, *Alpha* is in a position to mount publicity campaigns of a size and intensity far beyond the reach of other organisers of Bible study groups. Its approach is more broadly based than that of traditional Lent courses or Confirmation classes, being led by a team of church members rather than a single individual whose job is to teach those who have come in order to learn. Here, it is more a case of the congregation, or some of its members, acting as host to newcomers. A meal is provided and an atmosphere of relaxed friendliness aims at removing any nervousness caused by memories of classrooms and of 'having to learn things' which may still be left over from childhood.

So far as the local church is concerned then, *Alpha* represents learning for the purposes of evangelisation. This involves a good deal of Bible study on the part of the members of the congregation involved, who are cast in the role of mediators of the Christian way of life and have therefore to feel confident enough of their own familiarity with the message which it is their job to hand on. According to their insert in the Church of England newspaper for June 8th, 2010, *Alpha* stands for 'The evangelisation of the nations and the transformation of society.' Most Bible study, in Britain at least, takes place on a more piecemeal basis and consists of small groups of people who have gathered together to read and discuss passages from the Bible which have been chosen by a person with more extensive knowledge of the Bible than they have themselves, usually someone who is ordained or a senior member of the congregation. It would be almost impossible to assess the value of such groups or to draw firm conclusions about their contribution to church life. They are often quite informal and tend to come and go rapidly as circumstances change within the life of a congregation. They tend not to keep any records of their proceedings, and certainly function without guidelines or manuals.

They are regarded as being for personal use only, to get to know the Bible better. Some of the courses described in the next section appear to be attempts to regulate this kind of behaviour, as being too hit-and-miss for the Church's purposes in an age when Christians ought to allow themselves to be organised in defence of the Gospel on a more systematic basis.

The persistence of this kind of group Bible study across the generations is testimony to the enrichment which comes from simply reading it together, letting the words sink in, and maybe sharing something so you find it easy to pray. (Personal communication)

This correspondent describes how, year by year, such groups form and re-form as members of the congregation to which he belongs respond to the arrival of Lent and Advent. There will, he writes, be some new members each year as other members of the congregation decide to join in and some of the older ones will probably decide that, this year, they would prefer to 'give it a rest,' Consequently, when it meets the group will always be a new one, although the practice itself is exceedingly well established:

At these times of the year we give ourselves the opportunity to learn more about what the Bible has to say to us, preferably from someone who knows more about it than we do. (Alpha, 1993)

In between these two extremes — *Alpha*, which is organised, authoritarian and mission-centred, and the semi-official, congregation-based, optional Advent/Lent groupings which characterise church life in Great Britain — are groups modelled upon *Emmaus*.

This is less prescriptive than *Alpha*, and draws more on the spiritual experience of group members. For example, Stage I in the overall process is headed 'Contact: ideas for meeting people where they are;' Stage II is 'Nurture: a fifteen session course for growing Christians;' Stage III is 'Growth: growing up as a Christian: five short courses for growing Christians' (Cottrell et al., 1996). As with *Alpha* the infrastructure requires the provision of a handbook setting out the procedures to be followed so that all the course components are properly covered. Members are required to ask themselves questions regarding their spiritual 'journey through life' and to share the answers with the other members of the sub-group to which they have attached themselves during the session.

These 'buzz groups' play a large part in *Emmaus* which, as its title suggests, concentrates on the idea of Christian belonging as a journey through life. This kind of personal material is more easily shared in small groups than larger ones, as the sense of sharing among sympathetic listeners, themselves involved in the same process, is greater when there are a few people rather than a crowd. This kind of shared testimony is not the main purpose of the session, however, as the course guidelines make clear; in fact the 'buzz groups' are included within the structure as a way of personalising the teaching elements. The instructions remind whoever is leading the session that 'the timings allow for one brief "buzz break" during the teaching input' (*Emmaus* Sampler Pack, Section 2).

Like *Alpha*, *Emmaus* depends on a combination of personal testimony and scriptural exegesis, the first element intended to support the second. Like *Alpha*, it is highly organised and authoritatively presented. Those taking part

52

are encouraged to use their imagination — here more than in *Alpha*, perhaps — but original views or opinions must bow to the leader's superior knowledge, in this case her or his understanding regarding what it is that should be learned from the course material. *Emmaus* concentrates on 'life as a journey,' but the landscape through which those taking part are led has been very carefully laid out in advance. The course is intended to bring home what the Bible has to teach us about life, and so encourage those taking part to identify the events in their own lives as possessing significance from the standpoint of their membership of a Christian congregation. As such it claims to be 'a vision for evangelism, nurture and growth in the local church' (*Emmaus* Sampler Pack).

This vision is extremely detailed, more like a blueprint or a road map. The format for each session makes extensive use of action methods: these are workshops, not lectures or sermons. Their identity as Bible study is not immediately obvious, because of the dominance of the metaphor of the journey and the vivid scenarios suggested by it. Nevertheless the intention to teach is powerfully present, because the lesson is one which belongs to the very heart of the Christian message. We are urged to reflect each evening whether we have been 'on the way' or 'in the way' that day (*Emmaus* Sampler Pack). By concentrating on its theme in such a systematic way, *Emmaus* hammers it home.

Alpha and *Emmaus*, along with other courses which have since been modelled on them, are not primarily intended as Bible study groups but as 'process evangelism' carried out via the medium of group learning. In both cases, discussion in small groups is an essential part of the project, but the topics discussed are not confined to scriptural exegesis. Because they are intended to help group members explore what is involved in being a member of a wider group, that of the Christian Church, they have to be arranged in ways which will capture the attention, not only of enquirers, but also of those who already belong to the church but are conscious that their belonging is in need of refreshment. *Emmaus* in particular embodies a deep awareness of the part played in the growth of Christian involvement by active experiences of group membership. According to Mark Ireland the four principles underlying the course are as follows:

1. Entry into faith is a process of discovery.
2. This process is best practised as an accompanied journey.
3. It is a process that affects the whole of our lives.
4. Effective initiation affects the life of the whole Church (Booker and Ireland, 2005, 37).

For *Emmaus*, initiation is by nurture as well as instruction. Their 'process evangelism' works to deepen belief through real experiences of belonging together. This is an implicit evangelism, in contrast to the explicit approach offered by *Alpha*. It has more to contribute to the study of human groups than *Alpha*, which pins its faith on individual testimony and 'the friendship and personal witness of a Christian' (Booker and Ireland, 2005, 19).

Both courses use the Bible, in the sense of consulting it, but neither of them is actually about it. Rather, they are concerned with nurturing belief through the experience of belonging. This is also true of the course entitled *Christianity Explored* (2001), although this involves more Bible study and has been evaluated as having 'a strong engagement with both the Bible and contemporary culture' (Booker and Ireland, 2005, 50). Mark Ireland describes *Alpha* and *Emmaus* (and by implication those courses modelled on them) as having 'a strong didactic content that starts with the Church's agenda rather than the agenda of those who are beginning to ask big questions about the meaning of life' (2005, 39).

In other words, although such courses differ from one another in style of approach, which often reflects the tradition of churchmanship in which they originated, whether this be evangelical or sacramentally centred and whether these are intended for in-house or extramural use, with 'enquirers' or members of the congregation — or, as in most cases, both at once, these courses all represent the Church talking, in a variety of ways, about itself. A comparison of contents between *Alpha* and the central section of *Emmaus* illustrates this similarity-in-difference:

Alpha
1. Christianity: Boring, Untrue and Irrelevant?
2. Who Is Jesus?
3. Why Did Jesus Die?
4. How Can I Be Sure Of My Faith?
5. Why And How Should I Read The Bible?
6. Why And How Do I Pray?
7. How Does God Guide Us?

    Weekend Away
8. Who Is The Holy Spirit?
9. What Does The Holy Spirit Do?
10. How Can I Be Filled With The Spirit?
11. How Can I Resist Evil?
12. Why And How Should We Tell Others?
13. Does God Heal Today?
14. What About The Church?
15. How Can I Make The Best Of The Rest Of My Life?

Emmaus Nurture
    What Christians Believe
1. Believing In God
2. Why We Need God In Our Lives
3. The Life And Ministry of Jesus
4. The Death And Resurrection of Jesus

5. The Holy Spirit
6. Becoming A Christian

How Christians Grow
7. Learning To Pray
8. Reading The Bible
9. Belonging To The Church
10. Sharing Holy Communion

Living The Christian Life
11. Living God's Way
12. Serving The Lord
13. Your Money And Your Life
14. Learning to Love
15. Sharing The Faith (adapted from Booker and Ireland, 2005).

On the evidence presented here, then, it appears that courses like *Alpha* and *Emmaus* are mainly directed towards instruction rather than enquiry. They teach group members Church doctrine and Christian beliefs, using the Bible to do this. Except in very limited and carefully monitored ways, they do not really encourage exploration on the part of individuals or groups of people. As we have seen, *Emmaus* represents a more flexible and imaginative kind of course than *Alpha*, evidenced in its choice of metaphor to provide it with the structure required to 'present its case' — for all these courses are basically apologetic.

On the whole, *Emmaus* comes across as more imaginative than *Alpha*, which may be one of the factors in the slow but steady increase in its popularity (see Booker and Ireland, 2005). For those used to attending church, there is an attractiveness in discovering rather than simply being informed, and this is true about the Bible as well as other things in life. The growing interest in theological circles in the study of story-telling (Wiggins, 1975; Stroup, 1981) has given rise to a new kind of Bible study, one based on the concept of the story as a 'metaphor for living' in which fiction can be used to mediate truth, as in the parables of Jesus. This is an intensely focused use of biblical narratives, in which a session of groupwork revolves around a single episode in or passage from the Bible that comes alive as group members apply its message to their own lives. Such an approach depends on members' willingness to imagine in the way they are used to doing when they listen to a particularly vivid or gripping narrative. Whether the story being shared is history or truth-through-fiction, it strikes home with the vivid immediacy of parable, and they find themselves drawn into the story according to the measure of their willingness to become involved.

This is what the poet Coleridge described as 'the willing suspension of disbelief;' what is being concentrated on is not the thing itself but a vivid account of it, one made vivid by shared imagination. There have been several attempts at using storytelling as a way of enabling group members to find the courage to share their life experiences with one another (*cf.* Gersie and King, 1990; Gersie, 1992; Brun et al., 1993; Cooper, 1997). I myself have used this approach with the aim of encouraging personal involvement in biblical narratives. A workshop format is adopted 'in which people look at stories together, working as a group. The purpose of this is to allow us to compare our own life-experiences with those of other people, thereby encouraging us to get under the skin of some very familiar Bible narratives and helping us to rediscover things we have heard many times before and think we know all about . . . ' (Grainger, 2002, 1).

The aim here is to facilitate 'an adventurous kind of Bible reading, which might perhaps be called a "Bible sharing" . . . ' (2002, 2). There is a link here with *Emmaus* through the idea of sharing learning as a journey: 'What is valuable from the point of view of a groupwork approach is not so much the conclusions reached as the experience of *simply sharing a journey*' (*ibid.*). The authors of *Emmaus* would almost certainly take issue with this last statement as, for them as for *Alpha*, conclusions are all-important: the journey must lead to commitment, otherwise there is no point to it. I take issue with this evangelising stance, as it is frequently counter-productive:

> telling people what to look for and what they ought to find may not be the best way to do the Bible justice, because it doesn't let it speak for itself. (Grainger, 2002, 2)

Traditional ways of using the Bible to lead people into the Christian faith have sometimes prevented them from taking its message personally, the only way of actually hearing what it has to say *to them*.

Certainly, *Emmaus* takes full account of the power of metaphor to influence behaviour, even to the extent of changing lives, but the systematic spelling out of the implications of the Gospel message, to borrow a metaphor from Alexander Pope, 'breaks a butterfly upon a wheel' (Pope, 1734). In fact, of course, neither *Alpha* nor *Emmaus* is mainly concerned with Bible study as such, but with education in Church membership — the first by means of its own special brand of evangelism, the second by systematic nurturing. In contrast, *The Beckoning Bible* (Grainger, 2002) adopts a less authoritarian approach, without handbooks or guidelines issued in advance. The preparation of group members takes place within the workshop itself, so that there is no attempt to ensure that those taking part will know what it is that they are expected to learn from the session. The Biblical narrative presents its challenge at the median point in the workshop, when it is most likely to receive attention because of its obvious relevance to what has been going on before, i.e. the memories which have been shared and the experiences which have been recognised. The workshops are arranged in groups of three for each Biblical episode, as against fifteen for *Alpha* and*Emmaus* Nurture. An example of such a workshop follows.

Ruth and Naomi
(Workshop I)

(You will need: paper (writing and drawing), pencils,
crayons and paints, modelling clay)

- Say hello to as many people as you can.
- Paint/draw/model an image expressing 'exile'.
- Explore with a partner feelings and memories about being away from home.
- Circulate, looking at other people's pictures/models. Leave a note by each picture/model saying how it makes you feel. Don't sign your notes.
- Collect the notes and hand them out to group members. Read what you've been given. Share notes, reflecting together on the kinds of feelings expressed.
- Read Ruth 1:1–22 around the group.
- *Personal response*: Write a letter from Ruth back in Judah to her sister-in-law who has returned to Moab. Collect the letters and re-distribute them.
- Write a letter in reply to the one that you have just received. Return both letters to their sender, who now reads them to the group.
- On a large sheet of paper, draw an image or write a word expressing the experience of exile revealed in each pair of letters.
- Discuss the ideas and feelings in some of these letters. Reflect together on the workshop itself, and join in informal prayer.
- Stand in a circle and say the Grace together, then say goodbye to one another (Grainger, 2002, 17).

This is more like a game or a drama that the group members are engaged in acting out together than a traditional Bible Class using proof-texts. As with all approaches which are art (i.e. imagination) based, it is essentially non-prescriptive. This allows a kind of learning which actually leads to a more profound spiritual experience for those taking part (Grainger, 2010, 2002, 2009, 2003).[1]

(ii) Support and team-building groups

In the last section we glanced briefly at two group approaches, *Alpha* and *Emmaus*, both of which are mainly concerned with what Booker and Ireland (2005) refer to as 'process evangelisation.' It is quite clear, however, that courses such as these can also be used for purposes of support and team-building, and be directed towards the members of an existing congregation in order to reinforce their sense of belonging — within the Church — as 'members of the Body of Christ' (1 Cor 12:27). This aspect of evangelisation is more evident in *Emmaus* than *Alpha*; but there can be little doubt that seeking to bring others to a knowledge of Christ has a strengthening effect on one's own faith. 'I never really feel I believe in Jesus until I tell someone else about Him' (A psychiatrist: personal communication).

According to Booker and Ireland (2005), one third of the people involved in *Alpha* in the first years of the new millennium were helpers or leaders drawn from the host congregation. This kind of 'friendship-based evangelism' may be effectively directed towards fellow Christians as well as 'enquirers.' All the same, the *Emmaus* approach may have more impact within a church congregation than the more direct but less personal *Alpha* presentation for, as a local ministry advisor remarked to Mark Ireland in *Evangelism — which way now*:

> Sitting passively for virtually an hour to watch a tape 'lecture-style' is far less effective for adult learning than the interactive reflective method of the *Emmaus* course, which is far more engaging. (Booker and Ireland, 2005, 23)

Emmaus, in particular, has been used successfully as a congregational team-building strategy. An investigation carried out in 2003 within the Diocese of Lichfield showed *Emmaus* not only performing well among non-churchgoers, but also performing significantly better than any other published course in helping churchgoers to make a commitment of faith (Booker and Ireland, 2005, 36). The argument put forward in this book concerns group-work involving those who are already members of church congregations. In the case of initiatives intended to provide support and encouragement for existing members of a congregation by involving them more deeply in the life and mission of the Church, the influence of *Emmaus* is quite clearly visible, as we shall see in the following section. Although team-building as such is not usually mentioned in the various handouts provided, the aim of encouraging group awareness — the consciousness on the part of individuals that they also possess an identity as a group — is implied in *Alpha* and explicit in *Emmaus* and the courses inspired by it.

Booker and Ireland (2005) list several such courses, notable among which are *Christianity Explored* (2001), *Start* (2003), *The Y Course* (Meadows and Steinberg, 1999), *Catholic Faith Exploration* (1996) and *Foundations of Faith* (Hulsey, 2003). They point out that many local churches have followed suit by putting together their own versions of the 'nurture group' format origi-nated by *Emmaus* in 1996. Within the Church of England such courses have emerged at diocesan level so that they may be offered to parishes. The aim has been to promote solidarity and reinforce commitment, for which courses devised and run along the lines of *Emmaus* Nurture are considered eminently suitable. It should, however, be pointed out that *Emmaus* itself was not orig-inally conceived as a team-building group but as an exercise in 'process evangelism' aimed at increased understanding of the Church and its teachings. All the same, a sense of being securely held within 'the safe ark of the Church' is extremely valuable for those in need of support, particularly the emotional kind. All groupwork, as Brown reminds us, provides us with a method of helping groups as well as individuals, and it can help individuals and groups to influence and change personal, group organisational and community problems. (1992, 8)

In Great Britain awareness of the advantages of groupwork as a resource for Christian congregations goes back to the 1960s. In an article in *Contact* dealing with 'various types of church-related small groups,' Michael Hare-Duke writes:

Interaction in small groups is becoming a major preoccupation of contemporary society. It seems to offer a solution to many of our inherited social, educational and psychological problems, even to give promise of a new kind of society'. (1967, 1)

He goes on to claim that, in his view 'these small face-to-face groups are really the place in which Christian experience can most effectively grow.' The growth of the 'cell church movement' in Great Britain owes much to these early Christian groupwork enthusiasts (see Jackson, 2002; Booker and Ireland, 2005). In the same article, Hare-Duke points out that Christians, above all, have problems with coming to terms with unacceptable feelings about themselves and their relationships with other people. This, he says, applies particularly to hostility, which Christians have been taught to regard as unacceptable.

The more Christian we are, the more guilty we feel about our hostility and so the more we hide it. Yet the fact is that it is there in almost every group, and until it is acknowledged the way forward into a real exchange is blocked. (Hare-Duke, 1967, 4; see Ottaway, 1966; Yalom, 1995)

The blockage, says Hare-Duke, is removed by the confidence individuals feel as members of a group of people brought together for a single shared purpose, each of them exposed to and confirmed by her or his neighbour. This feeling of security has the effect of revealing to us the extent of our own defensiveness; we begin to be aware of the possibility of revealing ourselves to one another and of the peace of mind this would allow us to have.

Thus, both our self-centredness and our longing for engagement with other selves are highlighted by this focused experience of group belonging. The result is an embodiment of Tillich's paradigm of 'accepting acceptance because I am unacceptable' (1962, 159–163). In Hare-Duke's words,

Within the group a security is built up in the context of which it is possible to learn things about oneself which were previously too painful to acknowledge. (1967, 6)

The result is release of inner tensions, a sense of 'the courage to be' (Tillich, 1962, *passim*), an experience of relatedness to others which comes from the

(margin handwritten note: also gives access to truth that cannot be learned any other way)

permission to relax our defences, to relax into *ourselves*, by which is meant our whole selves and not simply that embattled space with which we are so familiar. It is of course always the other who gives us this permission. Freedom from what we have made of ourselves comes from other people and from God himself. After considering the emergence of 'cell churches' based on the life of small groups of Christians engaging in exploration and celebration of their membership of one another through and in Christ (Ro 12:5; 2 Cor 12:20, 27; Eph 4:25), Hare-Duke concludes as follows:

> When one considers the possibilities of life in a cell in these ways it becomes possible to wonder whether as, in our generation we have become increasingly aware of the meaning of human relationships, this may not be the most appropriate way in which we should endeavour to grow in the spiritual life . . . Such an experience would thoroughly revolutionise the life of many existing church members. (1967, 7)

These possibilities are still being explored (Malphurs, 2009; Gladen, 2011).

More than forty years ago, then, the possibility of a Church that used groupwork as a principal way of expressing its experience of belonging was being mooted in some circles within the Church of England. In the same issue of *Contact* Laurence Reading drew attention to the fact that this will certainly be a learning process, for groups work the same way for Christians as they do for other folk:

> It is a little shattering to discover that the forces which are released when men [sic] meet together are not suspended when the group is a specifically Christian one. (1967, 23)

Perhaps it is because a group, in order to run its course to best effect — to work satisfactorily as a group, that is — is bound on the way to run into a measure of turbulence. This will be more pronounced in 'process' groups, those in which the interaction of members constitutes the main source of learning, than in ones in which instruction is ministered to the group by someone who, however hard they join in the various team-building exercises, is definitely not themselves a member. One might even say that their non-membership is the salient characteristic of their relationship to the actual group: there is little doubt that they are involved in the process at every stage as teacher, not learner. In process-orientated groupwork, as we have seen, the group focus shifts between member and member — and as the focus moves, so does the distribution of authority within the group. Obviously, if the purpose of those in charge of the learning process is to retain control of the proceedings by avoiding all occasions of trouble, particularly ones which require authority to put itself in any danger of being undermined, this kind of group presents very real problems. In process-orientated groups, these may not concern matters of belief, which may not be directly questioned, but things to do with the experience of being human:

> The problems of acceptance and rejection, of conformity and rebellion, of death and life, would not be academic discussion subjects but aspects of their own experience together. (Reading, 1967, 26)

What Reading calls 'the facing together of the tensions inseparable from all real meeting' is almost bound to make this kind of group appear considerably harder to accommodate within a hierarchically organised church than traditional learning groups in which what the teacher says — or reads — is rarely questioned and never contradicted. Perhaps this is one reason why process-evangelism continues to make more headway than the cell church as the preferred type of groupwork in the Church of England (Booker and Ireland, 2005). In *Emmaus* and its successors, the need to discuss and consequently explore what it is that is being communicated is recognised and, to some extent, provided for, while responsibility for the truth of what is being taught is placed firmly outside the domain of whomever is occupying the leader's role. It is a case of following the script and keeping extemporisation to a minimum.

As we shall see in the next section, the underlying purpose of these *Emmaus*-type courses would appear to be support and team-building rather than evangelisation. The genre remains the same: groupwork that is prescriptive and directed, in which the Bible provides evidence for existing Church beliefs and procedures. These courses have as their aim the provision of support by reinforcing the terms of belonging: the re-evangelisation of an existing membership. In terms of the distinction made by Palmer, they are 'task' rather than 'sentient' groups. In other words,

> The effectiveness of the group is judged by its success in carrying out a task rather than by whether or not its members gain personal satisfaction from working in a group. (1972, 17)

A 'sentient' group, on the other hand,

> exists to meet the emotional needs of the members for a sense of belonging, acceptance, security, fellowship and purpose. (*ibid.*)

Palmer draws an important distinction between 'sentience' and Christian formation. Writing more than thirty years ago, he expresses a disdain for any kind of groupwork 'based on mutual gratification,' which may go some way towards explaining the Church of England's continuing neglect of the opportunities for personal growth offered by process-orientated groups:

> Such groups may meet an important social and psychological need in enabling men and women to relax some of the defences which prevent them from

[handwritten marginal note: what about TRUST?]

61

making human contact with one another. But to interpret this experience in one way or another as a redemptive encounter with Christ is to fall between flesh and spirit and thus to promote paganism in the guise of Christianity. (Palmer, 1972, 25)

In other words 'social and psychological need' has to be distinguished from the requirements of preaching the gospel. Judging by the current absence of process-orientated groups from the official groupwork provision made by Church of England dioceses, this distinction — between learning about oneself and receiving instruction in Christian belonging — still carries weight. It is, however, an invalid one, as there is no reason at all why the group process in itself should exclude the possibility of Christian testimony, and every reason why the introduction of such material into a free-flowing discussion about motives, feelings and anxieties, in which those taking part feel genuinely free to be honest about themselves and one another, should make such testimony valuable as a way of learning about Christianity.

discipleship

(iii) Current groupwork in the Church of England

In April 2003, the Archbishops' Council of the Church of England published a report which was to have a considerable effect on groupwork within local churches. This was *Formation for Ministry within a Learning Church: The Structure and Funding of Ordination Training* (Archbishops' Council, 2003). It was mainly concerned with the clergy, but its scope was to be wider than that: 'formation for ministry' necessarily involved addressing the ministry of lay people within the Church, and the contribution this must make to the work of its 'official' Ministers in promoting the Kingdom of God: 'We are convinced that collaborative ministry is essential both in principle and practice' (2003, 3.4). In line with this, 'academically accredited' programmes should be produced, focusing on 'deepening the knowledge and understanding of the Christian faith in order to inform discipleship, ministry and mission' (2003, 5.22).

The proposals issued subsequently as *Education for Discipleship* (Archbishops' Council, 2005) begin with the words from the 2003 Report: 'Learning is a task and gift for the whole people of God' (2005, 3). Clearly stating that they 'grow out of the aspirations of the 2003 Report,' they claim to represent a desire on the part of the entire Church to become what it calls 'a Learning Church.' In view of what is described here as 'a marked increase in the provision of enquirers, access and foundation courses in many individual congregations,' a blueprint is offered for

a structured 'Education for Discipleship' programme is offered so that, within the context of a Church engaged in the ongoing task of encouraging all Christians in their growing discipleship, opportunities are available to enable lay Christians to develop their learning further. (2005, 3)

In the wake of the 2003 report (usually referred to as the Hind Report after its Chairman, Bishop John Hind), several Church of England dioceses adopted their own versions of the kind of educational instrument advocated in *Education for Discipleship*. Generally speaking these follow the *Emmaus* pattern rather than the one suggested by *Alpha*, except that the educational emphasis is greater and the 'process evangelisation' one less pronounced. In some of them the aspect of mission and evangelisation has been changed into a concern that the laity themselves should be taught how to welcome enquirers. The contents lists of most of them include workshops combining instruction on various themes connected with membership of the Church in its universal and local manifestations with sharing of experiences among group members. The following is a partial indication of a scene that continues to develop. At present it indicates a tendency on the part of contributing dioceses to equate discipleship with 'knowing the Faith' as opposed to other qualifications for Christian belonging.

Out of 22 Church of England dioceses contacted who replied to the invitation to supply information regarding groupwork, 19 reported that on-going courses were provided by the diocese. (For a summary of these protocols see Appendix A: Groupwork provision in Church of England dioceses.) Some of these courses see 'education for discipleship' as enabling congregations to acquire new skills in ministry and hone their proficiency regarding ones they already possess (see Bath and Wells, Norwich, Oxford, Portsmouth, Worcester, York). They are concerned with passing on information rather than sharing experience. Several of the courses cited here see discipleship in the way it was presented by *Emmaus* — as a spiritual journey to be undertaken rather than a theorem to be understood. Thus Chichester, Coventry, Derby, Gloucester, Leicester, Lincoln, Rochester, Salisbury, Southwell and Nottingham, and St Albans all adopt the approach exemplified below by Diocese of St Edmundsbury and Ipswich (2002) and Diocese of Wakefield (2008) before and after the emergence of *Education for Discipleship* (2005). See, for example, the following extracts from the St Edmundsbury and Ipswich and Wakefield courses:

Way Ahead

Term I, Session I: Well-Trodden Faith

1. Gathering and Welcome:
    * Leaders will help you introduce yourselves to one another. They will briefly introduce 'Way Ahead.'
2. Meet the Saints:
    * With the Saints cards provided, build up stories of the lives of some East Anglian Saints and other Christians who have shaped the life of the Church. Share the stories in the whole group.

- Make a rough timeline on a large sheet of paper and write their names on it in the right order. You can add any other-local Saints that you know about.

3. Discuss together:
   - What makes a Saint? Try writing a list of desirable attributes under such headings as: Gender, Skills, Education, Personal qualities, Background, Experience, Age, Qualifications.
   - In the light of your list and the East Anglian Saints, write a brief definition of a Saint.

4. Reflect:
   - Maybe you are some of today's East Anglian Saints? Write the names of every group member. This will help you to pray for each other during the week. You might like to use the 'Way Ahead' prayer in your closing worship.

(Diocese of St Edmundsbury and Ipswich, 2002)

Transforming Lives

Lent, 2009 — Encountering Jesus
1. Welcome and 'ice-breakers'
   - You are given £100 as a birthday present. How would you spend it? Share your answer (no conferring).
2. Introductory prayer (provided in printed course material)
3. Bible reading
   - Listen together to the account of someone's meeting with Jesus (Nicodemus; the woman at the well; the man born blind; Lazarus; Jesus tempted himself).
   - Discuss and share questions arising from the Bible passage. How do these things affect *your* life?
4. Activities
   - Read something you think is related to the Bible passage OR Give an account of a change in your own life brought about by an important encounter.
   - Discuss how we cope with this kind of change.
5. Worship
   - Set form of service built round the Bible reading and its relevance to the lives of those taking part.

(Diocese of Wakefield, 2008)

These two sample groupwork sessions are dated six years apart, but the kind of groupwork has not changed. They are included here as representatives of the most common type of diocesan groupwork course current within the Church of England in 2010. Their principal characteristics are
- the use of imagination to produce involvement
- the use of structure to define process

64

- an authoritative approach with regard to content
- 'indirect directiveness:' a prescriptive intention communicated via metaphor rather than head-on.

These courses reveal an awareness of the power of small-group process first recognised by the Church in the 1960s, now used for a specific purpose: communicating the Christian world view.

To summarise then, the Covenant Principle, which underpins both Testaments and is implicit within the group as a human phenomenon, is made explicit in Christian groups which find their original model in Jesus's twelve disciples. The tradition of groups coming together in this way to study the Bible stretches back into history, but during the last twenty years large-scale groupwork initiatives designed for the purpose of building up congregations — both numerically and with regard to commitment — have become an important feature of church life within the Church of England. These are designed for straightforward evangelisation (e.g. *Alpha*) or for team-building among those who are already Christians and members of a congregation. This movement has become more pronounced with the emergence, at an official level, in investment in group experience as a token and pledge of wider belonging, so that 'the medium is the message' (McLuhan and Fiore, 1967).

Note

1   *Alpha* was published in 1993, although the course originated some years earlier, at Holy Trinity Church, Brompton, London. In 2008, 33,500 *Alpha* courses were being offered in 163 different countries throughout the world. *Emmaus* originated in the Church of England Diocese of Wakefield. Owing to its flexibility it has had an influence out of all proportion to its publicity and marketing resources (Booker and Ireland, 2005). Up to now, *The Beckoning Bible* (Grainger, 2002) has been used by four congregations in Yorkshire, UK.

3

The Structure of Group Learning

The place of structure in learning

In this chapter we take a closer look at the structure of Christian group learning, adding some empirical research involving the experiences of group members. We have been dealing in the last two chapters with the range of purposes for which groupwork of any kind, including Christian group-work, has been put to use.

Each particular purpose depends for its effectiveness upon its own variation of the basic format of the 'small group,' in which a handful of people interact in order to learn about things connected with the business of life in the world — on being taught by someone outside the group, by teaching one another through their interaction within the group, or by using the group structure as a safe jumping-off place for creative imagination. The group is always about learning in the broadest sense, which involves growing in faith, nurturing relationships and understanding oneself and other people better; what changes is the role which the group itself, as a corporate identity, sees itself playing in relation to whatever it is that must be learned, as pupil, researcher or artist.

St Paul reminds us of the necessity for Christians to be taught wisdom, 'So that we may present everyone mature in Christ (Col 1:28). 'Teaching,' 'wisdom,' 'maturity:' the three things go together. We talk about 'education in discipleship' (see previous chapter). It would be hard or even impossible to conceive of a process of education which does not involve the creation of structures for learning. Just as a growing child learns to walk because there is a floor on which to do it, so the human mind tests itself, and grows, by relating thoughts and feelings to one another to make concepts, the process which we call 'making sense of things.'

> Man looks at his world though transparent patterns or templates which he creates and then attempts to fit over the realities of which the world is composed. (Kelly, 1991a, 7)

In this quotation, Kelly uses structures (i.e. words) to describe the construction process whereby we arrive at words in order to present to ourselves, and hence to others, whatever it may be that we perceive, as 'each man contemplates in his own personal way the stream of events on which he finds himself so swiftly borne' (1991a, 3).

The amazing fact makes even a psychologist poetical, poetry itself being a supreme example of what is being described here; for it is precisely in poetry that the mind reaches out to make sense of what cannot be captured in prose. In poetry the pressure to discover the right structure for making sense is more intense than ever, poetry being, as Coleridge says, 'the best words in the best order' (1827) — the best word being the most expressive, not the one most rigidly defined. As Kelly points out, the action of 'tightening' perception in order to arrive at conclusions has to be relaxed in order to allow the possibility for new insights to be welcomed into the sense-making process (1991a, 378, 379).

As the Gestalt psychologists realised (Mackewn, 1997; Perls et al., 1973), human beings identify meaning with shape, and their need for contact with one another and the world which contains them is perceived by them as what May describes as 'a passion for form' (1976, 124), not simply a form, but form itself. The mind functions by imaging forth a series of pregnant solutions to the problems of living, thinking and feeling which it continues to perceive, creating as it goes along its own search for conclusions. This is the way we make sense of what happens to us, perpetually adjusting our immediate world-structure to take account of interior and exterior changes which must be brought into line with our master plan, the things about life and death which we experience as unchangeable. These things are fundamental to what might be called the 'general' sense we make of the situations in which we find ourselves; but in order to stay rooted in them we have perpetually to make adjustments to the sense we make of the 'details.' Kelly talks of 'superordinate' and 'subordinate' constructs within our 'personal construct system' (1991a, 353, 354), the point being that our way of perceiving remains a system, and consequently must be consistent within itself; but in order to achieve this self-consistency it has, at some level or other, to keep adjusting to take account of the flux of events, calling upon those central, pivotal understandings and values which are able to focus our experience of being human. For psychologists of the Gestalt and Personal Construct persuasion, perception is global rather than linear, in that the connections the mind makes in order to describe itself and its world emerge from and are organised by value rather than logic.

Personal Construct Psychology (Burr and Butt, 1992; Bannister and Fransella, 1971; Kelly, 1991b) demonstrates the pre-eminence of considerations about value in the way we process our thoughts: we do not simply have a 'sense of value' as though valuing were merely one of the many ways in which we perceive the world and what happens in it; it is our crucial awareness of value which actually allows us to make sense. Recognising what we regard as worthwhile guides the way in which we experience everything in life which comes our way. Valuing is what makes sense of sense.

Value is used to organise logic in order to create meaning in the form of experiences which possess value *because they mean something*. As such they can stand by themselves, as things or thoughts about things, which possess their own completeness. In other words, they are definite statements; they can be used to argue with — you might say that such was their main purpose — but they are not simply parts of an existing argument. In themselves they are propositions, ideas validated by their self-consistency as possessing meaning, and consequently available for the purpose of expanding thought and promoting action.

Learning depends on these things. Data must be both significant in itself and indicative of other significances. As May says, 'You can live without a father who accepts you, but you cannot live without a world that makes sense to you' (1976, 127). May is not suggesting, of course, that living without a father is in any way to be recommended and, in a sense, the two ideas are closely connected because having a father and feeling that life possesses structure march hand in hand in the psycho-spiritual awareness of human beings. In dreams, says Jung, 'it is always the father figure from whom the decisive convictions, prohibitions and wise counsels emanate' (1972, 92, 93).

It should be noted that Jung's view of paternal influence upon the developing child is considerably more positive than the classical psychoanalytic position, which often appears to regard the father's role as straightforwardly repressive, as the main instrument of what Freud identifies as the 'superego,' which 'restricts the activity of the ego by means of prohibitions and punishments and facilitates or compels the setting up of repressions' (1940, 52).

There can be little doubt that a growing human being is able to put 'convictions, prohibitions and wise counsels' (to use Jung's phrase) to good use, so long as they are communicated in ways which encourage her or him to work out who he or she is, and more importantly, wants to be — that is, with kindness, understanding and clarity.

Clarity in particular: mixed messages or, worse still, ones which are self-contradictory have a damaging effect in learning of any kind (Laing and Esterson, 1970; Laing, 1965; Bateson, 1973), a fact of which every teacher is aware:

> I find myself doing what I was taught at college, telling the children the same thing three times . . . (Personal correspondence)

Just as the business of making sense is a structured operation, so is the task of passing sense on to others. Incoming data is recognised, processed and included within the system whereby we know things (Gregory, 1974). According to this model, the most effective way of teaching is:

- by drawing attention to the opportunity to take in material of interest, to be used for purposes of extending the scope of sense-making
- by presenting this material as clearly and directly as possible
- by registering its identity as information received and capable of inclu-

sion within the network of inter-related ideas and judgements which comprises an individual's 'construct system.'

The way something is understood remains personal to the individual concerned. The way it is presented, however, lies firmly in the hands of the teacher. Both operations involve a three-fold system, that of the teacher being the most obviously tripartite: 'Tell them you're going to do it; do it; tell them you've done it.' This is the way we both learn and teach, but not the way we rationalise. Kempe points out that 'It is characteristically human to think in terms of dyadic relations: we habitually break up a triadic relation into a pair of dyads' (1889, 21).

In other words, in our determination to be precise and tie things down into simple cause and effect, we have a tendency to overlook the heart of the matter, the free-flowing centre, which is the part we cannot control without holding it firmly between things we have an intellectual grip on. To do this is to cancel it out, as an idea if not as a presence, by re-distributing it, dividing it up between ideas which we can grasp and manipulate. The problem is, that it is the middle part, the part we 'leave out of the equation' which drives the conclusions which we reach. It is obvious, of course, why we do this: it is simply because this is the unthinkable part, the stage at which we do not know, or don't know yet, and as such it is better forgotten. The model of actual human behaviour, however, is necessarily tripartite, as the one who chooses considers a particular course of action and wonders whether it is the right one, then decides either for or against it. It could be argued that the behaviour of men and women with regard to one another has the same shape, as we relate to each other within the context of all other relationships, and against a background of the whole universe of personal responsibility, what we usually refer to as 'being involved.' We are accustomed to choosing who or what we become involved with (or at least we think we are!), and the significance of this is brought forcibly home by the kind of situation we recognise as an eternal triangle in which all our awareness is directed towards the psychological struggle to find a way of reducing three to two and somehow rescuing our peace of mind.

As human beings, we are not looking for trouble, and the kind involved in not being able to think through things threatens our sense of autonomy — hence our tendency toward this particular kind of reductionism. Three-ness is hard to ignore, however. Whether we like it or not, our awareness remains a threefold phenomenon, consisting of two movements of intellectual control surrounding one of cognitive-emotional flux in which the hold exercised by our received ideas is unloosed and we are open to change, *when we eventually know what it will be like* . . .

The Christian Creeds present the historical facts concerning Christ in three distinct stages, revolving around the unthinkable ('He was crucified, died and was buried. He descended to the dead' *The Apostles' Creed*). Indeed, the Christian doctrine concerning God Himself is tripartite, although Spirit

Himself abides in escaping all attempts at definition (*cf.* Jn 3:8). Euclid is traditionally supposed to have called three 'the number of perfection,' perhaps because it is the prototype of putting things together to achieve a result. Certainly there can be no *betweenness*, and therefore no actual relationship without the presence of an activating absence. Ways of knowing what things are, or how they work, from plans of the human psyche to the arrangements we make for ordering the things which together make up our shared world, all conform to the 'rule of three,' as in 'before-after,' 'inner-outer,' 'above-below' etc., each of which relies upon the median position (located here as a hyphen) in order to be thought of as both connected to and separate from the other. The human experience of change involves this intervening condition, which occurs between 'before' and 'after,' and so does any effective learning about life and death.

Jung sees three-ness as an archetype, symbolising a truthfulness which is transcendental, 'which from time immemorial, and particularly in the Christian religion, has been regarded as a symbol of the pure abstract spirit' (Jacobi, 1942, 47n). In practical terms it signifies a situation actively changed, a finished gesture or statement, bearing the weight of authority. 'What I tell you three times is true,' says Lewis Carroll's Bellman. Thus what is achieved in the three-fold learning process is a real change of mind, however slight this may appear to be. In some way or other, the way we think or feel is now different. The structures we use to make sense of ourselves and other people, to draw our conclusions and guide our actions are altered, even though the change may only be incremental, but this is the way structural change takes place and traumatic reversals are avoided (Kelly, 1991b).

In the following pages it will be argued that each of the three types of groupwork we are considering — directive, process-orientated and creative/imaginative — conforms to the basic learning paradigm according to the process whereby, in Piaget's words, 'the organism changes by assimilating the external and accommodating itself to this assimilation' (1953, 7). It does not do this immediately, simply by being brought into contact with a new experience, giving rise to a new way of organising the available data, but in a series of stages, each of which alters the conditions under which perception comes about, relating what is new to what has happened previously and at the same time distinguishing it from it. To use a metaphor, the picture changes from frame to frame, moving from an initial impression to an established conclusion, the recognition of an identifiable object of perception, via an intermediate phase of searching for stability and definition.

If this is the case with regard to individuals, we should not be surprised to find it so with a group's perception of itself. It is a common theme among groupwork specialists that changes in people's awareness of themselves which have occurred during the course of a group's progress do not happen at once, and certainly not easily; when they do happen it is as a result of a process of working through conflicts which have arisen and barriers to progress which they and the other members have succeeded in overcoming, conflicts and barriers which have emerged as a result of their experiences within the group milieu, concerning feelings about and attitudes towards both themselves and other people. Groupwork is characteristically described in terms of a process of 'before' and 'after,' in which the inevitability of some degree of intervening conflict is stressed as an obligatory stage to be passed through before a group can begin to achieve its full potential in fulfilling the purpose for which it was formed in the first place. Writing in 1965, Tuckman distinguished three stages which he saw as preceding the 'performing' stage: 'forming,' 'storming' and 'norming', the latter representing a return to stability in the form of a stronger sense of group identity. Corey and Corey throw light on 'storming' which they see as the emergence of resistance, caused by individuals' 'defensive behaviour' during the stage of 'transition' between a group's 'initial' and 'working' stages (1997, 134–162). Jacobs et al. identify the central stage as the actual 'working stage' of the group, precisely because it gives rise to the thoughts and feelings from which new attitudes emerge:

> This is when the members should be working, learning and drawing maximum benefit from being in a group. (2002, 257)

However, there is general agreement that they do not emerge without struggle. Ottaway describes this central phase as the occasion when 'emotional learning' is born. For him the stages in the group's life history facilitate maturity not only in the group itself, which is now able to see itself as a kind of unity, but in the emotional life of its individual members:

> I am describing a teaching method from which the students learn more efficiently than by other methods . . . Emotional learning is beginning to take place. (1966, 40)

What he is describing here is the transition from Stage I ('Orientation') to Stage III ('Emotional Involvement'), the point at which, he says, the group process begins to work as defensiveness gives way to genuine sharing and the way the group functions is noticeably changed. Thus the structure of the group, its organisation into beginning, middle and end, corresponds to an inner change taking place within the hearts and minds of those taking part which both allows and reflects it. All of which corresponds to Yalom's opinions regarding the value of groupwork for the growth of personal relationship (Yalom, 1995; ch. 1: Types). The movement between stages in the process is not something which can be tied down, particularly in process-orientated groups. It is important for an understanding of this kind of group to recognise that Ottaway did not set out to design a three-part process; at some point, however, he felt the ground move beneath him as the structure of the group readjusted to the changes taking place within it (1966, 40ff.).

Directive groups

The following is an examination of the structure of a session taken from *Transforming Lives* (Diocese of Wakefield, 2008, Study group material, Lent 2009).

Format of Week I
1. General introduction
    This is the first of five sessions looking at some key areas of church life: our worship, the way we care for each other (and others); how we grow in faith; how we share our faith; and how we engage with our communities.

    Through each week we will be exploring some of the connections between God, 'me' and others . . . and the difference faith makes (Diocese of Wakefield, 2008, 57).
2. Introduction to Week I (*Look to God together*)
    Today's session looks at worship. Much of this is about what happens when Christians meet at church (or elsewhere). But remember that 'worshipping God' is not something we do only in a special place or on a special day. It is something we are called to do with our whole lives (Diocese of Wakefield, 2008, 57).
3. The session itself
    1. 'Worship'
        (Leader and members recite an appropriate psalm together antiphonally, followed by two prayers, the first said by Leader, the second said in unison.)
    2. 'Introduction'
        This being the first session, and it may be the first time people have met one another, they are instructed to turn to their neighbour and ask them about their earliest church memory and also their attitude to church at age twenty. This information should then be shared with the rest of the group.
    3. 'Opening activity'
        The Leader asks members to arrange strips of paper, each of which bears the name of a particular part of the communion service, in their 'proper' order. He/she then asks the group to discuss the following questions: why these particular sections? Why in this order? Which part is the most helpful to you? Have you any tips which would make any of the parts more helpful?
    4. 'True worship'
        The Leader cites Rom. 12 to underline the central importance of worship for Christians. He/she then asks the group questions about what Paul's words signify for members; which one of the five other quotations (non-Biblical) included here is most helpful or interesting?

5. 'Worship changes lives'
   The Leader asks members to imagine coming to church for the first time in 3 separate sets of circumstances: aged 6, with parents for cousin's baptism; aged 86, not having attended since much younger; aged 36. He/she described the different functions worship performs for different individuals, asking the group what they would say to someone who came to church in order not to have to think at all (i.e. after a very busy week), and then asks, Why do *you* come?

6. 'Fresh expressions'
   The Leader describes the strategy of some churches who offer their members 'worship options' by having a range of services on consecutive Sundays. He/she invites their comments. Leader informs members about 'Fresh Expressions' as an emerging movement within the Church: "new styles of worship to try and appeal to different people and their needs." Does the group approve? Would members approve if their church started something along these lines? Two 'extra' sections included here draw attention to suggestions "included in Appendix I. Hopefully during the session you and your group will have spotted a number of things that might be done to strengthen your church's worship . . . Tell your church your ideas."

7. 'Worship'
   The Leader conducts a short act of worship to close the session. This is included in the written instructions provided for those taking part, Leader and members. It consists of an antiphonally-recited psalm and a choice of 2 set prayers whose theme is Lent.

8. 'Homework'
   The Leader gives the practical advice provided to encourage members to continue thinking about what they have learned in the session: "During Lent be more aware of how you take part in worship."

This first session provides information about the course. Consequently, sections A and B distinguish between the entire five-week process and what is going to happen now, at this, the first meeting, Section C constitutes the structure of the actual session, in which the first three sub-sections ('Worship,' 'Introduction,' 'Opening activity') are the pre-liminal phase, preparing the way for the next three, in which the main learning activity is located ('True worship,' 'Worship changes lives,' 'Fresh expressions'). The workshop ends with 'Feedback,' 'Worship' and 'Homework', three sub-sections making up the last stage of the teaching process, in which what has been learned is celebrated and taken out into the world so that it can be used as part of members' equipment for living.

The shape of the other sessions is the same (only without 'A' and 'B'), the second, fourth and fifth having three sub-sections per stage of the process, while the proportions for Week 3 are 3-3-2. There is no tripartite division within the text itself, where the only sectional markings are the sub-sections. In every case, however, the underlying structure falls into three parts as the action moves from introductory material to final summation via material which represents the main message of the session, and consequently its purpose within the course as a whole.

Courses of this kind, however, are to be regarded as directive in nature, not so much because their shape embodies an experience of learning (which it does), but because in them the process of communicating information is spelled out in advance in the form of a written text. Such courses carry on the time-honoured schoolroom procedure of working from 'class books' under the direction of the teacher — or in this case, 'Leader.'

The books were handed out well in advance, as is usually the case in diocesan projects of this kind (see chapter 2), the material for groupwork accounting for roughly half the pages, the rest being taken up with 'Daily Bible Notes' and 'Notes for Group Leaders.' *Transforming Lives* is issued in a conveniently sized ring binder so that more pages may be added, in order to build up a compendium of resource material for study use and educational groupwork among congregations, 'to help you and your church explore our faith and the ways in which God changes and transforms us so that we can then help change and transform the world' (2008, 1).

The systematic use of groupwork as a way of changing individuals' lives and so helping to transform the Church itself is certainly a new one, at least on the scale attempted by current diocesan strategies within the Church of England. The approach adopted by these *Emmaus*-style courses is, however, a well-established one, in line with centuries of ecclesiastical procedures aimed at 'education in the Faith,' which have concentrated on passing on information in the time-honoured way, that is, by addressing groups of people rather than individuals. The 'educational' tone of these courses reflects their origin in various Diocesan Departments of Education. As we saw earlier, *Education for Discipleship* draws attention to the academic shortcomings of some attempts at, or attitudes towards, congregational training, and the groupwork courses which are current within the Church of England show a high degree of skill in marshalling the information which they aim at passing on as efficiently as possible.

It is not intended to criticise this way of instructing congregations, which is in line with a great deal of training carried out in other areas of life. Business management, for example, has depended on interactive groupwork carried out under the instruction of professional teachers for many years, as have larger organisations concerned with the provision of other kinds of service such as local government, transport and general utilities, health, the armed forces and, of course, education itself — every area of life which requires training to be undertaken in as speedy and efficient way as possible. This kind of head-on approach to education, in which whole numbers of people may be brought into contact with a particular skill and thereby equipped to pass this

74

on to others in ways which are considered to be logistically (i.e. economically) advantageous, is both approved and recommended. If people are to learn properly, they must be properly taught; this way they can co-operate by trying out the ideas they receive on one another, thereby increasing their own hold upon them. Certainly they should be taught by those who know, even if it is at second-hand, which may even be the best way of teaching them. Judging by the popularity of intensive group-learning projects, this quantitative attitude towards education sometimes appears to be the received wisdom within training circles.

Some groupwork writers, however, have questioned the fundamental value of teaching of this kind for the promotion of genuine learning; that is for its ability to bring about permanent changes in the way individuals make their own sense of life, what Gavin Bolton refers to as the 'modification' of values as distinct from the mere transmission of information (1979, 45–60). If the prescriptive approach is to take root so as to 'bring forth grain' (Mt 13:8; Mk 4:3), there must always be a willingness to be in some way affected by what is heard. The 'good ground' referred to in the Gospel parable is the predisposition towards learning which it is the responsibility of teachers to encourage in order to do their job properly. Without the desire to learn there cannot be change at a personal level, since our understanding of phenomena is dependent upon the importance we give to them; in other words, changes of mind are always changes of validity (Kelly, 1991b). Those who crowd business seminars and lectures given by experts from other parts of the world seek validation rather than knowledge; the questions asked are about practice rather than purpose, because they already know the direction in which they have chosen to move.

This is also true of the women and men who make up the congregations of churches. Those who organise educational courses of a prescriptive kind are well aware that they will be preaching to the converted. If the course structure involves group discussion there will be room for exchanging information regarding the way individual people approach the problems involved in life as distinct from those set out in examination papers. So far as this kind of prescriptive groupwork is concerned, these sections are the most effective source of learning, for in them the group members teach themselves within the context of an understanding already arrived at beforehand, a shared Christian identity. These are the parts of the educational procedure which are not prescribed, in the literal sense of having been written out beforehand, where understanding arrives through the exchange of personal testimony, whether or not this is overtly spiritual in nature. Here, as in other forms of groupwork, we learn by inspecting our own and others' attitudes and experiences, and grow both emotionally and intellectually in the process (Erikson, 1985).

From this point it is apparent that directive and interactive learning need not be seen as in opposition to each other. The model of groupwork recommended by *Education for Discipleship* certainly does not require them to be mutually exclusive. Provision must be made within the structure which would allow the group the scope it needs to be itself rather than simply a collection of individual learners, something which cannot avoid being at odds with traditional understandings regarding what it is that discipleship requires. The problem here is not structure itself, which is something every group must have in order to exist as a group, but directiveness as an entrenched attitude towards learning: that it begins and ends with those who know imparting knowledge to those who do not.

Process groups

As we saw in Chapter 1, there are other ways in which groupwork demonstrates the relationship which exists between structure and learning. Several authorities on working within a group format draw attention to the structural importance of the processes involved in the formation of the actual group itself (Ottaway, 1966; Corey and Corey, 1997; Douglas, 1993; Yalom, 1995).

Process, by definition, refers to a particular order which is observed to take place within a course of events. Small groups which identify themselves as 'process' groups are directed to concentrate their attention on observable changes in their experience of self and other which take place as they work in the context of the group because that is the particular context in which they have agreed to work. In other words, it is the process of group membership which gives rise to changes in group identity. 'Process' and 'structure' belong together, each being responsible for the other. If, as Douglas maintains, the basic function of group formation is 'the promotion of directional interaction' (1993, 26), then the direction taken by the group will be dependent upon the type of personal interaction taking place within it, the type and the quality.

According to Douglas, groups concerned with the welfare of those taking part in them proceed in the direction of support through mutual identification (1993, 120). Yalom, of all group specialists the one most closely associated with therapeutic groups, claims: 'Why are these groups potent? Precisely because they encourage process exploration!' (1995, 137) Yalom is concerned specifically with group therapy. What he has to say, however, is generalisable to other kinds of work with groups of people, which is orientated towards well-being. The principle is clear:

> By focusing on process we mean focusing on what members are doing or feeling in the group. For instance, a member may constantly be trying to one-up everything that is said . . . Or a member may ramble and the leader or another member may point this out to the rambler in hopes that the rambler may get some insight on how he comes across to people. (Jacobs et al., 2002, 30)

Jacobs et al. list other examples of the necessity for group leaders to concentrate on how the group is interacting *as a group*; members may be frightened to let others know what they are thinking and feeling, or they may be excluded anyway. 'The skilled leader,' they say, 'is always paying attention to process as well as content, and will focus on group process when it seems necessary and valuable to do so' (2002, 301).

In groups concerned with exploring and facilitating personal relationship it is the interactive process which is worked on; however the structure itself remains the active element in the process, because this is what allows it to be worked *through*. Corey and Corey remind us that every kind of group has its own behavioural norms and that these constitute its structural identity: 'Group norms are the shared beliefs about expected behaviours aimed at making groups function effectively' (1997, 150).

Norms develop as the structure develops; they change and are changed at each new stage within the process whereby the group attains its maturity as a group. In process groups these structural changes represent shifts in authority, as members seize the opportunity to move things in a new direction, and the centre of gravity changes. The Leader's task in a process-orientated group is to maintain equilibrium in a way which allows minority opinions and attitudes to be expressed and discourages attempts to dominate the group, whatever direction these may come from. In any group which sets out to allow freedom of expression powerfully counter-vailant forces operate, as each person involved, however committed they may be to the idea of being in a group and therefore doing their best to co-operate with one another, is still more or less aware of being themselves, each a person in her or his own right. In fact they are more rather than less likely to feel it because of the presence of so many other selves who can so easily be seen as competitors for the attention of the group and the approval of the Leader.

The latter's task in such groups is to facilitate interaction and avoid intervening in order to exercise his or her control over what is being said by whom (Ottaway, 1966). Burnett distinguishes two 'broad categories of groupwork':

- group *task* functions concerned with the accomplishment of group tasks, and
- group *maintenance* functions, concerned with improving and maintaining good relationships within the group, promoting its cohesion, and meeting the individual needs of its members (1972, 76).

In directive groups the function of the leader is to do his or her best to ensure that the group's purpose is understood and carried out. There is only one Leader (apart from his or her Deputies), whose task is to instruct the group as to the most effective way of achieving a specified goal. In process-oriented groupwork, however, leadership is more diffuse, as 'an effective process-oriented group must look to its membership as a whole rather than a special leader to accomplish its tasks.' In process-oriented groupwork, the Leader's task is to enable this kind of leadership to take place. The same thing applies, as we shall see, to groupwork that is art-based.

Very obviously this is a more difficult undertaking than simply keeping order and intervening in any exchanges which might lead to some degree of confrontation. Such groups aim to set in motion a process of change, both within the group's awareness of itself as a group, and consequently of members' own experience of themselves as individuals in relation to others. The conflict which this is bound to stir up cannot simply be suppressed — at birth, so to speak. If this happens, it will certainly never function as it should, and the group itself will be stillborn. The Leader attempts to facilitate the process of group formation by containing its dynamism and not merely discounting it. Rivalry, resentment, defensive withdrawal, anger itself are there to be lived through, not 'sanitized away' (Wilson, 1975, 4). These things, which are avoided outside the group conditions, are brought into focus within it so that they can be acknowledged and survived, so that the members may themselves have the experience of surviving them. As a group becomes more aware of its own identity as a group, so it grows more able to live through the disruptive forces threatening its existence, the interpersonal tensions which 'impel them to invest most of their energy in a search for approval, acceptance, respect or domination' (Yalom, 1995, 295).

The Leader of a process-orientated group consciously avoids the directive, prescriptive approach associated with the leadership of other kinds of groups and actively required for conventional teaching groups. This does not mean that the role of authority is abandoned, however. Instead it is exchanged for the more onerous task of containing the emotional conflicts which its refusal to dominate has promoted within the group, one of which centres around what the group itself identifies as a culpable dereliction of duty on the Leader's part in his or her apparent refusal to do their job properly, so that 'doubt begins to grow about the efficiency of the method in which the session in conducted' (Ottaway, 1966, 38).

At the same time, however, by focusing conflict, the group structure creates a sense of shared purpose to work towards its resolution. Leader and group co-operate to meet confrontation head-on and use it, as Corey and Corey recommend, 'to help members make an honest acceptance of themselves' (1997, 184). This focusing action operationalises the group's structure so that it may begin to function more consciously as a group and work together to try to solve its own inner conflicts, Thus, indirectly, the role of Leader as facilitator draws strength from flexibility and its own refusal to dominate proceedings as, in accordance with Lewin's (1948) theory of group dynamics, the group itself conforms to the model of living organisms which strive to achieve their potential by working with blocked connections in order to make new ones.

Two things contribute to the structuring of process-orientated group, the first of which is the changing interactional pattern as leadership shifts from member to member as individuals become, for a time at least, the centre of attention and the second, the space-creating action of the facilitator/leader as she or he holds the process together. Here, as in the other kinds of groups to be considered, the Leader is responsible for the group in the sense that he or she is the one who asserts and manipulates the form it will take — in other words its structure. The main structural difference between prescriptive and process-orientated groups lies in the rigid nature of the structure imposed by directive (and direct*ed*) learning compared with the self-created order derived from the process of group formation involved in those groups permitted to do their own structuring as they move towards creating a sense of belonging together as a group. In the first case, of course, structure is received. In the second, however, it is encouraged to evolve.

Structure is essential for groupwork, simply because no group of people can dispense with rules and remain recognisable as a group, either to other people or itself. Process-orientated groups are 'group-centred rather than teacher-centred' (Ottaway, 1966, 10), but this certainly does not mean that they lack direction. The identifying characteristic of this kind of group is that it is basically self-directed; not by individual members as within it they exchange the roles of 'teacher' and 'taught,' but by the group as a whole, the living organism which takes form in their emerging relationship with one another. This, of course, is what Ottaway means when he says that 'members learn by studying their own experience rather than by formal instruction' (1966, 10); their experience of their relationship with one another and those aspects of themselves — what psychoanalytic groupwork identifies as 'inner' relation-ships (see chapter 1) — which impact on their ability to reach beyond themselves and really encounter one another within the framework of an iden-tity structure which is genuinely shared.

A group where the members have been encouraged to develop in this way by the freedom afforded by a structure established to promote the interchange of personality is identified by Corey and Corey as one possessing 'group cohe-sion'. They describe such a group as one with the following characteristics:

> . . . a climate of support, bonding, attractiveness, sharing of experiences, mutuality within a group, the togetherness that unites members, a sense of belonging, warmth and closeness and caring and acceptance. A group char-acterised by a high degree of cohesion provides a climate in which members feel free enough to do meaningful work. (1997, 254)

Corey and Corey refer to cohesion as 'a multi-dimensional, interactive construct that can be studied from various perspectives' (1997, 254). The group specialists we have been considering represent differing psychological traditions: Rogerian, Existentialist, Psychoanalytic, Behavioural, for example. However they all agree that this degree of cohesion within a group is some-thing which takes time to show itself. As Yalom puts it: 'Mutual caring and concern develop late in the group: in the beginning members are likely to view one another as interlopers or rivals' (1995, 307). The structure gives its members strength to confront the obstacles which hamper their progress towards mutual acceptance, not by avoiding them but by learning how to survive them; actually using them as sources of insight. By being given permission to express themselves, and by gradually discovering how to make their own personal sense of the *sequelae* of their acts of self-expressiveness, the members of a process group learn important things about themselves and other people from a structure able to contain information of a kind which remains outside the reach of verbal or written instruction about what it is that should be learned.

As we saw in the last section, learning groups of the kind categorised by Booker and Ireland (2005) as 'process evangelism', which make up the greater part of the groupwork carried out within the Church of England, are highly structured, permitting only a very strictly controlled degree of divergence from the prescribed format. It would be misleading, however, to assume that the process-orientated groups we have been considering lack structure, or that the structure they possess is loosely permissive of variation. In fact this is far from being so. The structure of a process group, because it is harder to impose, requires more vigilance from the leader/facilitator than a more rigidly structured one would ever do. Keeping a balance among opposing tendencies, staving off the threat of anarchy, calls for greater self-control on the part of the person in charge of proceedings than they would require for the job of acting as representative of an authority whom all present regard as unquestioned, if not unquestionable.

Each of the two categories of groupwork looked at thus far has its own well-defined structure, the apparently unplanned process group as well as the pre-planned directive one. Before moving on to consider groupwork based on various forms of artistic presentation, it is important to draw attention to a fundamental difference between these two kinds of structure, one which reflects their divergent purposes. Structure gives definition to distinctions, and directive groupwork is recognisably different from groupwork aimed at enabling free participation. A markedly directive intention presented in advance in the form of a comprehensive procedural blueprint, even if this is scrupulous in including sections set aside for 'free discussion,' signals its nature and purpose very clearly as the use of structure to produce conformity. Ottaway's purpose is obviously opposed to this, and he uses the group format to provide an opportunity for individuals to express their personal uniqueness:

> I felt I had to give a little explanation. I spoke on the difficulties of understanding human behaviour — which was our task . . . That we should try and see how far personality develops differently in different people . . . I was not going to set a topic for discussion. The general subject . . . was 'personality development'. A short silence, then somebody asked for a definition of 'personality'. (1966, 24, 25)

Ottaway does not say whether he proceeded to give one, but we may presume he did not, it being against his stated intention to do so.

Creative/imaginative groups

In groups reflecting artistic experience, the group structure forms itself in accordance with the artistic medium. In other words, it allows itself to be shaped by the artist's imagination, in this case the shared imagining of the group, who all together represent the artistic impulse at work (McNiff, 1998). As was pointed out earlier, the art form which seems most appropriate for groupwork is drama, which is a way of structuring time by giving shape to a series of events. In drama the meaning of events, what the play is about, is disclosed not at the beginning, nor yet at the end, but in the middle. Hence to understand a play one must allow oneself to become involved in it; to really understand it one must be willing to be drawn into it (Grainger, 2010, 41).

This is something that applies to all art-based groups: they are all story-groups. The medium, whether it be visual or tactile, musical or choreographic, draws those taking part to involve themselves imaginatively with it. For art to be experienced as itself and not used as a manipulative illusion — a trick, in fact — there cannot be any kind of coercion. Describing poetry, Coleridge speaks of disbelief 'willingly suspended' (1817, ch. 14). We have already remarked on the epistemological significance of three-ness. In artistic experience this is expressed in terms of approach, involvement and retrospective interiority, as the totality of what has been perceived comes to be enjoyed as Wordsworth's 'emotion recollected in tranquillity' (1800). The emotional charge, however, lies in the encounter itself, the experience of involvement.

However, if we confine ourselves to thinking of art in terms of finished products — pictures, plays, pieces of music etc. — we run the risk of over-looking the fact that improvisation, too, is a form of artistic activity, just as an artist's sketches express her or his creative impulse. Art-based groupwork makes considerable use of improvised art of one kind or another. Creative self-expression subsists in the action itself, not in any single stage of it (Jones, 2004, 99, 100).

The art form in groupwork is used to contain what happens in a session but not to direct it. For example, Jones, writing about the use of visual art in therapeutic groupwork, describes how by not taking a directive approach to starting or stopping painting, or by giving specific subject matter to the group directly, areas of group and individual process open up (2004, 29). He goes on to say that:

> The issue of directive to non-directive approaches is one that receives a good deal of attention in [visual/tactile] art therapy writing and definition. (2004, 30)

Among other arts therapists, he quotes Dawes:

> Music is used as a catalyst for discussion and emotional out-pouring, a vehicle for emotional expression ... Sessions tend to follow a pattern of confrontation,

81

followed by reflection, then recreation . . . expressed by music. (1985, 6 quoted by Jones, 2004, 38)

Thus,

Music can offer safety because of its complementarity to words; it can contain and express powerful feelings; music can link to spiritual matters. (Jones, 2004, 39)

Dance Movement Therapy (DMT) uses dance for

- Expressing and managing overwhelming feelings or thoughts . . .
- Testing the impact of self on others . . .
- Developing trusting relationships (European Association Dance Movement Therapy, 2010).

The 'containing-in-order-to-release' function of artistic experience is dramatically present in dramatherapy itself, as the structure of all kinds of drama, whether performed as theatre or read as literature, or simply lived through in personal relationships and private experience. It has been pointed out by dramatherapists that the shape of one of their sessions corresponds to a tripartite initiation ritual (Van Gennep, 1960; cf. Grainger, 1995; Pitruzzella, 2004; Jennings, 1987; Cattenach, 1994; Grainger, 1990). Two outer stages enclosing a more spontaneous and free central one is an almost invariable dramatherapy structure. As in a rite of passage, the first and last movements are considerably less challenging than the middle one, being of a more controlled and consequently less alarming kind. The first may consist largely of games and exercises performed under direction, and involve some hilarity and a degree of relaxation of people's nervousness of one another; the last will be quieter and more reflective, the uncertainties of the central section having been survived and a recognisable framework for discussion re-asserted.

Because the heart of an arts therapy session is devoted to an opportunity for members to give free rein to their imagination, and the session itself is specifically structured for this to happen, art-based groupwork can be the most liberating of the three approaches investigated. The most democratic, however, is the process-orientated because of the directive stance which the Leader of an arts group must take in introducing an artistic medium into the proceedings in the first place, and then persuading members to allow them-selves to become involved in it. In art-based groups, closure is built into the structure, just as in directive groupwork it is often written into the instruc-tions which have been provided for potential group members. In process-orientated groups, however, members may be left to decide among themselves just how a session should close.

We have been looking at three different group structures serving three kinds of overall group purposes, each of which represents a particular aspect of learning which takes place within a small group setting. My argument regarding all three structures is that they represent identifiable areas of educational opportunity within the life and structures of the Church of England. Just as members of congregations may be regarded as benefiting from instruction regarding the Biblical sources of Christian belief and Church practice, so they also benefit from the learning about human relationship afforded by groupwork designed to provide focused experience of the ways in which human beings characteristically interact with one another, and the symbolism involved in opening minds and hearts to realities which lie beyond literal description. Knowledge, experience and imagination are all essential for full human-ness; the use of small groups allows them to be experienced at a personal level in community.

As we have seen, process-orientated and art-based groups are mainly concerned with learning about relationship, what it is that is actually happening between and among those present within the learning group, either explicitly as a process which is currently under way and can be experienced by — and pointed out to — the group members or implicitly by means of the mediating presence of imagination given artistic expression. Directive groups involve this kind of learning-through-involvement because of their group structure, but their actual way of working depends mainly upon the systematic transmission of information *about* relationship. Of these approaches, the art-based one may at first appear to be the least useful because it is the least definite in drawing conclusions. Many people, in fact, would probably claim that art has no practical value whatever; how can it have when any message it presents is subject to so many individual interpretations and variations in meaning?

This, of course, is why, when selecting strategies for educating individuals and groups, literal-minded people tend to leave artistic experience out of the equation or they use art as a visual aid in order to make a particular point in an argument which has already been shown to be unquestionable — art used to back up the argument, certainly not art as the argument (McNiff, 1998). Art-as-argument is a plea for the importance of seeing through phenomena, viewing the mundane as a doorway to the as yet unknown and un-experienced (Butcher, 1951), for using our imagination to evolve new structures instead of depending on techniques which are well-tried and capable of achieving the kinds of results which we expect — and which are expected of us.

Any kind of artistic activity is, from the point of view of those committing themselves to it, a risky undertaking. This is because it sets out to be itself, its own structure, not the repetition of something else. A group which creates an imaginative structure does so to express its own individuality, making a statement about itself without actually saying so. The structure created by their shared imagination speaks for them, to use Wordsworth's phrase, in 'thoughts that do oft lie too deep for tears' (1800).

Art-based approaches come into their own when signifying things unspoken yet deeply felt. Their simplicity and directness are able to cut through the world of the provisional and the contingent which is why art and symbolism go together so closely (Peirce, 1958). McNiff describes 'artistic knowing' as 'different than intellectual knowing' (1998, 36). He cites Richards who speaks of it as 'an underground river that gives us life and mobility' (1995, vii). Artistic knowing, says McNiff, is 'intuitive, mysterious and renewable' (1998, 36). In art-based groupwork, the art evolves from the group's decision to share imagination and inhabit the structure which emerges. However ramshackle and *ad hoc* this may be it provides the basis for some kind of artistic creation, as its various elements come together and the finished work arises — whether it be drama, music, dance, or some kind of pictorial or symbolic representation. In it, the life invested in it is revealed to the world and it is able to stand on its own as the living symbol of the whole group in its identity as an expression of sharing which takes place at a personal level:

> People chose to use the medium of bodily expressiveness to create a living sculpture of how it had been for them to take part in the group. Looking back it seems a strange thing to do, not very logical; at the time, though, it was the most natural thing in the world. (G. Pagnoncelli. Personal communication, Milan, May 5, 2010)

The following section contains material from members' records chosen to illustrate how each of the three structures we have been considering functions and is remembered by those taking part.

A comparison of examples of members' experiences of three groupwork structures

A: Directive group
We met at 7.30 p.m. in the room at the end of the church. About seven or eight of us were there I think. The Vicar was in charge of the session, although he reminded us about what he said in church about people taking it in turns to lead the group. So far as I remember there were three men there and the rest women. [This was written by a woman. RG] Only one of us was under 30, one under 40 and the rest over 60. The Vicar took us through this week's session in the workbooks we all had. I can't remember everything we did (although I could probably if I looked in the book), but it was all interesting and I think most people enjoyed it. I particularly enjoyed an exercise we did in which we had to turn to the person sitting next to us and try to arrange some slips of paper to make up the Communion service, each slip having the name of part of the service on it, and we had to put them in the right order. Also, there was a time when people were encouraged by the Vicar, who was leading, to say how we thought our church worship could be improved. We wrote our own opinion down on the paper provided, not adding our names. Then we each

84

folded our paper over in half and someone else read it out, not saying whose it was. We took it in turns to comment on what was read out. There was a space included in the session for people to give their own experiences of church services in our church, and someone present took the opportunity to talk about how they had been treated in another church. (This went one for some time, probably longer than the Vicar had counted on it doing, because people kept chipping in with stories of their own. I enjoyed this and I think he did, too.) This person was obviously angry about what had happened to them and I think they appreciated the chance to get things off their chest, but the Vicar had to draw their attention to the next item on the agenda, which was Bible examples and prayers. These were written down for us in the book we'd been given, and I remember thinking how nice they were. The things I remember most are the story which the person told and arranging the strips of paper — and the drawings in the work-book, of course! I appreciated some of Mrs ___'s comments and thought the Vicar was very skilful in the way he kept is all in order and helped us to concentrate on the matter in hand and not let our attention wander too far away from the workbook! (Group member, female, aged 67. Wakefield, 2009)

B: Process group
(The following are extracts of 'process recordings' from Ottaway, 1966. Two groups were involved: A and B.)

1. *Eighth Meeting* (A) Commenced with the usual rather trivial pseudo-relaxed conversational gambits . . . When the subject of murder was brought up the discussion veered to prison as a deterrent or as a process of rehabilitation, which to my mind did lead to a divergence between the prison officers and the probation officers. Mrs G then expressed the view that these things were only a type of cure when the whole point lay in prevention. Depression was also brought up and its various causes. Most of the group participated, apart from one member who had shown concern at the way the group was being handled. Throughout the entire time this gentleman made no comment whatso-ever. (Mrs E, Group A, Ottaway, 1966, 29. 30).

   (These notes come from the last phase of a succession of meetings which lasted over a period of months, in which members were encour-aged to keep 'process records' in order to remind themselves of what had been happening within the group since they first met. The rules governing group procedure are those applying to all process-orientated work, whether long or short term, and are aimed at learning through the resolution of inter-personal differences. These show up clearly during the initial stage of the process, but only come to a head later on, before being largely resolved:)

2. *Twentieth Meeting* (B) Miss J came back and made quite a difference to the life of the group. It began slowly. J started by asking did I really mean it was a 'sophisticated' group, that we were worldly wise but on a superficial level. I said yes, we were not prepared to tell our experiences except superficially and we often deceived ourselves . . . They were soon bothered again by how can we know what we are really like, and why do people like people. Seeing the good and bad in people . . . Something started E off to attack P, and she said she would hate to be one of his clients, and she could not stand his 'goodness' and his taking on the role of judging people . . . He tried to save the situation and remarked that 'goodness' seemed to upset the group. I said that 'good' people might do much harm, and that one should always suspect people who were trying to do good especially on firm religious principles. It was asked why we had not discussed religion before. (Leader/facilitator, Group B, Ottaway, 1966, 73).

(The Leader/facilitator, in this case Ottaway himself, was acting here as a group member, joining a discussion started by two other members. The extract provides a good example of the way the initiative with regard to choice of subject shifts between participants. It comes from the second stage of the process described by Ottaway, 'The Move Towards Emotional Involvement.')

3. *Reflections on 2nd Year* (A)
On the personal side I feel I must have presented the group with something of a problem. It may be true to say that in retrospect I hope I did! It is not my way to bare my soul, but I was prepared to respond to any reasonable approach . . . In my view the group failed miserably so far as I was concerned, i.e. in the opening up process. Or could it be that nobody was even interested in the whys and wherefores of yours truly being in the probation service, for example? Coming into this work was for me a very important move . . . and had someone the initiative to press on this . . . my defences would have been down with a vengeance . . . Curiously enough the very failure on the part of the group to put the screws on me drove me back on to myself and there was quite a process of self-examination over a period, especially during the latter part of the group's life. (Mr R, Group A, Ottaway, 1966, 133, 134).

(This passage has been chosen because it clearly shows the ability of the group process to encourage self-understanding in a paradoxical way, by going through times in the group's life when it works in the opposite direction. Group A continued to support Mr R, even when they had difficulty understanding his point of view owing to his wariness about disclosing his personal feelings. The result was a sense of frustration on his part which eventually broke through his unwillingness to contemplate his own difficulties in sharing important things about himself, either with himself or other people. It was involvement within the group process which had this effect of breaking down what had previously been an embattled attitude, reinforced by the initial hostility of another group member.)

C: Art-based group

We started by playing a game suggested by Andy, whose turn it was to lead the group this time. It was cold in the room (the heating had been turned off as it was still officially summertime) so we took it in turns to say what our Christian name was and how we personally would describe the weather. We all had more than one go at doing this, inventing a new name for ourselves each time. It started seriously but soon got ridiculous, so that we needed some time to stop laughing. Then somebody said something about having to wait until next spring for the weather to improve. Andy said, never mind, we can take shelter here.

There was a big table against the wall, so we pulled it into the middle of the room and all seven of us huddled together under it, wearing as many pieces of clothing as we could lay hands on — heavy sweaters, baggy trousers, multiple pairs of gloves, scarves over our faces, woolly hats, anything we could find anywhere in the building. Lack of space to move kept us almost motionless apart from the occasional twitch. Meanwhile Andy just watched from the sidelines without saying anything. Where do we go from here, I thought? We clambered out and sat around the table, hugging ourselves to keep warm. Someone offered someone else something to eat, which was almost grabbed out of their hands (and would have caused a riot in 'real' life). People rubbed hands and feet, their own and each others' because it was colder out than it had been huddled together under the table. Most of the time we just sat like statues; then somebody got up from the table and went to stare out of the window. To everybody's alarm she began to open it. (The window, like the table and the chairs, was real.)

In the fresh air rushing in, people started to revive. The impact on the group was amazing. Someone said, Look, it's Spring! and everybody repeated it: Look, it's Spring . . . People got up from the table and began unwrapping themselves and moving their arms and legs to get them going again. We joined hands and danced around the table. Then we sat down in a circle and talked about what we'd been doing and what it was like. (Group member, adapted from Grainger, 2007).

(This is a description of a dramatherapy session which took place in Summer 2006 and involved guests of Holy Rood House, a Christian healing centre in Thirsk, Yorkshire, England. The members of the dramatherapy group were self-selected and had never been involved in this kind of group-work before. Whether they have been since, I have no way of establishing; as can be seen from this example, dramatherapy values spontaneity highly and runs counter to the scientific delight in precise specifications.)

In this chapter, then, we have been looking at three different approaches to working with small groups of people, regarding them as alternative structures for learning. Each approach, we have argued, is appropriate for sharing a particular kind of understanding which can be seen as relevant for church congregations. These are:

1. the teaching of doctrine, whether biblical or ecclesiological; learning how such knowledge affects understanding
2. learning about the self through focused interaction with others; taking notice of one's effect on other people
3. the use of shared imaginative experience to discover truth in a way which goes beyond the literal.

The three group structures are distinguishable on three dimensions: purpose, procedure and process:

1. *Purpose*: directed learning, about particular subjects set out in an academic syllabus.
   Procedure: provision of texts and guidelines; dependence on exterior validation; text-led.
   Process: working through a series of lessons presented within the framework of a teacher–pupil relationship.
2. *Purpose*: exploratory learning about personal relations mediated by group membership.
   Procedure: group processes working towards more acceptance of self and other; interior validation; leader as facilitator.
   Process: evolution of group towards a sense of its identity, via the resolution of inter- and intra-personal conflict.
3. *Purpose*: the discovery of personal and social truth by means of shared imagination.
   Procedure: the establishment of conditions in which group members share an imaginative experience; leader as director/facilitator.
   Process: the artistic creation of an emotionally secure place for personal encounter.

The final section of the chapter contained testimonies regarding each of the kinds of group we have been considering included here for purposes of comparing actual experiences of differential groupwork structure. During the remainder of this book we shall be examining such experience in a more systematic way, using a phenomenological paradigm to do this.

4

Investigating Contrasting Group Structures

This chapter describes an investigation into three kinds of small group structure. Most of the chapter consists of accounts of the actual groupwork itself, which gave rise to the data concerning group experience to be examined in the next chapter. Each session of groupwork is reported in three different ways: first, a description of the order of procedure for each of the twelve sessions; next, the Leader's report for each session; finally, the report on each session submitted by the group member who acted as Scribe. The same group of people was involved in the three different group structures. In the first sections of the chapter the circumstances regarding the group's formation are described, preceded by a summary of the methodological approach.

Designing the Investigation

An experiment was designed in order to determine whether the division into three different kinds of groupwork structure — directive, process-orientated and art-based — might be considered legitimate in terms of its association with discernible differences in actual groupwork experience. Would a small group of people who had expressed willingness to be involved in groups designed in these three separate ways, and to say or write down what taking part in them felt like at a personal level, provide information regarding their differential value for the purpose of continuing congregational training within the setting of Church of England parishes (or any similar circumstances concerning Christian education)?

In other words, would it be possible to use an experimental approach designed to take account of the quality of experience rather than simply setting out to measure its behavioural effects? Any attempt to do the latter would simply have undermined the integrity of our original intention, which was to assess the impact on individuals of an experience of sharing something which happens *between people*, and resists attempts to reduce it to its constituent parts. In any case, the aim would not be to prove anything, but rather to point Church education towards a wider interpretation of its task.

From my point of view it seemed particularly important to find a way in

89

which my own long-lasting involvement in art-based groups might be set alongside other ways of working with small groups. Obviously this had to be done in as open and unbiased a way as possible, taking care to allow the people concerned to ask their own questions without laying down rules concerning the kind of questions someone else would consider appropriate. In other words, the enquiry would be one we were all making, and its results would reflect each individual's prejudices, not simply those of the experimenter!

The aim, then, was to design an experiment to *explore* rather than *demonstrate*. The experimenter's thesis that 'directive and existential groupwork has a differential effect upon group members' would be supported (not proved) or undermined (rather than disproved) by any results obtained. Obviously, because this is the nature of experiments, it was hoped that the conclusions eventually drawn would be definite enough to add weight to the proposal. Even if this should not turn out to be the case, however, my argument is that it was worth putting things to the test, particularly as this is an area in which, so far as I can see, there has previously been no systematic attempt to explore different kinds of small group structure in a way which strives to be impartial. This book is addressed to a particular situation existing within a single Christian denomination; whether such situations exist elsewhere within other church groupings is a matter outside the scope of the research being carried out here. All the same it certainly seems likely that Church authorities in other parts of the world and other denominations both at home and abroad may decide to limit themselves to one particular groupwork format and ignore the opportunities presented by other approaches; in which case the work carried out here will be relevant to them as well as to the English Anglicans to whom it is primarily addressed.

Conclusions drawn from the investigation are likely to be lacking in precision because the clarity demanded when making scientific judgements evades attempts at understanding the psychological processes involved in interpersonal experience. During the last thirty years a good deal of effort has been made by psychologists working within the 'human sciences' to loosen the grip of the scientific paradigm when it comes to the conclusions we are able to draw with regard to what actually happens between people within the sphere of human relationship, a grip which, for most of the twentieth century amounted almost to a stranglehold (Popper, 1972; Grainger, 1999; Polanyi, 1969; Shotter, 1986; Reason and Rowan, 1981; Robson, 1993). Writing in 1986, Shotter points out that

> We now realise what the empirical and behavioural sciences call data are not simply given us in the data, but are theory-laden, i.e. they only appear to us as the facts they are in terms of a theory constructed by us . . . rather than being given us by nature we in fact take them out of a constantly changing flux of events. (1986, 95, quoted by Murray and Chamberlain, 1999, 6)

Whether or not this is true of things in general, it is certainly so of our perception of other people, and theirs of ourselves. Social Constructionists

(Gergen and Gergen, 2003; Garfinkel, 1967) describe human beings' under-standing of one another as something put together (i.e. 'constructed') between them according to an agreement about what is involved in being alive as a person which is somehow negotiated between them. The Constructionist approach is one which 'abandons the notion of traditional psychological vari-ables and views them as changeable constructions, historically and socially located and serving particular functions' (Murray and Chamberlain, 1999, 7). Mathers, writing about the Pastoral Care function of groups, had this to say:

> To study a matter scientifically is to adopt a detached and dispassionate atti-tude towards it. This works well enough when we study aspects of the non-human world, but the social sciences deal with human beings. To be detached and dispassionate about one's fellow men is to cut oneself off from them; and such an affirmation of separateness carries an implication that one is either being anti-social or asocial, or, perhaps, superhuman and god-like. (1972, 99)

If groupwork is concerned with learning how to be more humanly aware, and Christian groups are seen as intended to allow their members to set about doing this within the particular circumstances of their shared identity as Christian, involving as it must do an understanding of themselves and the world in which they live from a specifically Christian viewpoint, any research undertaken by and for members of the Christian Church must concern itself with human beings in the fullness of their humanity and not any 'scientifically' reduced version of it. If the need to regard human relationship as a phenom-enon itself rather than the mathematical addition of theoretically isolable phenomena applies to all human beings, then it obviously applies to Christians and consequently to any research undertaken with regard to their personal experiences, of which learning is surely one of the most important.

In the case of this enquiry, the research paradigm chosen was ideographic, which may be described as involving the attempt to discover how people make sense of whatever it may be that is happening to them in a particular context. Individuals and the circumstances in which they find themselves placed interact in ways which make the setting as important as the act of interpreta-tion. To allow what is being learned to be communicable to others, the interpretative function, however, is equally important. Circumstances and interpretation are experienced together. This is qualitative research, concerned with trying to establish how something was experienced by those involved rather than seeking to confirm its existence by measuring its dimen-sions or those of the effects it produces.

The qualitative research paradigm used here is known as 'interpretative phenomenological analysis' (IPA). Effectively this is a reversal of quantitative psychological research procedure, in that an interpretation is derived from studying people's experience of a state of affairs (the phenomenon) instead of starting with a possible explanation (an interpretation) and manipulating the circumstances surrounding the phenomenon in order to determine the exact conditions for the explanation to be seen as the correct one. In IPA data consists of recorded experiences of a phenomenon using a range of techniques involving open-ended enquiry and depending on personal testimony, the stance of those conducting the enquiry being curious and facilitative (see Colaizzi, 1978). Certainly this seems more appropriate for research into Christian experience carried out by Christians.

Because it is concerned with what is happening rather than if it may be happening, IPA comes under the general category of 'action research' (Reason and Bradbury, 2008), aimed at dispensing with theories about the nature of research which have a limiting and restrictive effect on attempts to discover what in a particular situation is really happening. According to Curtis et al., action research

> . . . embraces a world where control of variables and outcomes is no longer possible. The action researcher must employ iterative, collaborative processes in order to generate precise knowledge in a specific setting . . .
>
> The 'data' sought in action research are the meanings and values that participants attribute to activities and social relationships in which they are involved. (Murray and Chamberlain, 1999, 218, 203)

This, then, is the attitude towards the nature and purpose of research applicable for real human situations embodied in Interpretative Phenomenological analysis, where the 'expert researchers' are all who are investigating whatever it is that is taking place between and among them:

> The aim of interpretative phenomenological analysis (IPA) is to explore in detail the participant's view of the topic under investigation . . . it is concerned with an individual's personal perception or account of an object or event, as opposed to an attempt to produce an objective statement of the object or event itself. (Smith et al., 1999, quoted in Murray and Chamberlain, 1999, 218)

Smith et al. go on to point out that although the approach aims to discover the views of individuals who are themselves involved in a particular situation, those who are observing others' reactions or listening to their testimonies regarding the quality of their experience are equally subject to their own ideas and attitudes of mind, and actually need these in order to make any sense of the personal universes to which they are being granted access. Interpretation is always necessary in order to make sense of anything which we intend to learn about. This, they say, is why analysis is also 'interpretative' and must always admit to being so. IPA represents a conscientious intention to make sense of what people are actually saying in the way that those people themselves actually mean it, which is why any theorising about what they mean must wait until what they have said or written down has been analysed in order to find out what they themselves are actually intending to convey. Although this can never be done precisely, owing to our own pre-conceived ideas, it is preferable to using those ideas in advance, trusting in our own ability to demonstrate that we have been right all the time. So far as human beings are concerned, 'educated guesses' should wait upon the attempt to understand what it is that we are actually dealing with, when there is a possibility of drawing realistic conclusions about what people were thinking and feeling within an actual situation. IPA, say Smith et al.,

> while recognising that a person's thoughts are not transparently available from, for example, interview transcripts, engages in the analytic process in order, hopefully, to be able to say something about that thinking. (1999, 219)

In the first place, material for enquiry is generated by a systematic accumulation of first-hand accounts of an experience given by those involved in it. Projects for IPA may be single case studies or involve more participants than this, although concentrating on a single example or the protocols produced by one individual is advised before turning to study other people's material concerning the situation as they experienced it. The research itself involves a process of thematic analysis in which researchers look for clusters of related themes which gives rise to a 'super-ordinate concept' (Smith et al., 1999, 222), expressing the dimension according to which separate items can be seen as related to one another, and hang together as an identifiable motif within an individual person's protocols over the period being considered. Working along these lines with all the individuals concerned, it is then possible to identify themes which are shared and estimate the extent of agreement on particular points or within specific areas in order to gain an informed impression of the thoughts, feelings and attitudes of a group of people subjected to the same kind of social and psychological pressures. Obviously this applies to any kind of shared human experience which is registered as personal, whether or not other people are actually present at any particular place or time; a group of people waiting together to be seen by a doctor have a definite sense of belonging together as do all those who have ever suffered a period of solitary confinement.

The essential point, however, is that no conclusions regarding the salience of particular themes emerging from people's reports should be drawn until all the evidence is in or, if they are (and it is difficult to see how they can avoid being to some extent, the mind being necessarily involved in an attempt to make sense of things so that it finds it difficult, in the process, always to bide its time), then they must always be held provisionally and constantly be adjusted or modified, as they become either more or less important. It is out of these conclusions, however, that the raw material for some kind of final judgement emerges, as our previous idea about what a respondent is intending to get across is, *must be*, the key we will be using to unlock whatever follows. Somehow, the quality of an experience has to be interpreted, rather than its presence being simply noted. The effort put into carrying out this kind of research consists in making sure that conclusions drawn are kept flexible until all the evidence has been considered as a totality and the appropriate cross-currents within it can be included within the account which finally comes to be drawn up. Smith et al. remind us that 'Analysis is a cyclical process,' going on to say that investigators should 'be prepared to go through the stages a number of times, dropping a subordinate theme if a more useful one emerges' (1999, 224).

In drawing conclusions from the exercise it is important to realise that the themes which are identified are not actually present in the material being studied in any concrete or objective sense; it is the process of identifying them which gives them significance. This may sound suspicious to those who depend on things being dependent upon their own concreteness, but our understanding of one another is always far from literal and Interpretative Phenomenological Analysis parts company with nomothetic approaches in order to take account of this fact, which is vitally important for understanding human experience in a realistic way. Thus Smith et al. invite us to consider the fact that

> the themes that are identified . . . come from your *personal* interaction with and interpretation of the interview data, regardless of the particular strategy you choose to employ. (1999, 230; authors' italics)

The categories distinguished must be ones which apply to all participants in the enquiry, which means that generalisability takes precedence over precision, and material which the scrutineer identifies as evidence regarding the state of mind of one particular person, but which finds no echo elsewhere in the group, must not be allowed to affect the choice of themes regarding the group as a whole although it remains part of their data for the experiment and its presence must be mentioned when the exercise is written up. Whatever seems important for the experiment, even opinions, feelings and attitudes which only impinge on one or two members, affects the state of mind of whomever it is that is drawing conclusions regarding the investigation as a whole and this, in the long run, is the salient factor, for

> However systematically a qualitative method is presented, the crucial part of the analysis remains the particular interpretative analysis the investigator brings to the text. (Smith et al., 1999, 238)

The investigation aims at arriving at a final 'master list' (1999, 226) of themes which corresponds to the overall experience of the group, revealed in 'the identification of shared themes across participants' accounts' (1999, 229). The emphasis throughout is on meaning rather than measurement which, as Lyons points out, is the identifying characteristic of qualitative as opposed to quantitative research:

In general, qualitative research is concerned with explanation and under-standing, and its primary aims are to elicit meaning and to gain understanding rather than to predict and control. (Antonia Lyons, in Murray and Chamberlain, 1999, 242)

This kind of research paradigm, when applied to groupwork, is particu-larly effective in studies involving up to ten participants, so that whoever is carrying out the investigation is able to retain a mental image of each person and of particular themes emerging from individual contributions.

Operational strategy

Before starting the practical, i.e. experimental, part of the investigation, proce-dural guidelines were drawn up. These are outlined below:

1. General procedure for recruiting group members
   - A group of around 9 adult churchgoers, which is to be selected on grounds of interest in groupwork and instructed as to the purpose and conditions of the investigation on a one-to-one basis.
   - The investigation to be led by myself (RG) with a co-investi-gator (IH) to act as 'Group Scribe.'
   - Protocols to be prepared summarising the three types of group to be compared, given to group members and then discussed with them as a group.
   - Group members to prepare and submit protocols recording
     - memories of previous group experience
     - conclusions about groupwork drawn from these
     - expectations, hopes and anxieties about the projected investigation.
   - A group discussion to be held of the ground rules proposed by the leader and adjusted according to group consensus.
   - Leader to explain the ways in which these are adjusted to fit the three different group formats.
   - One-to-one discussions to take place between members regarding the coming activity.
   - A final preparatory meeting (whole group) to be arranged, in which the main purpose (that of exploring the relevance and suitability for church members of alternative structures for group experience) will be underlined by the Leader.

2. Directive group work
   - This is text-based, form and content being received in advance by each member, and the proceedings directed by the

Leader in accordance with the requirements of the prepared text.

- Apart from her/his own copy of the material on which the session is based, the Leader provides written instruction as to proceed by the provision of 'guidelines.' He or she will act as the 'group instructor.'
- There is ample material, including sections which are signified to be of lesser importance, but which may be used if time permits.
- Consequently the amount of material actually used in any one session may be varied according to the length of session decided upon by agreement with the group members.
- The written instructions specify a formal procedure for beginning and ending each session.

3. Process-orientated groupwork
    - There is no set text, the subject matter being thoughts and feelings expressed by group members regarding an aspect of life (announced by the Leader) which in some way or another involves them personally.
    - There are no rules regarding what may or may not be discussed, but members are asked, by the Leader, to try not to cause distress by continuing to pursue a topic which a member finds offensive.
    - Members are urged to take part, and to trust one another enough to express themselves with confidence in areas which concern themselves personally.
    - No member is to be put under pressure to join in, either by the Leader or any of the other members.
    - The Leader to act as 'facilitator,' making sure that no single member, or sub-group member manages, however unintentionally to dominate the discussion, and that shy or emotionally vulnerable members are given an opportunity to express their feelings and register their opinions without being bullied in any way.
    - Members to agree on a formal procedure for beginning and ending each session.

4. Creative/Imaginative groupwork
    - There is no set text, the action emerging from a scenario, or scenarios, devised by the group itself.
    - The Leader is responsible for the framework of the session but not its internal structure and content which emerges from the group, with him/her as 'director'.
    - The session overall has three sections or movements, the main

action occurring in the middle one, which constitutes an acted exploration, or artistic image, of the theme decided on by the group.

- The central section is to be preceded by an introductory one, in which members introduce themselves and meet one another in the form of a game. The more hilarity the better as the aim here is relaxation, encouragement: 'we're all in it together.'
- The final section is reflective, as members share the experiences they carry with them from the central enactment. The imagination which has been at work continues to be expressed in inventing ways of saying goodbye to one another and the group itself.

The above procedure was followed throughout. In the event, the last four items of a) were combined into two introductory sessions. At the same time provision was made for one of the group to make notes on the course of each session (the 'group scribe').

(i) Defining the investigation operationally

The following operational definition is offered at this point:

> If a small number of people (i.e. around 9 or 10) are willing to be members of a group aimed at exploring alternative types of group structure and to keep their own individual records of their impressions of the exercise, these records will constitute data which can be scrutinised to see if it provides evidence of any differential effect on group experience associated with the differences in groupwork structure.

(ii) Enlisting group members

In the investigation which follows, members of three Church of England congregations, all in South and West Yorkshire, were asked individually whether they would be willing to take part in an investigation such as the one outlined in the above definition. Because those approached had all expressed some interest in groupwork or had themselves been members of small groups in the churches to which they belonged, everyone approached agreed to do so, apart from one person who preferred not to leave home in the evenings. This was the oldest person approached and because the work responsibilities of the other members made it necessary for the sessions to be held in the evenings, the withdrawal of this person was accepted by the group.

In the present group, ages ranged from 45 to 80. In other words, the preponderance of those aged over 60 which exists in the country as a whole was reproduced in the group. All participants were approached personally rather than by letter or e-mail and given a verbal description of what would be involved in taking part. It was considered necessary from the very beginning to make it as clear as possible that group membership entailed adjusting to a double change in the kind of group format being used. This point was also clearly expressed in a form sent to all the members shortly after this first conversation. This, however, was quite brief, being intended simply as a way of formalising the position reached in the more personal interchanges, the majority of which were conducted on church premises, apart from two which took place in the homes of prospective group members. The wording of the form was as follows:

Independent Enquiry into Congregation Learning by Groups

This is an exercise aimed at comparing three different kinds of groupwork:

- Directed learning (3 sessions)
- Group process learning (3 sessions)
- Art-based learning (3 sessions)
                    (i.e. nine sessions in all, conducted alternately)

Members of a small group undertake to attend 3 sessions of each of these kinds of group approach. (Sessions will be an hour and a half in length.) They will then be asked which approach they liked best and gained the most from, and why.
I would be willing to take part in such an exercise and would try to come to group sessions.
No pressure will be put on you to attend every session, even if you have ticked this box!

Because it was generally felt by the participants that they should know more about what they were committing themselves to, two explanatory sessions were held to which everybody was invited. The first of these was poorly attended as only four people (apart from the Investigator) actually turned up; the second, however, attracted eight of the nine prospective group members, the ninth sending his apologies. The Investigator had asked those attending to jot down in advance their reactions to being asked to take part in the project ('What do you feel about working in a small group?') and most of those who came did this, thus starting off the data collecting process.

(iii) Data collection

After spending some time explaining something of the background to the groupwork project, the Investigator described its nature and purpose as action research, in which the group itself would be responsible for the thinking behind any results achieved in the way of conclusions drawn regarding the three types of group structure. The intention would be to generate an understanding of what the groups had to offer rather than testing any pre-existent theory about this. This was why they, the members, were being asked to 'write up' their own impressions of each session after it had been taken place. They would likewise be asked to do the same when the course was completed, so that each member would have her or his summary of how the experience had been for them.

An effort was made at this point to bring home to the participants that they should try to say what they had thought and felt about the session they were reporting on, because this was really what the investigation was about: their experiences and opinions were the data itself, not simply additional 'background' material of any kind. The Investigator him/herself needed to know who had written what, so that changes and developments would be recorded, but the actual identity of those taking part would remain confidential. Members were given exercise books so that they could write down what they wanted to say about each session. These would be collected by the Investigator at the end of the series of sessions which made up the experiment. The results, in the form of a series of themes which had emerged regarding the experience of the group *as a group*, would be shared among all who had taken part. The Investigator briefly described the IPA research paradigm. Finally he repeated his assurance that individual group members' depositions would be regarded as personal and treated confidentially. Nothing would be included in the final report of the investigation without the permission of everyone involved in it at every stage. The question of disguised identity led to some discussion as to whether or not people involved should be distinguished by letters (Mrs A, Mr B, Ms C etc.) or assumed names (Mrs Brown, Mr Smith, Ms Jones etc.). No formal decision was reached and the matter was shelved for the time being, some members protesting that they saw no reason why they should have to be disguised at all. The Investigator pointed out that people would feel safer saying what was really on their minds if they knew that nobody outside the group was there to hold them accountable for whatever they might find themselves saying. In the event, an arbitrary system of capital letters was used for written recording of the investigation.

Members were provided with some written suggestions regarding the kinds of thing which they might include in their post-session reports. It was stressed that the following was not a questionnaire and need not be strictly adhered to in any way. The important thing was that group members should put down what it was they wanted to say about the particular session. This could be as long or short, vague or precise, as they chose to make it.

Notes (to help you write your own notes on each session)
YOU
- How do it feel on the whole?
- Was there anything which you found helpful?

- Was there anything you found unhelpful?
- Did anything remind you of anything happy?
- Did anything remind you of anything unhappy or disturbing?

THE GROUP
- Was there anything about being in the group which you enjoyed?
- Was there anything about being in the group which you found unpleasant or disturbing?
- Did anything which happened in the group arouse strong feelings in you?
- Was there anything you said which you're glad you said?
- Was there something you said which you wish you hadn't?
- Is there something you didn't say which you wish now that you had?
- Was there anybody who annoyed you in the group? (You should try not to say who.)
- Did you find anybody reassuring?
- OR ANYTHING ELSE YOU WANT TO SAY . . .

Prospective group members were not required to produce written material concerning these two introductory sessions which were designed for the communication of information and resembled seminars. The question arose as to how the sessions should be recorded and the investigator pointed out that the nature of the research would suggest a way of doing this which would be more personal than merely recording the session electronically. The suggestion was made that someone should take notes of the proceedings 'and just do their best to be as accurate as possible'. The volunteer who took the job on got to work immediately producing a short report of this same session. An extract from this appears below:

21st August 2010 (Scribe's notes)
The meeting took place at St John's Church in Wakefield. 8 people were present. One arrived later (having been informed of a later start time). Total 9. Roger took most of the leadership role by explaining what he wanted to achieve in his research: He explained about Interpretative Phenomenological Research [and went on to explain] the function of 3 different groups:

- Directed — using written material
- Process group — enables people to work through stuff of their own; it usually has a theme and individuals can make unique contributions
- Art-based group — uses a theme to explore ideas through imaginative processes.

The aim of this is to examine what is actually going on in a learning environment. The Church is the body of Christ, we often worship and pray in Church but we do not always know what is going on for other people. This is a chance for people to say what is useful for them.

Aims and objectives of the research were set out:

- to examine group experience
- to provide written evidence
- to examine the purpose of different types of group
- to compare three categories — directive, process and arts-based groups — that is the differences and function of learning where there is a structured content, where the leadership moves from person to person, and the inventiveness of a freer imaginative process where space is allowed to explore more personally and playfully.

A handout was given to all the group members to consider their own personal feed-back.

Members were given questions to ask themselves and to examine their role in the group. The first set of questions on the handout is personal to the individual participants; the second relevant to the group. It is vital that after each group session the participants write down or record in some form what their emotional and cognitive thoughts about the process are. Roger gave everyone present an exercise book to record these.

Finally a discussion ensued of different congregations, of whether the structure of male and female participants will influence the outcomes of the group experience, and that the thesis is Anglican based groupwork. Spiritual awareness will be of paramount importance. [Meeting times were arranged.]

The meeting closed with a sense of anticipation and co-operation.

The author of these notes distributed them to members before the first actual group session began, two days later.

The investigation itself

This consisted of nine sessions of groupwork, each session lasting for one and a half hours and arranged in accordance with one or other of three types of group structure:

1. Directive
2. Process-orientated
3. Art-based.

The sessions took place in the following order: A, B, C, B, C, A, C, A, B.

Session A   **(Directive) (August 23rd, 2010)**
This session used the approach described above. The theme was 'Caring for

each other' and the text used was Week 2 of 'Study Group Material, Lent 2009' in *Transforming Lives* (Diocese of Wakefield, 2008, 65–72), the published guidelines having been previously distributed to group members by the investigator, who led the session in the way set out in 'Study Group Leaders' Notes week-by-week' (2008, 123, 124) and adopted the recommended 'pick-and-mix' approach:

> Do *not* attempt to start at the beginning of a session and plough through to the end. Be selective in the light of what interests your group to try something that might be outside their comfort zone. (2008, 124)

As a result the session covered seven out of the nine groupwork activities, including the acts of worship prescribed for the beginning and end of the session i.e. 'Introduction,' 'Looking back,' 'Let us!' 'The Revelation,' 'Issues to think about.' Members sat in a circle.

Leader's Notes
Because of the heterogeneous nature of the group concerned (different ages, congregations, traditions of churchmanship and degrees of personal involvement in, or commitment to, the Christian faith), the sections of the programme calling for discussion were noticeably lively. The group leader was conscious of the need to move discussion along before it became polarised around the issue of Christian exclusiveness, on which two members held opposing views which the formal structure was designed to contain rather than fully accommodate. On the other hand the provision of definite 'subjects for discussion' encouraged members to feel able to take part; and it may be that this incident had as much to do with temperament as it had with anything else. The shyer members certainly seemed to appreciate being told what to do next and encouraged to find their own way of doing it. The group went away in a cheerful atmosphere, assuring me that they intended to come to the next session, although they understood that the way it would go would largely depend on themselves.

Group Scribe's Notes
The written material [*Transforming Lives* (2) 'Caring for each other'] was followed led by Roger. 9 people present, composition the same, apart from 2 members being absent and 2 new members joining the group. There was a genuine sharing of reflections of times when the group members felt cared for. Scriptural passages were read as directed. Pastoral care was discussed honestly and openly — most group members contributed animatedly to the discussion. Many individual incidents were described in a free and honest manner, the group felt safe and inclusive. The material was adhered to and several people commented that they had found the session interesting. People were

beginning to make connections and complement each other. A volunteer was quickly forthcoming and the issues around 'The Revelation' conjectured upon. The basis of shared faith brought considerable consensus, while instituting a space for consideration. Issues to think about and feedback to the church were discussed quickly and the worship carried out with due reverence. The grace was said as we all held hands, making us a concrete group. A coffee/tea break had been mooted at the beginning of the group. After what seemed like a short time, Roger asked if people wanted a tea-break. The consensus was that we should continue to complete the piece and forego a tea-break. When the session was finished — people were talking and sharing. The group has gelled and become a unit. The general feeling was positive and co-operative, with individuals looking relaxed and affirmed. Roger announced that the next meeting would be concerned with the theme of sharing: what we actually feel about sharing.

Session B   (Process) (September 2nd, 2010)

This session used the approach described earlier. Group members had been reminded at the end of the previous session that this one would be directed by the group itself, and the Leader repeated this at the beginning of this session. He said that his job this time was to facilitate the proceedings, encouraging people to express themselves on matters they themselves brought into the conversation. The aim, he pointed out, was to allow the members to develop a sense of working together as individuals with their own ideas and feelings who had expressed a common willingness to embark on the process of developing a sense of identity as a group. Because the final aim of the investigation was to compare people's experiences regarding three different kinds of groups, it was important to have the same overall theme as last time — that of 'Sharing burdens.' In order to get things going, he invited members to take turns saying their first names and 'one thing which has stood out for me during this last week.' When everyone had done this, he invited any members who might like to do so to start a discussion on the subject of sharing, so that others could comment on what was said. The session was divided into two forty minute periods, with a short tea interval. Ten minutes before the end there was a time for open prayer, and the session closed with everyone saying the Lord's Prayer together. Members sat in a circle.

Leader's/Facilitator's notes

Members were perfectly willing to describe events which had taken place in their lives during the past week. Most of these were of a cheerful or celebratory nature, except for Mrs J's contribution which concerned a family crisis. Once permission to speak freely had been given, proceedings became slower. At first it seemed as if people couldn't think of anything to say or didn't want to 'take the plunge' until others had prepared the way. Miss Y, whose account of a recent train journey had aroused a good deal of interest from the rest of the group, myself included, was the first person to take the opportunity to tell everybody something which she obviously needed to talk about. This concerned obstructive behaviour on the part of a relative whose co-operation she felt she should have been able to take for granted. Miss Y was considerably upset by what she was describing, and this brought a sympathetic response from several people, notably Mr and Mrs N. Seeing Miss Y was angry about what had happened, and sensing that anger was a subject likely to give rise to varied reactions from the group, I said that I thought it was a pity that this should have happened when Miss Y was trying to perform a worthwhile task for someone. Almost immediately someone (I think it was Mrs K) brought up the subject of betrayal, and this idea was seized on by Miss H, who reminded the group of Peter's failure to support Jesus in his hour of need — something which she said she had difficulty in understanding. Mr L said that he thought it was necessary for Peter to behave like this and afterwards be forgiven: this was God's purpose and Peter had to do it. This turned out to be a controversial opinion, and several people appeared to be taken aback by what Mr L had said. Miss H complained, forcibly, that 'that kind of attitude makes us all puppets', and there were murmurs of agreement.

I reacted by trying to combine the opposing attitudes, saying that both these things were true, but Peter's human response was part of the story we had been given and try to live by. Mrs J said, 'I don't believe in predestination,' adding that she was 'an Evangelical not a Calvinist.' She said this rather defensively, as if she was aware of having a reputation as a fundamentalist, and went on to say that she thought differences of personality and temperament affected our views as Christians. Mr L said, 'I know this is going to be an unpopular thing to say, sexist or something, but the fact is women are better at sharing and caring for others than men.' There seemed to be a good deal of agreement about this, and when I pointed out that I had come across examples of mothers whose supportiveness was directed towards their sons at the expense of their daughters, Mr N was eager to say how his wife (who was also present) certainly never showed this kind of partiality. He went on to remind us about the ability that groups of men have to look after their comrades, pointing to the situation in Chile, where a body of miners were trapped underground with no prospect of immediate rescue. Mr N jumped in to remind the group of the camaraderie which develops among fellow combatants when the common danger binds them together. Someone said that this could happen even in peacetime, in situations where 'people feel they're all in the same boat.' I told the group of an experience of my own as a National Serviceman when my fellow 'squaddies' felt that I had been given favourable treatment which broke the bond of solidarity previously existing among us. (I realise now that I was reverting to the theme which dominated the earlier part of the session, that of 'betrayal'; and in fact I had a sense of having let myself down by telling this study as it involved a suicide attempt on my part. I had never spoken about it to anyone outside my own family. Was I 'facilitating' myself at the group's expense?) After what I felt was an embarrassed pause, the discussion continued. Mrs J said something about the limitations of our attempts to be unselfish: 'Only God can really care.' As we were approaching the end of the session, I suggested that people might like to spend a few moments in 'open prayer'. Several of those present offered prayers, and we finished by saying the Lord's Prayer together. During this latter part of the session I was aware of developing warmth within the group. Although some people had said very little, Mrs A and Mrs K, for example, there had been a sense of people's presence which contributed to an overall feeling of community. The session left me feeling unsure of my own contribution, feeling that I should have been more discreet. By showing too much of myself, had I damaged any authority I might need with regard to my role in the other kinds of group format? Mr L had the last word, delivered to me personally after the others had left the room: 'Remember, confession is good to the soul . . . '

Scribe's notes
There were 12 people present; one new member and one back from holiday. The beginning was a small recap to inform the new member and the rest of the group of the purpose and function of the session: to build a group, by coming together and drawing strength from being in a group. The first task, then, was to talk about something interesting since we last met. Everyone in the group participated, some with serious concerns that seemed difficult to solve practically, some with genuinely happy and joyous situations that they felt they could share. Everyone was intensely interested in each individual's participation. The theme of the session, Roger said, is going to be about sharing and bearing each other's burdens. A discussion took place reiterating that it is often necessary to accept that there is no answer to life's trials, but at least we can empathise and understand the perspective of the individual. After several contributions the general consensus was that it is really important to receive permission from others to express what we feel. This led on to trusting in God and giving it all to Him. The fundamental question of betrayal was then aired — people sometimes let us down and betray our trust: Jesus was betrayed by the people He loved. Several members of the group were in awe of the fact that God, through Jesus, can feel as we do, yet still forgive and reinstate people in the previous relationship. A break for tea occurred here, and Roger was quite firm in allocating time for a change in focus. This allowed people to break into smaller groups and talk animatedly about issues that had been brought up for them in the previous discussion. Then, the issue of male and female contributions in sharing emotions was discussed, with different contributions and perspectives on the norms and mores of society. Consideration of mother-daughter relationships led on to the bond the miners who are trapped in Chile are displaying. Also the Army, Navy and Air Force: the

special understanding of people in extreme situations. Accepting the power of the group experience in many areas of life enabled us to share some of our deepest feelings. The discussion then went back to betrayal, forgiveness, pre-destination and free will: 'Peter the disciple of Jesus' was just 'an ordinary bloke.' A time of open prayers then concluded the meeting, finishing with the Lord's Prayer. (Dates were agreed for the next meeting, which will be an art-based one. People were asked to bring their diaries/calendars to make dates for the next 3 sessions.) Again, the feeling at the end of the group was that we had been part of a very healing experience and the commitment to the group was solid.

Session C   (Art-based) (September 8th, 2010)
The session was adapted from Grainger (2002), the Leader acting as artistic director of the group.

- People were asked to use the space available to wander round, trying to keep as far from anyone else as possible. (The meeting space had been left empty of chairs, and members were given permission to move out into the church and explore it if they wished to do so.)
- Now they were invited to say hello to the people they knew very well, at first ignoring the others, then greeting them and bringing them into the central space.
- Dividing into two 'casts' of five, the groups were asked to invent their own scenarios on the theme of 'Offering help and being rejected.' These would then be acted out in turn, with the other group as audience. The scenes could have dialogue, or be shown in mime, with or without a narrator.
- After a refreshment break, members were summoned back into the circle to share their experiences as actors and audience members.
- The group read the Parable of the Good Samaritan, going round the circle, each person reading a sentence before passing the book on to her/his neighbour.
- The group members were given paper and pencils and asked to write down what they imagined the Priest, Levite and Samaritan giving as excuses for not going to the assistance of the man who had been robbed (or in the latter case, being tempted not to do so). They took turns to read out what they had written. Open discussion followed.
- There was a pause for reflection and/or listening to music.
- Everybody said the Lord's Prayer together. They took hands to say the grace.

Leader's notes
Nobody seemed particularly surprised at being invited to wander round, perhaps because the empty space and absence of the usual ring of chairs had already prepared them for something out of the ordinary. Likewise there was very little resistance to the idea of having to create scenarios

to be performed before an audience. Mr M pointed out that rehearsing the scenes would interfere with their spontaneity: surely improvisation would be better? I said that improvisation was certainly an option; it was up to the cast to decide. I stressed the fact that we were not looking for good performances but for imaginative treatments of the theme, which was 'trying to help and finding it hard'. As it happened both groups produced at least one notable performance: Mr M's own as a Saturday night kerb crawler and Mrs K's as the young mother of a dead child who refused to allow anyone into her house, where she knelt clutching a doll and comforting it as if it were alive, a really moving scene which members of the group continued to discuss during the coffee break and for several minutes after, when we had re-convened. I remarked on the fact that Mrs J hadn't been one of the actors and Miss Y, who had been a member of the same group, said that the scenario had come from a suggestion from Mrs J: 'I'm afraid I don't do acting, Roger, but I told them about the women in Holbeck, and that gave us the idea for the drama.' Mrs J went on to describe her work among prostitutes in Leeds: 'They do what they loathe doing in order to make a living.' What she said, like Mrs K's performance, had an emotional impact on all of us, making it possible to move on from the heightened atmosphere of play-making and performance into a deeper appreciation of the message for each one of us contained in Jesus's parable. So the session ended quietly in a reflective atmosphere.

Scribe's notes
There were 10 people present, two members having sent their apologies. The intention was to have no chairs and to explore the space. Roger (the Leader) asked us to walk around not speaking to anyone, then to say 'Hello' and begin to make contact. People entered into this — grounding them, then making contact with the group. Next, two small groups were formed. We were to think up a scenario and present it to the other group.
The theme was offering help and having that help rejected, or being helped ourselves.
There were five people in each group, and the process of deciding on a scenario and putting it together was obviously different for each group. Two group presentations took place:

1. A young mother with a child, refusing to answer the door or accept any help. Many different officials summoned and attempts made, but eventually both mother and child were dead.
2. Two young prostitutes approached by a person trying to make contact and offer help. Although the girls took the chocolate he pressed on them, the girls refused to connect or interact.

107

(At this point we had a break, during which we were not meant to discuss the previous depictions. This proved very hard!) Next, discussion took place of the circumstances presented in the depictions. Roger brought in the theme of the Good Samaritan and we each read out a sentence from the story. Roger then asked us to write down two excuses or apologies which the Levite or the Priest might have made along with what the Samaritan may have had in mind before helping. All the group members participated, using their imaginations to pull the situation in the parable into a contemporary context. This involved some spontaneous prayers and we finished with the Lord's Prayer, holding hands to say the Grace. Group commitment was obviously very strong and there was a high degree of interaction.

Session D   (Process) (November 12th, 2010)

This was the second of the sessions described earlier. Group members had been reminded at the end of the last session that this one would be directed by themselves, and that the Leader would form part of the group while keeping a watchful eye on the proceedings to make sure that everybody would have a chance to say what she or he really wanted to say without being 'crowded out.' As before, in Session B, the aim was to develop a sense of being together as a group. The overall theme of this and the next two sessions would be 'Growing in grace.' There would be a pause after forty minutes for a ten-minute refreshment break before the final part of the session. This time we would start with a few minutes' silent meditation instead of taking turns to say our names. As before, however, we would allow some time at the end for open prayer. The session would end with our saying the Lord's Prayer together.

Leader's/Facilitator's notes

After the short silence I reminded everyone what the theme was. Almost immediately Mr L said, quite forcibly, that in his opinion it was harder for older people to change their ways than younger ones. (He is over 80 years old.) The older you get, he said, the more trouble you have with fixed ways of thinking. Mrs J (mid-40s) immediately said that she believed real change only came from God, who had given her the help of the Spirit to change her life. This aroused a high degree of interest within the group, as people seemed to want to agree with her in ways which were less forthright. I said that I felt I knew what Mr L meant, and some others seemed to agree with me. Mrs J had mentioned that St John's Church (where the sessions are held) was not the kind of church she was used to, but she came because she liked 'the people and the atmosphere'. Mrs Y (whom I have been calling Miss Y by mistake) followed this up by saying that St John's had been 'a real home' to her; she didn't know how she could have coped without it: 'It's like a new world to me.' Mr L said that he found some of the ways the service had been changed disturbing ('I like real hymns, not "Jack and Jill" songs.').

Mrs J took issue with the statement, saying that what happens in church is unimportant compared with the truth of the Bible message. Mrs D said she had known many church congregations and it was important to keep a balance. Mr M broke his silence to say that the Christian tradition was older than the NT writings. At this point I said that I thought there were opposing attitudes among Christians, some seeing faith as unchangeable, others as a developing experience: 'I think we all of us feel that by ourselves we can never get it right.' (I seem to remember saying something about Pharisees . . .) Mrs H said, quietly but firmly, that it was all about 'accepting being accepted.' I suggested that 'growing in grace' and 'developing as a person' were closely associated, and we broke up for ten minutes. When we sat down again, Mrs Y, still clutching her coffee mug, said that she would like to say something. She spoke for a few minutes about what it was like to suffer from occasional times of deep depression. This had started when, some years ago, she had been divorced by her husband 'out of the blue'. She described her anger and the way she had turned it against herself: 'It doesn't go away, you know, and this is why I come here.' She said that she had recently emerged from 'a really bad time.' There seemed to be a feeling that people wanted to say something, but didn't know what to say. Instead of waiting for someone else to speak, I said that I thought Mrs J and Mrs Y reminded me of John Newton and William Cowper, both of them hymn-writers, but with very different experiences of being a Christian. Encouraged by Mrs J's warm smile, I went on to say that I thought that souls and minds, although connected, weren't actually the same thing. This unlocked something in Mrs A, who said that she found her mind was always getting in the way of 'things she knew were OK' — things which she actually wanted to do and enjoyed doing. 'I'm bothering with trivial things, and the families I'm trying to help have *real* problems.' (She is a probation officer.) It turned out she was describing an experience familiar to other group members. Mrs S (the Scribe) said that she had been 'conscious that we seem to be more aware of being a group,' and Miss H agreed that this certainly seemed to be happening. Somebody, I can't remember who, said that this was rather surprising since there had been such a long gap since our last meeting (10 weeks). I suggested that we should not leave such a long time between the 3 session courses in future and this was agreed. The prayer time was largely silent, but I was conscious of everyone taking part whether or not they actually said anything aloud. We said the Lord's Prayer together. During this session every member had made a definite contribution to the group process.

Scribe's notes
Ten people present. The group took place at the back of the church with seats arranged in a circle. Roger brought in a heater, so no-one was cold,

even though it was a dark and miserable night. The theme of 'Growing in Grace' was announced by Roger, who reminded us that it was a 'process' group. Initially a silence was maintained that set the theme and ambience. The theme provoked an immediate response from several members of the group: 'old habits die hard'; 'the Holy Spirit empowers us to do what we cannot do on our own'; 'it's like growing up into adulthood'; 'we often try to operate in our own strength, and the Holy Spirit is much more powerful.' Individuals were immediately able to reveal their innermost thoughts without reticence; discipline and obedience were discussed and shared. References were made to the way we often stagnate, and then have a time of moving forward, of being able to feel God's presence and being able to grow again. People agreed about the importance of fellowship — no-one has to do things on their own. Roger brought up the notion that perhaps gender makes a difference to being able to express ourselves regarding our feelings. The discussion moved onto discipline and theology, with some current issues related to Christianity, tradition and worship. Faith-life may reflect psychological-life and yet transcend it. Anger and depression were revealed and aired. The whole group were engaged in this discussion, although two people participated less than the others. Everyone seemed able to share their thoughts, challenge others without animosity and listen attentively to individual contributions. We finished by praying the Lord's Prayer and saying the Grace. Next week's session was mentioned (by Roger) as being an 'art-based' one, and this provoked some discussion about role-play and drawing. However the group has been re-kindled and the mutual support and group commitment is high.

Session E (Art-based) (November 19th, 2010)

Again, the session was adapted from Grainger (2002). This time it was directed by the Scribe, with the author taking part as one of the group members.

1. Members were asked to stand in a circle, close enough to hold each others' hands. Then, they were invited to move closer still, so they could put their arm round their neighbour's shoulder and start to sway slowly, first to the left, then the right. They could say hello to one another while they were doing this.
2. Everyone sat down in a circle of chairs, while the Director explained that the session theme was people's journey onwards. She asked them to draw or paint some dramatic change which had happened to them personally, each sitting at one of the small tables and using the materials laid out on them.
3. Next, members were asked to find a partner and talk to them about their pictures.
4. The pictures were collected together, shuffled, and laid out on the

tables, one of them on each table. Members were invited to walk round looking at them. If they wanted to, they could jot down comments on the blank sheets of paper accompanying the pictures.

5. The Director asked members to write a story about one of the pictures (not their own) and place this by the picture. (At this point there was a ten minute coffee/tea break.)

6. The Director read the story of Jonah to the group.

7. She invited members to discuss what she had been reading, with particular reference to the story's ending.

8. She asked the group whether Jonah's story related to anything in their own one? Were there times when they found it hard to deal with change? Did it take a long time? Would they like to be able to 'forgive the past'?

9. She invited members to read out the story which had been placed by their picture.

10. The group said the Lord's Prayer together, holding hands.

Leader/group member's notes

Eight people were present, three group members being unwell. I had asked the Scribe to be Director, and she had seemed quite happy to play the role. She explained the situation to the group, saying she was going to direct from 'Roger's book' so if anything went wrong it would be Roger who was to blame! I admit to feeling slightly unnerved by this, but the members relate extremely well to the Scribe, and so things got off to a good start (although Mr L, who is 80+, was alarmed at the idea of having to put his arm round the neck of the tall lady standing next to him). Because she was working from the structure I had provided, and I was present, the Scribe was less confident in the suggestions she made to the group, but they seemed to have no difficulty in carrying out her instructions. As a group member freed from the normal responsibility of 'being in charge' I appreciated being allowed to give scope to my imagination. In fact, the picture I produced was a surprise to me because it turned out to be about a 'dramatic change' which until then I hadn't identified, usually being more preoccupied with the more obvious ones which I think and talk about almost automatically. My partner obviously enjoyed creating an image which would give me some idea of the significance of a spiritual discovery which had confirmed her allegiance to Christ (if not always to the Church!). Mrs J, who opted out of acting during the first 'art-based' group, declined to produce a picture and wrote an account of her experience instead. Despite being determinedly non-artistic, she gives a lot of herself to these sessions. The fact is that members enjoyed both the pictures and the stories, spending some time working on them, which accounts for the session's running over time. Another reason for this, however, was the decision to read the whole of the Book of Jonah (which I hadn't intended, having origi-

111

nally divided it up into 3 parts). This meant that the last part of the book, the part we were asked to discuss, had to be read twice. In the event, this part of the evening was very powerful, despite the Scribe's nervousness: 'Am I doing this properly?' Mr L said that he couldn't see why Jonah was so angry with God, and Mrs E said that Jonah felt that the Nenevites should have been punished: his job had been to warn them of God's wrath 'and here was God, letting them off!' I said I thought this was a very human reaction; Jonah's whole story was intensely human. Someone (the Scribe) said, 'It shows that God is so much more loving than we are.' As it turned out, I was the only person to read out the story to someone who had written about my picture. The way the story ended reminded me of an incident in my own life, and I thought it was significant. I realise now I shouldn't have done this because there was no time left for other people to read theirs if they wanted to. So we said the Lord's Prayer and then said goodbye. I told the Scribe how pleased I was that she had agreed to direct the session, and she said, 'I'm glad that's over.' I think that we were both unsettled by the reversal of roles, she at the time, I during the rest of the evening when I kept thinking I hadn't done my job properly. At the same time, at a deeper level, I had been deeply moved in a way I can't really explain; or at least, not yet.

Scribe's notes
There were 9 present, with no apologies received. The group took place at the back of the church, in the reception room. Initially while music played we all stood together in a circle and swayed to the right and to the left, getting a little closer together and making clear connection while centring ourselves. We then sat in a circle before moving into separate spaces to depict, by drawing or design, a time in our lives when we had experienced a dramatic change. We then moved into pairs and described our own picture or story to our partner. The pictures (depictions) were placed separately, each one with a blank piece of paper. As if they were in an art gallery, we looked at them all and made written comments on the sheets of paper, before choosing one to them to write a short story about. We left our stories by the picture we had chosen and joined together again to have a cup of coffee or tea. After the break, the Leader read the story of Jonah in its entirety to the group, explaining that there really should have been three workshops attached to the story, but we were simply doing the final one. Then she read the last part of the story again (Jonah in Ninevah) and asked us to make connections with our own stories and pictures of the time in our lives when we had experienced dramatic change. Individuals were then asked to collect their own depiction and the comments and stories (where there was one). Little time was given for people to read out the comments and stories left by other people about their depictions. We closed with the Lord's Prayer

while holding hands. Group commitment was very high, but feedback to the group was much more limited. Individuals appeared to be processing their own individual journey — perhaps needing more time to respond. People could participate very privately without being exposed to the group. The final prayer was heart-felt and very meaningful. The Leader announced that the next group would be a directed one.

Session F   (Directive) (November 29th, 2010)

This was the second directive session. The theme was 'Growing in God.' Material was taken from that set out in Week 3 of *Transforming Lives* (Diocese of Wakefield, 2008, 73–82). As before, the guidelines provided for the complete course had been issued by the investigator who led the session according to the approach described in the 'Group Leaders Notes' (2008, 123, 124). This time, however, the session proceeded as set out in the handbook, all sections being dealt with in order ('Introduction,' 'Stories of Faith,' 'River of Spiritual Life,' 'Lessons in Spiritual Growth'). The sections which dealt with a specific church congregation were omitted as this group is drawn from more than one local church. The session began and ended with the sections provided for worship. As before, the group sat in a circle around a central table, and the session was led by the investigator.

Leader's notes

There were 7 people present, several having been prevented by the weather from making the journey to the church where meetings take place. There had been a heavy fall of snow during the past few days, so that I was expecting to have to cancel the meeting. The people whom I contacted were enthusiastic about coming, however, so we went ahead. As it turned out the element of challenge gave the session a sense of adventure, so that this turned out to be a very lively and productive session, with everybody present involved in the discussion, so that the time passed very quickly and I have a feeling that things were shared at a level which we did not manage to reach in Session A and have rarely done since we started the course of sessions. The fact that the format encourages those taking part to try to respond to questions asked and directions given in the text, and that group members are normally willing to do what is required of them is, I think, partly responsible for keeping things going; but it needs more than this to produce the level of self-disclosure attained on this occasion, as people engaged with the suggestion presented in the text that they should each try to remember 'What has most helped you grow as a Christian?' Each of us tried to answer. For Mrs J it was 'the warmth and fellowship of fellow believers', something which Miss H identified with; for Mrs A it was the repeated experience of being rescued from failures — something which Mrs E said she recognised in her own life; Miss H found that time spent for spiritual refreshment away from the pressures of life had brought her most refreshment and helped her to grow as a Christian; and Mrs E said that the most important thing was 'silence'; Mrs K (and also myself) described the experience of coming out of a time of alienation and disillusion into the knowledge of acceptance and hope; Mr M said that it was the discovery that spiritual fulfilment did not depend on being a Christian. I expected Mrs J to come back strongly at this point, but she didn't. Perhaps in the atmosphere of sharing which had been created, she was able to allow herself to understand something of what Mr M had meant. We concluded the session by arranging dates for the next 3 sessions, to take place during the month after next (i.e. after Christmas).

(Deputy) Scribe's notes
8 members were present. The session began with worship from the material supplied. Members of the group were directed to work in pairs. They were asked to think about their own schooldays, what they liked or disliked, and to tell their partner what lessons they had learned in terms of what messages they absorbed about themselves or life in general. All sat round a large table. Significant time was allowed. Contributions seemed animated and people seemed to be offering a high level of personal disclosure. Next, each member of the group took it in turns to read different people's accounts of growing in faith from the handout, and the group was asked whose story they most related to. Before answering, the group discussed the account of Stephen (from the handout) who recounted: 'I haven't changed my mind about anything. I still believe what I was taught forty years ago.' After considerable animated discussion about Stephen's story, group members went on to share with the group which of the accounts from the handout they themselves most related to, sharing valuable personal experiences often shedding light on their choices. Some people related specifically to one story, others to bits of several. The quality of the contributions was high, indicating a high level of trust, awareness and engagement. Next, the question was asked 'What has helped you grow as a Christian?' Members of the group were invited to share experiences with the group as a whole about what in their lives had produced spiritual growth. An extraordinarily fertile discussion followed in which people described significant points of processes in their lives which they felt had resulted in spiritual growth. Some of these had been dark and painful at the time. One person's account often triggered another person into sharing a similar or related experience. Some accounts told of apparent road-blocks to development, which might appear differently from another perspective. This discussion was very personal, open and animated. Drivers for Christian growth included: fellowship, people in different ways, prayer, the Word. (Time had begun to run out so the group didn't get on to discuss a series of questions.) Members were encouraged to say one thing about their journey. Comments included: 'Wish I wasn't

114

so selfish'; 'Still on the journey'; 'Lots of help from retreats and retreat guides'; 'Full of surprises'; 'Permission to doubt, and it's OK for me'; 'Questioning and frustration'. The session concluded with the act of group worship (from the handout).

Session G   (Art-based) (January 21st, 2011)

The session was adapted from Grainger (2002), the Leader acting as artistic director of the group.

1. People were asked to stand in a circle and say who they were. Then they were asked to go round again, this time saying three things about themselves: what they like doing, what they don't like doing, and what they would like to do.
2. Leader announced the theme of the session: 'Evangelism and sharing faith'.
3. Group members were asked to walk across the circle and say hello to someone personally.
4. Members were invited to think of a gift which they would like to give someone in the group, based on the three things they said about themselves. They should write this down and keep it with them until later in the session.
5. Having found partners, people were asked to exchange memories of times in their lives when somebody they didn't know had given them something unexpected which they had found of value.
6. Leader asked members to find new partners in the group and act out a scene with them in which one person was sitting on a park bench and the other person approached and sat by them without being invited. They should try to show how they felt about this by the amount of space they left between them, varying this as the conversation developed (or didn't develop). How did they feel? What did they think the other person felt like?
7. After a break, members sat in a circle and took turns to read from Jn 4:5–15, the Leader reading the whole passage and then passing the book round so that everyone could read a verse.
8. Leader invited members to say what they felt and thought about the story of the woman at the well.
9. He asked them to share their feelings about the 'park bench' experience. Were the two related? What did they think?
10. There was a pause for prayers said silently or aloud. Everyone said the Lord's Prayer.
11. Members were asked to give their 'gift papers' to the people they were intended for, making sure that no-one was left out.
12. The Grace was said together.

Leader's notes

This was the first of the final group of 3 sessions. Only six of us were present as four people were too ill to attend and 2 more sent their apologies. Those who came threw themselves whole-heartedly into the session. Two things stand out very clearly: the 'park bench' exercise and the discussion regarding the Samaritan Woman. Perhaps because it was a very simple idea and left a lot of scope for imagination, 'strangers in the park' produced some fascinating scenarios. (Mrs S said that she found herself understanding, for the first time in her life, 'what it must be like to be gay and feel guilty about it'.) People had not been invited to share with the group what it was they said to their partners in the first half of the session, so the discussion about the Samaritan gave them an opportunity to see their own experiences that more vividly. It also opened up a lot of intense feeling regarding the treatment of foreigners and refugees. Mrs J with whom I associate a tendency to be very sure where she stands on most subjects, told us about her new friends, the Polish family who had moved in next door to her and whom she found she liked very much, 'and there's a Russian lady just down the street.' (Although by no means bigoted, Mrs J is very strongly Protestant. Her friends, she revealed, are Roman Catholic and Orthodox, however.) During the course of the session there was a growing sense of sharing in a process of discovery which made the story of the 'Woman at the Well' very vivid for us — and also made the exchange of gifts seem particularly significant. I am beginning to wonder whether it might not be possible to carry on the group for another 3 sessions, but as yet I haven't asked members what they think about this.

Scribe's notes

Six people were present, with apologies from three. Initially we all stood in a circle and said three things about ourselves. No-one had any trouble with this and we were able to go quickly and clearly round the group. Pairing with another person, we talked about when we had received an unexpected gift from someone, describing the feelings. We each wrote down a gift to this person and kept it till later. A situation in which two people sat on a park bench not knowing each other took place. We took it in turns to be already sitting there, and the second person experimenting with sitting further away or nearer on the bench. Each pair had a conversation, some of these interested and animated. A tea break occurred here with the wonderful addition of cakes and biscuits brought by one member of the group. We read John 4, the Samaritan woman at the well. Roger read out the first section of the reading, then we read one sentence each to reinforce the reading. A very interesting discussion ensued of the situation of the woman at the well and the living water. Everyone spoke, and people clearly asked for clarification, alongside some theories based both on research and conjecture. It is interesting that the group is now totally accepting of anything said, and individuals support each other. Next, the earlier gift was given to the recipient. Much affirming and convivial discussion ensued. Finally, informal prayers were said, finishing with the Lord's Prayer.

When clearing up after the session a lot of conversations and exchanges took place concerning the session. This is informal but extends the interest and continues to validate individuals. (We were given a hand-out regarding the next session, which is directive.)

Session H   (Directive) (January 28th, 2011)

This was the 3rd Directive session. Its theme was 'Evangelism and sharing faith' (Week 4, 'Study Group Material, Lent 2009'; *Transforming Lives*, Diocese of Wakefield, 2008, 83–91). The published guidelines for this had been distributed beforehand. The session was conducted by the investigator as Leader, in line with the 'Group Leader's Notes' (2008, 123, 124). The order of procedure followed that of the handbook: 'Worship,' 'Introduction,' 'Role Play,' 'Your Journey,' 'Good News to Share,' 'Worship,' omitting sections which did not include all of those present. The group sat in a circle round the table.

Leader's notes

There were 8 people present, four being absent owing to illness. (Two of these, Mr and Mrs N have only been able to come for two of the sessions up to now.) This session was marked by a degree of spontaneity which was considerably higher than that attained by either of the two preceding Directive sessions. The game at the beginning in which we had to present arguments in favour of the fruit we liked best was a lot of fun for everybody, and established the theme of persuasion very effectively. The role play was included as an example of how not to evangelise someone, and succeeded in doing this without having to spell it out. Everybody certainly seemed to get the point, and there was a lot of discussion regarding counter-productive evangelisation strategies. Mrs J, who is probably the group member whose evangelising experience is most recent, described her work in a health agency where she frequently has the opportunity to share her faith with those to whom she is employed to help in medical ways. (This, of course, is not an easy thing to do in a society as secular as ours.) Faced with the question, 'What has helped you learn about God and Jesus?', most people said something abstract in reply, but Mrs Y launched into what promised to be a long, detailed story. I was about to bring her back to the point when she arrived at it. It was certainly worth waiting for. Mr M, who as a former Church Army Captain was actually trained as an evangelist, pointed out to me that the Church was responsible for making Christians (whereas I and Mrs J had been talking about the experience of liberation itself . . .). Altogether, the evening passed very enjoyably. Before we dispersed we talked for a short time about the possibility of carrying the group on for a few more sessions.

Scribe's notes
8 people present. The format for the session had been given out the week before and we went through the written material as presented. The descriptions of fruit were lively and highlighted each individual's commitment to the group. The fruits chosen were pear, lemon, banana, kiwi, raspberry, tomato, strawberry and apple. The most votes were collected by the lemon. The written material was followed and questions after each section discussed. Each member of the group joined in without being asked, and understood the rules of the session. Discussion ensued about jargon, formulae, trite responses as opposed to listening and responding to individuals' needs. The discussion was animated and interested: all members of the group were involved. A tea break occurred. The text was taken up again and 'the hope that is in you' seen as crucial. References were made to a television programme and the outcome of a spiritual programme discussed. [This was the BBC's Christmas serial about Jesus's birth — R.G.] When the discussion began to get more animated, Roger redirected the group back to the worship. The worship was completed. Roger suggested that possibly three more sessions could be included and asked the group to consider this. The last of the present series is going to be in two weeks' time, on February 11th.

The session was lively and showed considerable differences of opinion. It was, however, difficult to move away from the scripted piece in order to explore the themes that had arisen. There was some of the work-sheet which asked individuals to respond by discussing their own church. Because we are from several churches we were able to leave these sections out. A very cohesive and united feeling was present at the end of the session, with people taking up previous points and continuing to debate them. The weather was cold outside, but the group seemed unaware of outside influences. All members were able to communicate and everyone was accepted and affirmed.

Session I (Process) (February 11th, 2011)
The third 'process' group aimed, like the two previous ones, at group building, with the overall theme ('Evangelism and sharing faith') to be approached in a way that was group-directed, but facilitated by the Leader whose job would be to take part while trying to make sure that all members would feel encouraged to take part and to express what they really felt and thought without being 'crowded out' by anyone. The session would start with a few minutes' silence and end with a space for free prayer and the Lord's Prayer. There would be a short tea/coffee break halfway through, and members could bring their drinks back into the session in order to allow more time for discussion. Afterwards we would consider whether to arrange any further meetings of the group.

Leader's/Facilitator's notes

There were 9 members present. One member did not turn up and two more were absent through illness. (Mr and Mrs N have only managed to attend twice.) The opening silence went on for a few moments after I had announced its termination, so I explained that this was what often happens with open groups, as nobody wants to be the first to speak. I said that someone had recently described to me a meeting where the facilitator simply held the silence in order to see how long it would go on for. Realising they didn't want me to do this, I reminded them of the theme of the session, and this started some discussion about people who get into conversations with you on trains. Mrs J said that she seemed to attract people who wanted to talk to her on the train and she had to move seats: 'Your duty is to look after yourself.' She was fierce about this. When Mrs A said something about liking to get into conversations, Mrs J said she had been badly harassed on one occasion. Mrs E spoke sensitively to her about this and the rest of the group reacted sympathetically. I asked if anyone had had a good experience talking to a stranger, and described a conversation I once had when I was hitchhiking. Mrs Y told us about an encounter which began in a threatening way but turned out to be good in the end. She added that there had been a time in her life when she felt 'completely abandoned'. Mrs J said that since being a Christian she had never felt like that. I said that perhaps other people may have done, and Mrs A nodded. At this point, feeling I might be in danger of taking over the session, I suggested that we take a short break. When we sat down again I asked if anyone had had any thoughts during the break which they might like to share. Mrs S said, rather timidly, that sometimes things happen, 'quite ordinary things', which made her feel that God had had some kind of message for her — that he was looking after her. She said that these were things she felt she could tell other people about. Mrs E then told how she had done this and been told by somebody that they had no idea what she was talking about. Mrs H said that she felt God was looking after her when she avoided something dangerous, but what about the person that the dangerous thing happened to instead of her? Mrs A said that try as she could she wasn't able to work out the way things work out. I said I thought that we work out about God through our story, i.e. looking back over things rather than puzzling about God when we're in the middle of them. Mr M said that thinking that God helps some and lets others be harmed may be a complete illusion. Had we thought of that? He didn't put this forward very forcefully, 'only for the sake of the discussion'. The consensus seemed to be that we believe in God because of what he has done and does for us personally, and this we should share with other people if we have the opportunity. In this session there was a high level of participation, and everyone spoke at least three times. When I asked about having three more sessions, only Mr M said he couldn't manage the time.

119

Scribe's notes

9 people present with one apology. The theme of the group is 'sharing faith'. The group started with silence, then a prayer. A very general discussion began, considering the nature and focus of groups. Three themes quickly emerged. They were: trust, confidentiality and safety. Everyone in the group made a contribution, with some very serious issues of safety and threatening/abusive/violent behaviour being considered. Travelling on a train or coach enabled the group to share some positive and negative experiences. Faith was discussed in these contexts. A reference was made by Roger to the Ethiopian in the Acts of the Apostles, and one group member talked about the importance of fellowship. Generally the discussion was quite open. People were contributing well and the discussion seemed varied in focus. A break occurred. After the break, one person wanted to bring into the group what God had been doing in our lives. Another member contributed about a further conversation with a family member after a previous group. This seemed to focus the group in a different way: 'There but for the grace of God go I!'; 'speaking in tongues'; 'a clear conviction that God is there' can sometimes be interpreted negatively, with the person speaking seen or perceived to be superior, thus inhibiting further investigation and silencing some people who have become intimidated. Some very profound feelings were shared of the magnitude of God and how Jesus was sent to be the human face of God. Roger interjected at various points and concluded the discussion with a point about stories being really important. We are trying to make sense of an evolving story: Jesus is our guide, using stories to illustrate the path of a Christian. Finally, an exchange took place about different forms of group, the merits and detractions of the three types of group we have looked at. We said a prayer, 'Our Father' and 'The Grace' and finished the session. (Three further groups were arranged for 4th, 11th and 18th March. Everyone agreed to give Roger their personal questions and answers as near as possible to the 18th March.)

Session J (Directive) (March 4th, 2011)

This was the first of the 'extra' sessions, and the fourth directive one. Its theme was 'Working with God in your community' (Session 5 of *Transforming Lives*, Diocese of Wakefield, 2008, 92–101). As before, the material was distributed in advance so that members would have an opportunity to read it beforehand in preparation for the session. We dealt with each section in the order prescribed: 'Introduction,' 'Worship,' 'Communities: Who Are We,' 'Salt and Light,' 'Wise Words,' 'Some Practical Ideas' and 'Worship.' As before, we omitted the section requiring feedback to a host congregation. The group sat round a table on which members were able to place the written material involved. The investigator led the session.

Leader's notes

Six members turned up out of the eight who had opted for a further 3 sessions. I felt a bit annoyed at this but the group worked well together and found the framework provided stimulating enough to overrun the time set for the session. Because there were three congregations represented, the number of local organisations and groups whose life affected or activities impinged upon our own church activities turned out to be greater than it would have been for a single congregation, so this part of the session dragged a little and things didn't really come to life until we reached the section entitled 'Wise Words'. Mrs J was particularly moved by the quotation from St John Chrysostom: 'Don't tell me "It is impossible for me to influence others". If you are a Christian it is impossible for you *not* to influence others! It is impossible for a Christian's light to be concealed.' She said she found this a great comfort, and so did others, particularly Mrs A. At this point the quality of people's contributions seemed to change, and some of the helplessness which members had felt when we were considering the effect their own churches, and they themselves, had on the other groups of people in our local community, seemed to grow less, so that by the time we arrived at the final worship section there was a real feeling of God's presence among us. The first section, in which members said where they would like to live if they were given the opportunity to choose, had proved more of a distraction than a help, although one or two people — Mrs J, Mrs S, Mr L in particular — said they would chose to live where they did (which may, in fact, have been the purpose of the exercise). Throughout the remainder of the evening we were moving towards the clarity which only came at the end, helped by Archbishop Romero's prayer — which is probably why we never made time for our usual tea/coffee break.

Scribe's notes
7 people present, with one apology. The group tonight worked from 'Week 5 — Working with God in your community — *Transforming Lives*, Lent, 2009'. The text was followed completely as set out. Several minutes were explored with thinking where we would each like to live. Several people said they would like to continue living where they are now but have several acres more land — be living in a nature reserve, or by the sea. This provoked some memories of previous houses and places of residence. Other continents were mentioned as well as relationships with people and animals. The poem was read out and a good discussion ensued. The relationship of communities and their inhabitants brought the situation of ethnic minorities to the fore. Chinese people, mental health groups and asylum seekers were especially focused on. Individuals then wrote into their worksheets their own responses to questions asked. Specific groups that individuals were involved with were mentioned and catalogued. This led to a discussion of salt and light, and the fact that we have a responsibility of stewardship. One member of the group challenged the group to be specific about the role of individuals in glorifying our Father in heaven. The 'wise words' from various Christians provoked a

spirited discussion. Someone from the group commented on each of the quotes — except for the quote from Archbishop Desmond Tutu. Practical ideas for the Church to try would be to be more involved with people with addictions, and the pastoral care of older people, who often seem to be abandoned after they have served their usefulness. (The words 'Hot Potato' were used to good effect.) Local parishes were mentioned in the conversations about changes in the current welfare system. Each individual contributed well, and the text was adhered to with no deviation. The prayer at the end of the worksheet was read out and we said the confession together, finishing with holding hands and saying 'Thank you, God'. No tea-break occurred this week but the discussions were focused and each individual was clearly putting in their own perspective. The overall feeling was that of being quite challenged to be thinking about our own particular communities. (Two people said they would be unable to come next week, March 11th.)

Session K (Process) (March 11th, 2011)

This was the final process-orientated group, aimed at allowing members to express their ideas and feelings about the subject ('Working with God in your community') and also about the group itself, with the Leader as Facilitator. As before, the session would start with a time of silence and end with an opportunity for open prayer. There would be a short break halfway through for a cup of tea or coffee, during which members could continue the discussion if they wanted to. Members were reminded of the theme for these last three sessions: 'Working with God in your community.' As before, the chairs had been arranged in a circle.

Leader's/Facilitator's notes

When we had sat down in the circle of chairs I announced the theme. The recent news about the earthquake disaster in Japan was on everybody's mind and I suggested that we might use the time of silence to pray about this. The discussion itself when it started, centred on the idea of Japan as part of the wider community of people throughout the world, one which cuts across all national boundaries. Mrs S asked what the Japanese religion was, and Mrs J said it was Shinto. Nobody seemed to know much about this and Mrs J said that she thought it was a form of ancestor worship. I said that I had read that Japanese people are very aware of social rules about living in community. I said that there were many Christians in Japan, too. Did the group think we were good at dealing with differences among us? This seemed to cause some consternation. Mrs E said that she didn't think there had really been any differences among us, and several people agreed with this. Mrs E went on to say that she had belonged to groups in which there was 'always someone who was determined to bring every discussion round to themselves, a kind of group *prima donna*.' Nobody had tried to do this in our group, she said, and Mrs S agreed with her —

she, too, had suffered from being a member of a group like that. I was about to point out that one of the purposes of groups was to try and work through difficult situations among the members, when Mrs E suddenly said, 'Perhaps Roger is our *prima donna*.' This brought me up sharply, and I said that I realised that I liked the sound of my own voice. Mrs E said, 'Yes, but you are the group leader, it's *your* group', and everyone agreed with her. Rather defensively, I pointed out that the difference between this kind of group and the ones based on *Transforming Lives* was that members were free to take the discussion wherever they themselves chose to take it, without being governed by directions laid down in advance. I had tried to help people do this. Mr L said, 'Yes, I know you have, Roger, but you are the one in authority.' At this point I tried to change direction by asking if anything anyone had said or described in these groups had had a particular impact on the way they thought or felt about anything? Was there anything that they now saw in a new light? There was no immediate response to this, and Mrs S asked me to clarify what I meant. I said, 'Well, for instance, I prefer a more formal kind of worship, and you (Mrs S) come from a Pentecostal background. The kind of worship we like can be a barrier, but things you have said in the group have made me feel differently about this.' Immediately Mr L said how much he personally preferred a traditional form of worship. Mrs S replied by saying that the form of worship doesn't matter: 'It is Christ's presence which counts.' Mrs Y said that she didn't entirely agree with this. Now that she was approaching retirement she had thought of going back to live in Wales. What stopped her, however, was the fact that, not being a Welsh speaker, she found it hard to worship in a language she didn't really understand. This brought us back to the subject of life within a community. Miss H described a TV programme in which well-known people from the UK had undertaken to work with deprived and poverty-stricken families in another part of the world. What had moved her so much was the way in which a famous comedian, known for his light-hearted outlook on life, had burst into tears and admitted his own inability to cope with the anguish around him. Others in the group had seen this programme and shared their feelings of respect for the comedian's honesty and humility (Miss H, Mrs S, Mrs J). This led into our prayer time, in which several people offered prayers about life within a community of other people. We held hands and said the Grace together.

Scribe's notes
7 people were present. Roger began the meeting by having a period of silence for the Japanese people in the wake of the earthquake and tsunami. A discussion of the culture and differences of the Japanese people led us into the topic of 'other communities' and differences. The relationship to church traditions and rituals was likened to literature through the underlying narrative. Very quickly the topic of discussion turned inward to the

group itself. A slight discomfort was expressed about the group not having any arguments and perhaps getting on too well, but this was quickly dispersed. Other group behaviour was compared to this group and a comment made about the group not having a *'prima donna'*. It was confirmed that everyone felt very comfortable in the group and is affirmed and listened to. The process group itself was examined as, although differences exist in the group, people have become cautious yet have proved to tolerate differences well. Learning is taking place from each other and there is a willingness to keep to the guidelines of group behaviour. This is the penultimate session and Roger asked what we remembered from the previous weeks' discussions. Last week's poem at the beginning was a splendid example of all group members getting something from the study. It makes clear that direction taken reduces chaos. The differences in atmosphere of different church services and different church structures was pointed out, with some pros and cons for variety of traditions and keeping elements the same in worship. The trust and confidence in the group provided the backdrop for some members of the group to share their thoughts and feelings about specific issues in their lives. (A coffee and tea break occurred here.) A television programme of some celebrities being in some poverty-stricken areas of Kenya had been seen by several members of the group, and a point about 'not taking hope away' from children mentioned. To make a difference the price has to be paid, was a comment from one member. The structures of the church and issues which we get hung up on do not matter at all to God. The poem from last week was discussed again as one member was not present last week. This led naturally onto relationships with neighbours and some very difficult situations. Advice and insight into the problems of trying to befriend and help people in difficult situations brought us all together again. The power of prayer is so important. We finished with the Lord's Prayer, held hands and said the Grace together. Next week, on 18th March, it is the last week and is the final art-based group.

Session L   (Art-based) (March 18th, 2011)
This session was adapted from Grainger (2002), leader and scribe acting as artistic directors of the group.

1.   People were invited to stand in a circle. Leader: *'Say the name of the person next to you, either on you right or you left. If they then say your name, you can either say theirs again or give in and say the person's name on your other side.'*
2.   Members were asked to find partners and compose a short scene in which one person visits the other at home and tells her/him the various problems he/she has on her/his mind. Members were invited to think of their own experiences of sharing and the people they shared them with: *'Who would you take something really important to?'*

124

3.   People stood in a circle, holding hands, and sang a hymn which everyone knew well.

4.   The group read 'The Last Supper' (Lk 22:7–27), each person taking it in turns to read a sentence.

5.   After the break for refreshment (and conversation) members stood in a circle, arranging themselves in pairs in order to exchange invisible gifts which they thought up with this particular person in mind.

6.   On a large sheet, people wrote down all the things in life which can and should be shared and which help us to feel we belong together. The sheet was placed on a table in the centre of the circle.

7.   The directors asked the group to imagine that these were things which they were bringing to Jesus's last supper with the disciples. There was a time of silence.

8.   The group leaders thanked the members for the work they had all done during the 12 sessions.

9.   Some prayers were said, including the Lord's Prayer and the Grace.

Leader's notes

I said first of all that the theme of this final session was to be 'Belonging together'. The game with names, after a tentative start, developed with a lot of imagination and caused a good deal of hilarity, so that things seemed to develop a party atmosphere (which was suitable for a final session, perhaps). The 'home visits' lasted rather longer than planned, as two of the couples were obviously engrossed in whatever it was that they were sharing. Mr L was the first person to choose a hymn, and led the singing with 'The Lord's My Shepherd'. I noticed that he missed out the verse which begins 'Yes, though I walk through death's dark vale.' I pointed this out to him and we sang that verse as well. I got the impression that people were quite proud of the performance. I introduced the 'Last Supper' reading, which we shared. After the break I became less conscious of the structure of the session although we still kept to the format; somehow I lost myself in thinking what I should give to my partner, who was Mrs S. (I finally decided to give her 'A calm and Heavenly frame', as in Cowper's hymn.) The sheet of paper was covered with the names of things to be shared, some mundane, like various household tasks (Mrs J), some inspiring (Mrs E, Miss H). The table in the middle of the circle reminded me very powerfully of what we had been reading together. I was suddenly aware of the reality of what we were sharing in Christ, and said that I would keep the sessions as a treasure for the future. We said the Lord's Prayer together. I sensed that people were moved. Mrs S said that we 'should all have a party when the research is all finished.'

Scribe's notes

7 people were present. We initially stood in a circle and spoke to people on either side of us; we could not speak to anyone else and only used first

names. After a few rounds we were asked to do the same thing with different emotions. This provoked some laughter and serious concentration. In pairs (and a three) we were asked to make up a scene where you call on a friend at home to discuss your day; afterwards we reflected on whom you would talk to and who would talk to you. This seemed to be productive in each small group. We sat in a circle and sang 'The Lord's My Shepherd'. Our tea break occurred here. On a large piece of paper we wrote all the things which can be shared and which help us feel we belong together. Everyone participated well in this task and there was some discussion of these things. Each person in the group read a sentence from 'The Last Supper'. This was very considered and serious. Personal response — in pairs again, we talked about what we would give to the person sitting on our left. All groups seemed serious and animated. Reflection of the points brought up from the material of the evening, plus reflections on the whole twelve, was very productive here; everyone spoke, clarified thoughts and were accepted by the whole group. Roger led us in a prayer of thanks, then 'The Lord's Prayer' followed by 'The Grace'.

As this was the last meeting some time was spent in analysing what we had all got out of the group. In addition, Roger was asked about his research. Everyone seemed keen to meet up again when Roger has finished his writing, to celebrate his work. Goodbyes were said, with clear instructions to return all comments on the whole twelve groups to Roger as soon as possible. Everyone participated in this final group with 100% interest and commitment.

5

Examining and Interpreting the Results

The analytical process

Members submitted their impressions regarding the group sessions attended. This was done after the final meeting (No. 12, Session L). The material submitted was then subjected to a phenomenological analysis involving a four-stage process of progressive interpretation in which underlying themes were brought to the surface:

Stage 1   Group members prepare their written depositions
Stage 2   Written material submitted for scrutiny
Stage 3   First analytical stage: themes identified (see Table B.1 in Appendix B)
Stage 4   Themes analysed to discover underlying structure.

The first member to submit her impressions of the course of sessions was Mrs S. The examiner's task was to identify the main themes which emerged from what she had written. Instructions had been given for submissions to be presented in the form of notebooks set aside for this purpose, but only half the members kept to this, the others using various ways of presenting their material. The material submitted by other group members was then treated in the same way, building on and extending the range of themes, so that a comprehensive picture emerged from the evidence as it accumulated. Attempts were made to include all the themes, and to see which of them fell into 'natural' groupings, each of which represented the underlying reaction to a particular human experience — in other words what Kelly (1991b) identifies as a 'personal construct' (see Table B.2 in Appendix B).

(i) The data to be analysed

In dealing with the data which gradually began to emerge as a result of this process, the Kellian notion of the 'cognitive construct' was a primary tool. A construct is not a concept, but a logical way of separating things as distinguishable ideas in order to give some kind of form to what would otherwise be perceptual confusion. They work in pairs, as 'dichotomous abstractions' (Kelly, 1991b, 218), the 'this-not-that' which we apply to every human situation in which we are involved, helping us to make distinctions at various levels of importance. Themes emerging from the written material produced by group members are thus presented in the form of constructs for purposes of comparison and assessment. Constructs act as building blocks for our personal ways of making sense of life according to the way that we and others perhaps, assess the importance and value of things we experience. In other words, they are themes which occur and recur in our discourse regarding our perception of the world we live in. Thus, the number of times a construct is used in connection with a particular category of event is an indication of the importance that is being attributed to it as a way of evaluating such events.

Kelly describes the grouping of constructs in order of their importance in the way we arrive at decisions about what is most important to us so far as life's meanings are concerned. A construct's importance is to be assessed by its position within a system of related constructs, which is itself based on the actual judgements made with regard to events and experiences interpreted in the light of a limited number of judgements which emerge as our principal ways of making sense of the entire system. Ideographically speaking a 'personal construct system' (Kelly, 1991a, 83. 84) takes the shape of a pyramid of personal values, with the ordinary, practical business of dealing with life's decisions on a daily basis forming the base and an inclusive judgement concerned with what life is really *about* at its apex (Landfield, 1971). The process is thus one of increasing degrees of abstraction, but the abstract principles are those on which we base our actual behaviour, so their importance can never be considered 'merely theoretical', divorced from the practical concerns of life.

It will be seen that the process of ordering is actually the same as that of evaluation, constructs being arranged in accordance with their value as ways of making sense of life. Looked at in such a way, the data involved in our assessment of human experience, our own and other people's, is never random, constituting as it does implicit evidence about major factors regarding the things which matter most to us in our encounters with life (Burr and Butt, 1992; Epting and Landfield, 1985; Fransella, 2005; Bannister and Fransella, 1986; Kelly, 1991b). Practically speaking, 'construct' and theme are interchangeable ideas, as both describe a bi-polar perception of a state of affairs — what it is in terms of what it is not and *vice versa* — so that its use can be either positive or negative, expressing either the presence or absence of a quality, as in the constructs 'strength/weakness', 'height/depth', 'foolishness/wisdom' (see Table B.3 in Appendix B). Constructs which concern the meaning, purpose and value of life are characteristically concealed by ones which appear to be more immediately relevant; however they exercise the profoundest effect on the way people think, feel and act. Kelly (1991b) calls these 'regnant' constructs.

They are not subject to argument, referring as they do to things which will

		Related constructs
1	Impact (20 times)	coherence. focus. relevance
2	Belonging (20 times)	acceptance. inclusion. unity
3	Sharing (18 times)	congruence. empathy
4	Open-ness (18 times)	open-mindedness. self-disclosure
5	Validation (18 times)	re-assurance
6	Depth (15 times)	commitment. self-discovery. thoughtfulness
7	Safety (15 times)	anxiety. containment. courage
8	Comfort (11 times)	serenity. facilitation. self-confidence
9	Freedom (11 times)	release. fun

Regnant Constructs — Synthesising the themes drawn from members' submissions

go on mattering to the person concerned whatever else may change. Although our construct system allows us to change our minds about the importance of some things, it stays anchored by regnancy:

> A regnant construct is a kind of superordinate construct which assigns each of its elements [i.e. the phenomena to which it is applied] to a category on an all-or-none basis. (Kelly, 1991a, 291)

(i) Searching for regnancy

If the emergent themes represent the group's combined construct system, the next task is to try to discover more about the principles on which it is organised (see Regnancy table above). The themes are given in descending order of the number of times on which they occurred:

All of the nine themes occurred in all of the three kinds of group — directive, process-orientated and art-based. Because of their apparent generalisability, the search for underlying concordance was extended to produce *four themes* perceived as underlying ones. Three of these were in the original list of themes: belonging, safety, and validation. The other one, also harmonizing with the rest, was enrichment, itself a synthesis of impact and depth. Two of these were in the original list: *validation* and *safety*. The other two, which also harmonised with the complete list, were *enrichment* and *belonging*. Constructs which had appeared to be discrete were drawn into accordance with one or other of the four categories (e.g. 'impact' and 'comfort,' 'openness' and 'depth,' 'freedom' and 'belonging'), which contributed to the regnancy of the four underlying themes, the fundamental significance of each to the whole group.

129

If we look now at the three kinds of group structure, the results are:

	Directive Group	Process Group	Art-based Group
Belonging	5	4	7
Sharing	5	5	7
Impact	4	3	8
Open-ness	4	4	8
Validation	5	4	6
Safety	7	4	4
Depth	4	6	8
Comfort	4	2	1
Freedom	3	4	7

Distribution of the principal themes at the penultimate stage of thematic analysis

The above list simply indicates the occurrence of particular themes. However it gives us no indication as to whether an individual group member remarked on the presence of a particular quality or its absence. Thus the scores here draw attention to the number of times a theme emerged, either as a positive judgement or a negative one. They tell us about groups rather than people's actual experiences in them. Each of the four constructs identified as regnant is, of course, open to negative as well as positive expressions; in other words it communicates absence as effectively as presence. More specific evidence regarding the group's experience is therefore necessary before conclusions can be drawn as to what actually happened within the group itself; certainly with regard to any variations in individual and group experience that reflect different ways in which the group material was structured.

In the following section the material produced by the nine group members is presented in tabular form, illustrating the comparative salience of the four themes or thematic dimensions:

- validation/rejection
- safety/danger
- enrichment/impoverishment
- belonging/alienation

In this way it will become apparent which of the two poles of the construct is involved.

Recording members' reactions to the three kinds of groupwork

([A], [P], [D] stand for 'art-based,' 'process' and 'directive' groups.)

Mrs A	
Validation	**Rejection**
Sept. 8 [A]	
The Rejected Helper is a poignant theme in my own life ... With God's help, however, I am receiving some insights into this area and I pray that they may continue.	
Nov.12 [P]	
The triumph of hope over experience. I have come away from groups where this approach has been used in a state of confusion and unhappiness — listening to other people's stories told very candidly made me feel relieved quite a few times — a positive experience.	
Safety	**Danger**
Sept. 2 [P]	I felt the 'hard' challenges about sharing were avoided. I missed out on the first week so missed a bonding and team-building stage. This meant I was cautious about contributing. Because I am always keen to avoid conflict and really do dislike hostility, negativity and criticism, I felt quite tense — there was a danger of hijacking by individuals.
Sept. 8 [A]	All sorts of distressing scenarios crowded my mind and I felt very high levels of anxiety. Just thinking about them before we even got into 'acting' and observing ... bothered about getting things wrong, being silly!
Nov.12 [P]	Daring to share is risky. Still not sure I should have done the labelling experience: you can have the experience without recognising the labels.
Jan. 21 [A]	A strong sense of awkwardness. Felt a bit was missing because there was no feedback to the discussion about form and content of approach.
Jan. 28 [D]	I think, as always, I want straightforward and clear answers, a sure-fire method that will work in terms of sharing truth — how to give everyone the right answer.

Enrichment	Impoverishment
Sept. 8 [A]	
High impact, as the issues were 'felt' in the body as well as the brain — gave rise to a massive number of connections and reflections in a short space of time, strong feeling — of trust best of all — compassion and understanding and insight — struck by the power and usefulness (of the 'points of view' exercise). Aroused strong feelings of an almost infinite range of possibilities. It felt more meaningful, transformational and in a very important sense, 'practical', that the heart is touched and this will translate into real action, although I don't know in what form.	
Nov.12 [P]	
I find I am beginning to enjoy any activity which is punctuated by periods of prayer. On my journeying home as I thought over the evening, I felt gratitude to God and the benefit of forgiveness — and felt blest.	
Jan. 21 [A]	
Wonderful possibilities	There could have been more discussion around these issues, more juice to be squeezed, more learning from sharing.
Jan. 28 [D]	
I loved the connections you could make, mythical and symbolic connotations. I get ideas and inspirations, 'aha' moments.	
March 18 [A]	
God works in mysterious ways. I am full of wonder and awe. How God has worked on my Soul, I don't know! It is beyond my comprehension and that is joy and not burden to me. The way we respond comes out of the situation. Why don't we simply do what we're told?	None of the 3 types of group has got to the heart of my problem (which is) the lack of sound factual grounding in the faith. I found all the sessions satisfying in themselves but I suppose all this really means nothing unless I love God or my neighbour and I can witness better for Christ. [Summary]
Belonging	**Alienation**
Sept. 2 [P]	I started to have feelings of doubt and loss of faith in the enterprise, wondering what good, if anything, was going to come out of it [i.e. being in the group]. Engaging mentally, but not really fulfilling my needs for 'hard' information, nor practical tasks, nor creative stimulation ... I did wonder, 'all very nice, but can anything come of this?'

Nov.12 [P]	Felt ambivalent about the value of this to my spiritual development. Does this bring me closer to God? It's very interesting but is it just a pleasant way to pass an evening?
Nov. 30 [D]	
Time and again I have come away from groups in which exchange of views and opinions have led to conflict, me keeping quiet, not wanting to be judged or criticised. This group left me feeling positive, if not elated. The group has already bonded. I was struck by how open people seemed to be. I was encouraged to share feelings and experiences which I am always very guarded about in group settings. Having a positive group experience with material I have previously found a turn-off is very interesting and instructive and hopeful ... and for me I felt privileged to be privy to this knowledge. I felt refreshed by people's open-ness. This is exactly the sort of discussion that I have found fruitless and disheartening on previous courses, but now I felt infinitely more positive — a great evening which, given my initial reservations was a big surprise and pleasure.	

Mrs E	
Validation	**Rejection**
Aug. 23 [D]	Started badly with hanging around outside because no-one had opened the front door. Very irritating, it made me feel unwelcome and unvalued.
Sept. 2 [P]	
I empathised both with [Mrs P's] anger and inability/unwillingness to express this directly to the person.	
Sept. 8 [A]	
I felt that (the different contributions) gave quite an insight into group members. Last week someone spoke about how Jesus was an example of someone who was betrayed by friends, yet not only forgave them but restored them. This resonated with a situation of my own, and I shared with them how helpful to me this observation had been.	
Nov.19 [A]	
I did my version of Jesus getting me to open the door to him. My 'pair' seemed apologetic that he had not had a Damascus Road experience, but I said the brief said 'life- changing', with no religious tag.	The introductory exercise didn't seem to have much relevance to what came after.
Nov. 30 [D]	
I felt we were all being listened to with great attention, and that is very affirming. Aspects of hurt and distress were met with empathy. I felt the evening had been just right, rather than feeling rushed or fore-shortened. I was struck by the intense 'vision' experiences several people recounted and could have added my own.	
Jan. 21 [A]	
We had to choose a present to give to our partners. I offered 'confidence and self-assurance'. We both came up with times when we'd been given words and/or actions that really affirmed us as valued individuals. The gift-giver had really seen us as ourselves and also offered an unexpected validation.	

Feb. 11 [P[	
When one person shared having been a Christian and then experiencing years of not knowing God before coming to faith again, I recognised that she still *knew* God in the dark time because she was aware of his *absence*. It was a different, painful way of knowing.	
Aug. 23 [D]	
By the end of the session I felt we were becoming more comfortable with each other. It was encouraging that people were able to share and also disagree.	
Sept. 2 [P]	Since people are sharing some personal situations and feelings (including Roger), perhaps the need for group privacy should be reminded; but I felt it was not a suitable time.
Nov. 12 [P]	
It was interesting how open people felt able to be, and how words were often inadequate to express clearly what people were trying to say.	
Nov. 19 [A]	I chose a picture of lots of people in a boat at sea, because I don't like not having my feet on the ground and the boat had no means of propulsion or steering, which adds to my sense of insecurity. ... The whole evening felt rather disjointed and it would have been better for me if there had been more time for sharing comments and stories.
Jan. 21 [A]	My 'pair' cannot use her imagination. When you do get into a scenario, things you never expected or realised can make themselves known, which can be exciting or scary. I wonder if my 'pair' sub-consciously chose not to take such a risk.
March 4 [D]	Our Biblical evangelical member gets quite 'preachy' at times. Her approach is so far from mine it is not surprising I feel as I do. I can admire so much that she does which I could not do — it is the manner of it that puts me off.
Enrichment	**Impoverishment**
Aug. 23 [D]	
The icebreaker worked well in giving more insight into one another --- lovely variety of revelations.	I found [Mrs J's] dogmatic approach very unhelpful.

Sept. 8 [A]	
Once we got to organising the enactment it was very collaborative. The actual performance brought out the best in people. I felt it went well because we were all caught up in the scene. It was very interesting how different contributions — some quite restrained and 'correct' otherwise — felt very imaginative and engaged. The whole evening felt more challenging for me than the previous two as I am less comfortable with bodily expression and action than the primarily verbal. However, because I was willing to engage with it, I coped OK. We were caught up in the reality behind what we were doing.	The wandering around at the start felt very unnatural.
Nov. 12 [P]	
I'm getting familiar with different people's style and approach which informs how I 'hear' and understand what they're saying.	
Nov. 30 [D]	
The material encouraged some sharing at depth, with most people recounting some very personal aspects of their faith journey — members of the group encouraged others to contribute or to expand what they had originally said.	
Jan. 21 [A]	
The evening was enjoyable and stimulating. The sharing was mostly easy and open, lots in common but enough difference to be stimulating.	
Feb. 11 [P[	
People were mostly willing to share experiences of talking to/being talked to in different situations and with very different outcomes.	
March 4 [D]	It was irritating to be moved on when the discussion was heading off at an interesting tangent. After the meeting I felt I'd not really got far with the topic: too *parish*-orientated.
March 11 [P]	
I shall miss interacting with [Mrs J] and [Mrs S] as they bring insights and energy I value.	I think I'm relieved the next meeting will be the last. The group feels as if it is meandering now.

March 18 [A]	
It was a fun exercise. After coffee we were invited to write on a long piece of paper things it is good to share. Lots of hope, a whole gamut from washing up to love and joy. I'm now more aware of how meetings can work and very pleased to have met some new and interesting people to share my pilgrimage.	
Belonging	**Alienation**
Sept. 2 [P]	
I enjoyed the fact that the initial sharing often resulted in laughter. I feel that this helped us relax and feel comfortable as a group.	
Sept. 8 [A]	Being disregarded/overlooked [i.e. by finding the church unopened on arrival] triggered bad reactions (on behalf of the group). I felt irritated as we gathered.
Nov. 12 [P]	
I was encouraged by the range of people's experiences of growing in grace. We are all on our own pilgrim journey, and sharing these journeys can enable further development or help us discern God's work in our lives.	
Nov. 19 [A]	Overall it felt less a group activity than an interactive session between individual people and things — didn't feel as if the group benefited as a group.
Nov. 30 [D]	The man member was clearly not keen to share much. I wonder if they would feel quite different with no women present?
Jan. 21 [A]	
The congruence of our sharing was very marked.	
Feb. 11 [P[	
We started just sitting in silence. It seemed very comfortable doing this. Once we had started talking there was easy discussion among the group.	For most of us, sharing with other Christians is affirming and encouraging, but in some situations it can make people feel inadequate. I chose not to say I find the very dogmatic, Biblical approach of one member very off-putting and judgemental. One man [see Nov. 30 for this person] seems unengaged: his body language an echo of his apparent lack of involvement.

March 11 [P]	
(Roger) seemed a bit disappointed that we hadn't quarrelled — but we feel we had too much respect for each other to do that. [Mrs J] and I could quarrel, but neither wish to; she cannot, rather than will not, understand quite a lot of what I say.	
March 18 [A]	
Later Process and Activity sessions were easier because we knew each other better and were literally easier with one another. We were asked to hold hands, look each other in the eye and give each a gift. I was given Friendship and I gave Affirmation. We talked as a group about how the last 7 months [the period covered by the sessions] had been. There was a lot of positive comment. It had been difficult for some, but everyone felt it had been worth it.	

Mrs J	
Validation	**Rejection**
Sept. 8 [A]	I simply cannot relate to what they describe happening within themselves.
Nov. 19 [A]	It's not the medium that's the problem; I just don't use these things to learn about God and my faith.
Nov. 30 [D]	
Hearing the testimony of others was wonderful. It was a revelation to hear stories of faith from people who are 'private'. Thank you, God, for all you are doing in my life.	
Jan. 21 [A]	
We all need to feel the validity of our own approaches is respected by others.	
Feb. 11 [P]	
I spoke to [Mrs A] about how God had spoken into my life the previous night. She actually wanted to listen to this and was encouraged by it. — Forget me, focus on God.	
March 4 [D]	
I was pleased that [Mr L] found spiritual stimulation in the group. It is very grounding when people are willing to be real with you.	Last week Roger cut me short when I said that, rather than being intimidated by the powerful testimonies of some very ordinary Christians, I chose to embrace the gospel and was converted. This shocked me ... I have felt throughout the discussion sessions that there was a reluctance in some quarters to accept the testimony that I have.
March 18 [A]	
I found grace to join in the first exercise, even though I really didn't feel comfortable with it.	Being rejected by Christians is especially hurtful.
Safety	**Danger**
Aug. 23 [D]	
The structured approach sat comfortably with me as a concept.	
Sept. 2 [P]	[The session] made me do some reading of Acts later on, which I needed to do.

Nov. 12 [P]	
[One person in the group] has a deep and mature-sounding faith. It makes me feel safer, less alone. [Mrs S] is gracious and generous to me, acknowledging how I feel about next week's [art-based] session. I am less worried about appearing stand-offish and unco- operative.	I daren't raise the Lord's view for fear of what? What am I afraid of? Upsetting people?
Nov. 19 [A]	
[Mrs S] was very sensitive and kind in her approach. I trusted her. I found the creative stuff we did non-threatening and I was very grateful for this.	I didn't want to share anything personal. Suddenly I didn't feel safe any more.
Jan. 21 [A]	Creative approaches just interfere with my learning and become an end in themselves.
Feb. 11 [P]	
Tonight God reminded me that nothing is impossible for him.	I realised that God's power frightens some who I would have thought walking in it.
March 4 [D]	I was right to hold back [previous session] on sharing what God had done for me that week. Some of the people said they felt intimidated when a Christian shared a spiritual experience that was not part of their own. When I converted to Christianity I shared my testimony with a vicar and a lay reader because I naively believed I was in a safe place. I was wrong. I was faced with silence ...
March 18 [A]	
In some ways it was a relief that the creative activities seemed to reduce the theological content — less chance for tensions and differences to arise ...	It didn't feel safe when [the member Mrs J doesn't recognise as a Christian] was there. I don't mind being with non-Christians — I welcome it. But I need to know that is the situation. Then we can proceed in a way that aims to be acceptable to all without making assumptions about beliefs.
Enrichment	**Impoverishment**
Aug. 23 [D]	The content of the material (is) not always especially helpful.
Sept. 2 [P]	
I have met a lovely person in the group. It's good being in the group with them.	I keep wanting us to look at the bible together and we don't. Sometimes it's easy to forget we are a group of Christians.
Sept. 8 [A]	Some people like acting. I don't. What did God make of it/me/us?

140

Nov. 12 [P]	
I enjoy one person's incisive way of putting their point across. It gives me hope. One person described how an exercise in artistic creativity was a deep spiritual experience. It sounded great.	I get the impression that one or two people had found the meeting deeply moving. But I don't know how or why.
Nov. 30 [D]	
It's so encouraging to hear what God has done for others in their everyday lives. This was the most helpfully encouraging and edifying to date for me. Tonight I have felt I was truly with Christians who have a living faith, and I'd not felt this before during any of the other sessions.	
Jan. 21 [A]	
I really liked talking to [Mrs S] and [Mrs A] tonight.	I saw the creative point of the (art-based) exercise, but I can't act and so couldn't engage with it. There was nothing spiritual in it for me.
Jan. 28 [D]	There seemed to be a reluctance to address in any deep way how we shared/didn't share our faith. No-one gave a living testimony.
Feb. 11 [P]	
This was for me the best session of the whole programme. How wonderful to see [Mrs A's] faith. There was a widely spread sense of a desire to share experiences of God — too much for the negative force in the group who backed out at the end.	
March 4 [D]	Roger cut [Mrs S] short when she was sharing a lovely testimony that filled her with such joy. You (R) directed us back to the perceived difficulty, yours not mine, of being faced with such testimonies. Perhaps there would have been more interest in looking at what the gospel was actually saying.
March 18 [A]	
I liked the welcome tonight. It was honest. I liked [Miss H's] surprise that I could choose something very specific to delight her. I was very encouraged to hear her belief that God was directing her and really wanted her to enjoy the sense of excitement she expressed.	I certainly wouldn't attend a group like this through choice. I was OK through this in order to support the research.
Belonging	**Alienation**
Aug. 23 [D]	Being with other Christians and not feeling common ground most of the time is not a comfortable feeling.

Sept. 2 [P]	I don't do group therapy and certainly don't share deep and personal things with people I hardly know.
Nov. 12 [P]	
How do I have unity with these lovely people?	
Jan. 28 [D]	I felt I should hold back. I didn't think I could bear it if no-one connected with what I said. I thought this was a group of Christians and yet now I'm not sure — there is someone who seems hostile to Christianity. God does so much for me and I wanted to share it (but) I have experienced being under-whelmed by a Christian's response to the most amazing acts of God in my life and others'.
March 4 [D]	I have felt I was in a club where some ideas were to be tolerated and others weren't. No matter what I said there were some people who would only hear what they wanted to hear. I was surprised at how defensive some people wanted to be. I felt I had done something deeply offensive, from a marginal position within the group.
March 11 [P]	
I felt in the place God wanted me to be at that time. I grew spiritually and matured, not because of the services or their structures, but in spite of them. I wanted to say this but couldn't find a way of saying it here.	I couldn't relate to a spirituality that was based upon forms and structures of church meetings, but I couldn't find a way of saying that without being misunderstood and causing offence. I want so much to hear the group affirm the love of God by their own testimonies. I fear our group is suffering from a kind of spiritual constipation. Our preference must be for God, not styles of worship!
March 18 [A]	It's weird proceeding as if we were all singing from the same hymn sheet and then finding we're not. I haven't liked that aspect of the group at all. It has really bothered me.

Mrs K	
Validation	**Rejection**
Sept. 2 [P]	Some very confident people who hogged it all at the expense of the shy ones. I didn't say much.
Nov. 30 [D]	
It was helpful for me to describe something.	
Feb. 11 [P]	
Perhaps I was hoping for something.	People were saying how great it was but I wasn't convinced and didn't feel able to participate properly. Was it just me? Was I trying to make it what it wasn't?
Safety	**Danger**
Sept. 8 [A]	The session made people take risks.
Nov. 30 [D]	
The structure made it safe. Doctrines were carefully avoided by the structure, which made things clear, but kept them shallow.	People were just trying to get things right. There as a sense of rigidity and restraint, stereotyping. People knew what was wanted. We knew what we were doing and what was expected.
Enrichment	**Impoverishment**
Sept. 2 [P]	
I think I managed to mention what the subject was at one point.	
Sept. 8 [A]	
I enjoy this kind of drama-based session. I enjoyed playing the part of a mother whose baby had died. The session showed there isn't an obvious answer to life and we should avoid stereotyping.	
Nov.12 [P]	No real sense for me that people were being allowed to be honest about their difficulties
Nov. 30 [D]	
It was clear.	I felt that the sharing was only on the surface. Again, it was the confident ones who took charge.

Feb. 11 [P]	I don't think we really had time to do this kind of group properly. I got a sense of people having to do things they weren't ready for yet. I had a sense of missed opportunity.
Belonging	**Alienation**
Sept. 2 [P]	Sense of people trying to 'get it right', not really pulling together yet.
Sept. 8 [A]	
I think people pulled together more and began to listen to one another.	
Nov. 12 [P]	I felt it hard to join in because of people who seemed to know what they wanted to get across.
Feb. 11 [P]	When people started to make dates for the next 3 sessions I felt excluded because there was at least one date I knew I wouldn't be able to manage. I felt on the edge of things – the odd one out.

Mrs S	
Validation	Rejection
Aug. 23 [D]	The general feeling I got was that maybe I didn't know enough to present my opinions.
Sept. 2 [P]	
I was very tired (but) very soon I was glad I was there, was a part of the group and accepted and affirmed. Practically everyone is reassuring. I could talk to everyone really closely.	
Sept. 8 [A]	
I found one member reassuring — because I had been honest, opened myself out, and was accepted for who I am.	
Nov. 19 [A]	
My own depiction of a dramatic change was quite stressful, but (the session) was really liberating.	
Jan. 21 [A]	
I felt accepted and comfortable with who I am by not trying to be anything or anyone else. I'm glad I said I enjoyed Rod Stewart 'cos I do, and even though others may not approve it is a very important part of me. Everyone in the group seemed to affirm me today — even the dominant and 'bolshy' personalities.	
Feb. 11 [P]	
I am glad about the small, almost trivial ways God influences my life.	I did feel strongly when one member said what a responsibility it would be to have received a conversion as St Paul did — it shook me because I have received a clear vision, and have not broadcast it is much as perhaps I should have.
March 18 [A]	
I was reminded of very happy feelings when at least one member of the group seemed to value the fact that I had been there.	
Safety	Danger
Aug. 23 [D]	
I felt quite comfortable in the group as a whole. I felt quite safe.	When there was a slight difference of opinion, I remembered the anxiety I used to feel when I was running groups, sort of jagged and uneasy.

Sept. 8 [A]	
I am feeling much more comfortable in the group.	
Nov. 19 [A]	
I enjoyed the fact that I could share with one other person some of my deepest and most traumatic hurts — plus it was safe to do so.	It felt quite scary. The issues were deep-seated.
Jan. 28 [D]	
I was quite surprised by (R's) clear boundaries, but it was reassuring and felt safe.	Slight uncomfortable feelings when two people began discussing an issue intently.
Feb. 11 [P]	
I felt safe in the group.	
March 11 [P]	
The whole experience tonight was very comfortable. R's leadership and control is democratic but somehow reassuring.	
March 18 [A]	
It felt very comfortable, relaxed. One member of the group talked about difference, but not in any hostile or difficult sense.	
Enrichment	**Impoverishment**
Aug. 23 [D]	
I enjoyed hearing the other members speak of their own individual situations. I felt quite emotional when people shared their stuff.	
Sept. 2 [P]	
[Mrs E] no longer looks dour to me, but very interesting and intelligent.	I'm having slight irritations if I perceive a closed mind, but I would say (I'm) annoyed ...
Sept. 8 [A]	I found the group a little slow, and felt a bit of irritation that they were being ponderous. One person was a little irritating tonight.
Nov. 12 [P]	
It had been a month since we last met and I was not sure I would remember people's names. In fact I had no trouble at all, and this gave me a slight boost of confidence. For some reason it felt more serious, sitting in a smaller circle at the back of the church. When anger and depression were mentioned I felt empathy.	

Nov. 19 [A]	
The picture I wrote a story about reminded me of finding peace. An honest and liberating session.	Strong feelings arose when I reflected on my own story and the stories of others in the group — quite stressful. We seemed rushed at the end, with little time to process the material.
Jan. 28 [D]	
I found R reassuring. He tends to pick up on most people's feelings, and then by becoming quite academic, manages to affirm everyone.	One person looked a little bit worried at a late stage in the group and I was concerned that everyone should feel comfortable.
Feb. 11 [P]	
The fact that I knew the group members was encouraging. I found [R] really reassuring.	It felt much vaguer and slightly frustrating. When one member disclosed being attacked I re-connected with disturbing feelings.
March 4 [D]	
The poem at the beginning made me feel I very much enjoyed being part of this group. It was very focused and worked hard.	
Belonging	**Alienation**
Aug. 23 [D]	
I felt affirmed as a member of the group.	I felt it was more academic than I could cope with and maybe I would be found wanting.
Sept. 2 [P]	
I really love being part of this group. I could empathise with every single person in the group.	
Sept. 8 [A]	
(I) now know everyone that is attending and get quite a degree of comfort from the fact that I am a member of the group. I was reminded of a happy feeling when I was allowed to take on a role in the small group. I really enjoy becoming 'another person' (so) I really enjoyed the role-plays, both in taking part and being in the audience.	
Nov. 12 [P]	
I was reminded of a happy feeling (connected with) being moved out of my comfort zone.	I sensed that one person was out on a limb and wanted to include and affirm them — they seemed to be disregarded by the majority. At the beginning it felt as though we were all individuals trying to say our point of view.

Nov. 19 [A]	
I am beginning to feel safe and comfortable with everyone in the group. I feel safe and cherished. As I was running the group and was quite nervous I found the support all the group members gave me really encouraging.	
Jan. 21 [A]	
I had not been for a few weeks and I was relaxed and looking forward to seeing people again. I enjoyed just being in the group and being missed.	
March 11 [P]	
I am glad I said 'the group is very profound' because it caused a laugh. I was reminded of a feeling of real inclusion, of being an important member of the group.	

148

Mrs Y	
Validation	**Rejection**
Aug. 23 [D]	
For many years I would not talk openly about my dyslexia, so I was glad I had mentioned it to the group.	Memories brought up (because) my church group not able to give me the support I needed.
Sept. 2 [P]	
Participation is the way I learn. The openness of the discussions brought to my memory things which were very positive.	
Sept. 8 [A]	
The plays reminded me of the work I did with groups of homeless people whom I much enjoyed helping.	
Nov. 12 [P]	
I've been thinking about my early church life and how I have developed. I have taken great encouragement from the people in the group.	
Nov. 19 [A]	
I've been thinking about my early church life and how I have developed. I have taken great encouragement from the people in the group.	Many times in this course I found myself remembering how unhappy I had been.
March 11 [P]	
One of two people, such as [Mrs J] have been able to express their commitment in more detailed terms, and I have felt this quite helpful personally.	
Summary	
I felt it very helpful that each group meeting followed its own theme, so I did not feel put off at any point by missing a session. If the Church is to be relevant, to young people in particular, it is important that church groups are able to be diverse. The people who made up these groups all had a great deal to offer in very different ways, so the learning experience was all positive.	

Safety	Danger
Aug. 23 [D]	
A mix of people I know well and others I did not know at all, so for me at first a formal setting was quite a good setting to discuss issues. I liked the formal structure. I was able to share some of my thoughts about my disability [dyslexia] and the group felt quite a safe place to do this.	It was important for me to look at the make-up of the group members a bit ... I did not fully open up with my thoughts in the first meeting. One or two people clearly had very different ideas ...
Sept. 2 [P]	I was reminded of my very unhappy marriage. I felt that many women or people who experience something like these experiences will go on being scared.
Sept. 8 [A]	There was a sense of being hesitant about starting work for this group.
Sept. 12 [P]	
There have been a mix of memories of being in a very bad space when I felt God was nowhere about and other times when I had great help. I have found it very interesting that there have been no real conflicts in the group as to what matters to people both in their spiritual life in a church and their commitment to the Lord.	
Enrichment	**Impoverishment**
Aug. 23 [D]	
A smaller church makes it easier to get to know people. Quite a lot of the discussion reminded me of events or things both in my church life and outside which have been happy. Very pleased that everyone in the group played a part in the discussions.	
Sept. 2 [P]	
Much of the discussion was really helpful as people did seem to understand each other. One or two people opened out to discuss really personal issues of faith in a manner which was really inclusive.	

Sept. 8 [A]	
I had not expected the Arts group to be like this. Not to be rigid is something that I have not thought about as much as I should, and the analysis of the last weeks has set me thinking about this. These meetings have left a powerful impression on me. It was a very moving night, all the plays were very well performed --- the whole experience was helpful and memorable. This is the group- work which so far I have found most moving. The whole session did give me strong feelings. Christians and church members can offer help in so many ways, and this is positive.	One or two people did not want to participate, and I found that irritating. Sometimes we are not as forthcoming as we could be; we hold back ... I know I could have said more.
Sept. 12 [P]	
	The group did not really spend enough time on gender issues. Time was a factor which did limit what one could say. One or two people could get a bit much.
Nov. 19 [A]	
Everyone opened up and talked more about themselves, so it was a really good session, with everyone in the main being quite open on deep issues. I found the hardship some of the group had come through to be very moving. This group worked better than I expected an art-based group to work.	I was reminded of unsettled times in my life; the group was rushed.
Nov. 30 [D]	
There was plenty to talk about and most people had lots to say. Reduced numbers but people seem very committed.	
Belonging	**Alienation**
Aug. 23 [D]	
(This was) not like the time when not being able to speak Welsh hindered greatly my church life and made me feel unhappy ... I was pleased that I had joined the group.	
Sept. 2 [P]	
People seemed to be comfortable in the group. I felt an overwhelming degree or pleasure that I have joined this group and that the whole group was a positive process.	Trust and trusting in people or situations is always a difficult issue.

151

Nov. 12 [P]	
I have taken great encouragement from the people in the group. Wonderful fellowship.	
Nov. 19 [A]	
Because we all know each other, so felt able to trust, which led to an openness which revealed a lot.	
March 11 [P]	
One or two people in the group have been very consistent, and this has been reassuring.	(Where I live) I never keep in touch with the neighbours on one side, and on the other the people do not speak to me.

Miss H	
Validation	**Rejection**
Nov. 12 [P]	I'm not quite sure what I was meant to come away with. I am finding I have to try to understand viewpoints which are completely alien to me and are not my understanding of the Gospel.
Nov. 19 [A]	
I thought the written comments and the story about my picture were fascinating. One person actually got the correct quotation. It was a life-changing episode but a fairly minor one.	
Jan. 28 [D]	Although my favourite format, it didn't really work for me this evening. I find faith-sharing a difficult topic. I hate soap-box or door-knocking evangelism.
Feb. 11 [P]	The session reinforced the feeling that this style doesn't really work for me.
Safety	**Danger**
Aug. 23 [D]	One person seems to have fundamentalist tendencies, and there is potential conflict there. There seem to be several damaged people in the group (I include myself in that). It will be interesting to see if they continue to personalise their experiences in a positive light.
Enrichment	**Impoverishment**
Aug. 23 [D]	At first it seemed rather stilted, people rather reticent. It seemed as though it might be hard work.
Sept. 8 [A]	
One person's contribution about teen challenge was very moving.	Some people seemed to find the drama more powerful than I did.
Nov. 12 [P]	I try to understand viewpoints which are completely alien to me.

Nov. 19 [A]	
I realise I am being unfair to certain members of the group in not respecting their reactions to the tasks. I will try to be more tolerant and accepting.	I still don't feel comfortable enough with all of the group to be able to share major events. This session has a very unfinished feel to it.
Nov. 30 [D]	
More in-depth sharing tonight — interesting divergences and many similarities. 'Allow God and He comes' seems to be a common theme. This was a much better session for me — structured! Began with experiences of school — very telling.	
Jan. 21 [A]	
It was good to see everyone again. This was a creative session, very good. As always, we didn't have time to draw threads together, but it is pretty obvious how the three exercises linked to the story.	
Feb. 11 [P]	I didn't feel this session worked too well because it was designed for a Church community to look at itself and its engagement with the local community. As we were from different churches it was difficult to apply the questions.
March 11 [P]	Oh dear, I feel very negative, but for me the process sessions seem aimless. Many of us need the structure to feel comfortable, 'at home'.
Belonging	**Alienation**
Aug. 23 [D]	I find the simplistic attitude to prayer and the limitations placed on God quite irritating. (I hope it didn't show.)
Sept. 2 [P]	Several people took the opportunity to share recent troubling experiences. I was conscious of having nothing to offer at this stage. I wondered how far one should go in refuting what one believes to be an untenable idea.

Sept. 8 [A]	
It is an interesting group of very different people, who probably wouldn't interact very much under normal circumstances so it is a learning experience.	
Nov. 12 [P]	I have to say I'm disappointed that people are not honouring the commitments they made; two others will only do what they want to do rather than what is asked of them.
Jan. 21 [A]	
The faithful are beginning to really feel like a group.	
March 11 [P]	
I'm not sure I'm feeling the 'depth' people keep speaking about, but I do like the group and have enjoyed getting to know individuals.	
March 18 [A]	
It was amazing how intuitive we were (or was it?). Sadly this was our last session and for me proved to be one of the best ... a strange unrelated ice-breaker which was actually great fun and had us all relaxed and laughing. We then did a shared activity, an in-depth sharing of something painful. It was good to feel the level of trust which exists between us. Hopefully we will be able to meet again to discuss R's findings.	

Mr L	
Validation	**Rejection**
Aug. 23 [D]	
In all it turned out to be a very stimulating evening for me.	
Sept. 8 [A]	This was a session I did not enjoy because I lack imagination.
Nov. 19 [A]	Once again I felt out of my depth.
Safety	**Danger**
Aug. 23 [D]	The group was balanced in favour of the female gender, which was at times slanted against male comment.
Sept. 8 [A]	I felt I had spoken out of turn on some of the ideas.
Enrichment	**Impoverishment**
Aug. 23 [D]	
Very good, as we tend to take so much for granted in our present society. Some members came up with some excellent ideas.	
Sept. 8 [A]	
The theme made me examine my own ethics — very thought-provoking.	
Nov. 19 [A]	
I tried to contribute as best I could. I felt sorry that the time had run out.	
March 4 [D]	
I felt at home with the evening's content and could relate to much of the topics discussed. Found this session spiritually uplifting. Didn't think I would — which just goes to show.	Missed [Mr M's] input, as I am the only male participant.
March 11 [P]	
I observed the discussion that took place was very relaxed.	Thought we might be running out of time.

March 18 [A]	Summary
Overall I found it very spiritually rewarding — which had its benefits. I was impressed by the deep commitment of some members in their knowledge of the faith, plus the spirituality they brought to the group.	During the months the group has been meeting I have found it difficult to take in the complete content of each week's theme --- I felt very much discomfort at times with the artistic evenings. Not my forte.
Belonging	**Alienation**
Aug. 23 [D]	
The group seem to be coming together as a unit.	
Sept. 8 [A]	Found (the role play) very difficult. Felt I had not contributed much to the group meeting.
Nov. 12 [P]	
The team seems to have come together well, though some have dropped out.	Began to feel I might be out of my depth. I have not the Christian commitment and knowledge that was being discussed.
Nov. 19 [A]	
I would have been willing to stay a little longer to discuss the stories behind our drawings. Felt we had been conned.	The sessions are becoming more intellectual and I find it hard to keep up, plus art is not my favourite subject.
March 18 [A]	
I did enjoy the coming together as a group.	
Summary	
I did enjoy the coming together as a group.	

Mr M	
Validation	**Rejection**
Sept. 8 [A], Nov. 12 [D], Nov. 30 [A], Jan. 21 [D], Feb. 11 [A]	
Summary: For me the art-based and directed group meetings seemed to work better. I felt more able to be engaged precisely because I knew what was expected of me.	
Sept. 2 [P], Nov. 19 [P], Jan. 28 [P]	When I advocated routine door-knocking and formulaic questioning as a viable form of evangelism, some members of the group suggested I was being 'sarcastic' when I was merely being facetious. I think there was a tacit recognition on the part of the group that I was not 'at home' in it, and the group leader said as much on severaloccasions to justify my inclusion in it.
Safety	**Danger**
Sept. 2 [P], Nov. 19 [P], Jan. 28 [P]	Because they were less free than their *prima facie* format would suggest, [these sessions] caused me some disquiet. What I had to offer or contribute would not be accepted by the group or could have the effect of taking the group off-course. It might even be regarded as an attempt to 'hi-jack' the meeting. It was better to say very little.
Enrichment	**Impoverishment**
Sept. 2 [P], Nov. 19 [P], Jan. 28 [P]	I think that there is sometimes a conflict of interest, even disingenuousness (in) discussing items of faith within a therapeutic setting, because what is important is how people behave in the group towards each other, rather than the presuppositions they bring --- and since those for the most part are never challenged, there is an absence of'truth'.
Sept. 2 to Feb. 11 inclusive [Ds, Ps, As]	There was far from sufficient range of people present, the over-whelming majority coming from not dissimilar backgrounds and (myself included) getting on in years.
Belonging	**Alienation**
Sept. 2 to Feb. 11 inclusive [Ds, Ps, As]	I was very much aware of an ideological gulf, hence somewhat out of my comfort zone. To take on the role of *agent provocateur* every week would have been asking too much --- fine for one week but in danger of becoming tiresome or causing offence if allowed to continue.

158

6

Conclusions Drawn from the Investigation

The Investigation as an experience

The use of Interpretative Phenomenological Analysis revealed a shared dimension of group experience within the three groupwork formats, one of which was directive and the other two experiential. The degree to which each of the four groupwork themes was represented suggests that different structures contribute in their own way to the group solidarity on which effective groupwork depends. Enough evidence of the value of experiential formatting in encouraging positive group experience emerged from this investigation for any assumption that only directive groups serve the interests of congregational learning to have been demonstrated to be at least questionable. This being the case, concentration on directive modes of groupwork must involve a restriction of the overall value of groups for both individuals and organisations. The research procedures employed required group members to concentrate on their own personal experiences within the group, resulting in a depth of participation in the group process which strengthened individuals' sense of Christian belonging. In this chapter we shall continue to examine the results of the investigation.

(i) Belonging ↔ Alienation

The analysis of members' depositions carried out in this chapter resulted in the emergence of four themes as salient dimensions of the groupwork experience so far as the members of a particular group of churchgoers were concerned. These have been identified as 'validation,' 'safety,' 'enrichment' and 'belonging'. In the kind of groupwork we have been considering here the last of these dimensions the most important. Perhaps this is true of all human groups. It is particularly salient in the self-awareness of individuals brought into contact with identifiable others with whom they have chosen, or in some cases have been required, to enter into a particular form of relationship, one concerned with belonging to a group which is itself identifiable. Church groupwork of the kind considered here is a special case, as the small groups concerned are formed within the parameters of a wider association, a relationship which is more extensive although equally personal.

159

Belonging, then, is what groupwork may be said to be about. Those who belong are extremely conscious of the fact, which underlies their actual group experience; those who, for one reason or another, do not, tend to be even more aware of their position than the 'insiders' are, as this kind of belonging relieves basic anxieties about oneself which make alienation an ever-present issue. Looking at the results of the analysis carried out here, Mr M's alienation, the expression of his awareness of not belonging — and consequently the importance of actually being a part of the group — stands out very clearly indeed. Mr L felt excluded for reasons concerning his own view of himself rather than of the group — he saw himself as limited in his ability to contribute through theological ignorance, lack of commitment and — most important of all — gender vulnerability. It was he, however, who was failing to belong properly, not the group which was excluding him.

The process groups
In the case of Mrs H, Mrs J and others taking part in the exercise, alienation is divided between individuals' attitudes towards the group itself and their own feelings regarding their role as participants. Because of the importance of phenomena concerning belonging it is necessary to take such attitudes extremely seriously by drawing attention to those aspects of the investigation which had proved alienating to group members. From the point of view of this analysis, belonging means *belonging to the group*; just as the group format itself functions as a tool for investigating the quality of human awareness, we experience group belonging as distinct from other kinds of inter-personal attachment. Those who, as a result of their own shyness or vulnerability or because they have had an unwelcome and aversive experience of groupwork in the past (Mrs A), are wary of becoming involved are also aware of positive benefits, both emotional and practical, of belonging and so work towards eventually being able to embrace membership more wholeheartedly. Although both had difficulty in accepting the group as a shared human presence to which they personally belonged, Mrs J and Mrs A formed genuine attachments to particular individuals. The same is true for Mr L, although his sense of alignment with Mr M appears to have been more to do with a fear of being isolated than any real sharing of views. In fact, Mr M and Mrs K appear never to have tried very hard to embrace the emergent group ethos. These are the genuinely alienated individuals within the group; but only Mr M chose definitely not to see himself as having a sustainable role within its life. Towards the end of the course of sessions, Mrs A, Mrs E, Mrs H, Mrs J and Mr L definitely saw themselves as belonging to the group.

What, then, in Mr M's eyes stood in the way of his letting himself claim membership? What, exactly, had he seen about the group which the others had either missed or chosen to ignore? His criticism focuses on the process-orientated group sessions. These, he says, signally failed to provide the promised opportunities for self-expression. His claim is borne out by the stereotyped responses provided by group members who, in Mrs K's words, 'seemed to be playing safe and saying what was expected of them.' The group leader was, of course, the same person who had been (and continued to be) in charge of the directive group sessions; not only that, he was actually an ordained clergyman. Both these things were almost bound to have an inhibiting effect on spontaneity and individuals' willingness to express views which might be considered in any way unorthodox or embarrassing, this despite all the assurances given by the clergyman concerned that such groups would be — more or less — permitted to run themselves . . . For Mrs J it was precisely the challenge to self-awareness offered by the process group, even in its restricted and compromised form, which presented the greatest threat: 'I don't do group therapy.' She saw the exchange of specifically religious testimony as the (comparatively) safe structure she knew she needed.

Experience of the process group appears to have drawn attention to feelings of alienation which were shared by at least four, perhaps five, group members who saw the group itself as having no role to offer them because what they perceived to be its understanding of Christianity, and the implications of Christian belonging, was not one which they themselves felt able to share. Mr M and Mrs K were made uneasy by what they saw as the conformist ethos of the group, Mr L by its intellectual demands, Miss H by what she saw as a fundamental distortion of Christian teaching, Mrs J by the unwillingness of group members to describe their own personal faith histories — something with which the group leader himself seemed to her to be colluding.[1]

- *What is important is how people behave in the group towards each other, rather than the [unchallenged] pre-suppositions they bring.* (Mr M, Nov. 19)
- *No real sense for me that people were being allowed to be honest about their difficulties.* (Mrs K, Nov. 12)
- *Began to feel I might be out of my depth.* (Mr L, Nov. 12)
- *I am finding I have to try to understand viewpoints which are completely alien to me (and) are not my understanding of the Gospel.* (Miss H, Nov. 12)
- *I keep wanting us to look at the bible together and we don't. Sometimes it's easy to forget we are a group of Christians.* (Mrs J, Sept. 2)

Members attempted to cope with these feelings of estrangement in different ways — Mr M by adopting a semi-serious role as 'devil's advocate' (which he was unable to sustain, however), Mrs K, Mr L and Miss H by keeping silent what they would have liked to express as what they were actually feeling, Mrs J by telling herself that experiences which she herself found distracting with regard to her own Christian purpose might actually lead others to God. In all this, Mrs A was the odd one out; although in no way alienated from her group belonging, she questions the ultimate significance and value of groupwork for a Christian:

- *I found all the sessions satisfying in themselves, but I suppose all this really means nothing unless I love God or my neighbour and can witness better for Christ.* (Mrs A, March 18)

Mr M and Mr L objected to the way in which this particular group was constructed, the former because it was unrepresentative with regard to gender, age and social structure, the latter finding the absence of male support occasionally alienating:

- *The group was balanced in favour of the female gender, which was at times slanted against male comment.* (Mr L, Aug. 23)

There were, however, other forces at work apart from the presence of alienation, and most of the reactions recorded above are evidence of an implicit wish, and sometimes a very positive need, to belong (*cf.* Mr M, Mrs K, Mrs J). Mrs J in particular found the groupwork more frustrating than aversive. For some members of the group, on the other hand — Mrs E, Mrs Y and Mrs S, and for most of the time Mrs A — the sessions gave a welcome opportunity to belong together in a purpose which was genuinely shared. These five people engaged wholeheartedly with the group.

- *We started just sitting in silence. It seemed very comfortable doing this. Once we started talking there was easy discussion in the group.* (Mrs E, Feb. 11)
- *I felt an overwhelming degree of pleasure that I have joined this group and that the whole group was a positive process.* (Mrs Y, Sept. 2)
- *I was reminded of a feeling of real inclusion, of being an important member of the group.* (Mrs S, March 11)
- *On my journeying home, as I thought over the evening, I felt gratitude to God [in contrast with previous experiences of groupwork elsewhere].* (Mrs A, Nov. 12)

The art-based groups
The most striking expression of unwillingness to take part was actually Mr L's reaction to the first of the art-based sessions:

- *This was a session I didn't enjoy because I lack imagination . . . The sessions are becoming more intellectual.* (Mr L, Sept. 8, Nov. 19)

Mrs J, too, had difficulty with imagination; in her case, however, art was a distraction rather than any kind of devotional aid:

- *Creative approaches just interfere with my learning and become an end in themselves.* (Mrs J, Jan. 21)

As time went on, however, she began to understand that they might well connect with other people's religious sense, but not with hers. She felt that the sessions contributed to her feeling of alienation from the group, as to some extent did Mrs E:

- *It's weird proceeding as if we were all singing from the same hymn sheet, and then finding we're not . . . it has really bothered me.* (Mrs J, March 18)
- *Overall it has felt less like a group activity than an interactive session . . . didn't feel as if the group benefited as a group.* (Mrs E, Nov. 19)

For Mrs Y, however, the art-based format brought her into closer contact with other group members:

- *Because we all knew each other and so felt able to trust which led to an openness which revealed a lot.* (Mrs Y, Nov. 19)

Mrs K echoes this growth in belonging, as do Miss H and Mrs S:

- *I think people pulled together more and began to listen to one another.* (Mrs K, Sept. 8)
- *It's an interesting group of people, who probably wouldn't interact very much under normal circumstances, so it's a learning experience.* (Mss H, Sept. 8)
- *I know everyone that is attending and get quite a degree of comfort from the fact that I am a member of the group.* (Mrs S, Sept. 8)

The directive groups

These were the sessions in which the church's message regarding the circumstances of Christian belonging were succinctly expressed and distinctly announced to group members. Miss H felt that this direct approach exposed weaknesses within the group's attitude to the Gospel:

- *I find the simplistic attitude to prayer and the limitations placed on God quite irritating.* (Miss H, Aug. 23)

Mrs J reinforces this judgement (from an angle which differed from Miss H's):

- *I have felt I was in a club where some ideas were tolerated and others weren't. No matter what I said there were some people who would only hear what they wanted to hear.* (Mrs J. March 4)

Mrs S found the first of these sessions *'more academic than I could cope with'* (Aug. 23); Mr L, on the other hand, remarks that *'The group seem to*

163

be coming together as a unit' (the same session). Mrs Y's verdict was unequiv-
ocally favourable:

- *This was not like the time when not being able to speak Welsh . . .
  hindered my church life and made me feel unhappy . . . I was pleased
  that I had joined the group.* (Mrs Y, Aug. 23)

All in all, the directive groups did not give rise to as much comment as the
other two group formats with regard to their effect — or absence of effect —
on members' sense of group belonging. This may have been because they were
perceived as presenting less danger that a person might perhaps be caught
unawares by unexpected challenges to his or her self-composure. In other
words, the directive groups were expected to be the safest. The relative absence
of comment reflects the fact that such turned out to be the case. This, after all,
was the kind of groupwork with which people were the most familiar, and
familiarity and belonging are close partners with safety. Whatever the reason,
however, in the present investigation the directive groups obviously aroused
less awareness of any kind of group belonging than either of the other
approaches.

(ii) Safety ↔ Danger

The dimension of safety/danger is, of course, closely associated with that of
belonging/alienation. Faith may be seen as release from deep-seated spiritual
anxiety and religious alienation, which we experience as being 'prisoners in
misery and irons' (Ps 107:10). Safety lies in knowing oneself to be released
from bondage. For some the group provided an experience of rescue from
oppression; for others it confirmed them in their anxiety. 'Safety' and 'Danger'
express the group's ability to provide a safe refuge, or its failure to do so. All
the group members record a degree of anxiety as to whether or not they felt
the group in one or other of its three forms — or in fact in all of them (Mrs
A, Mr L, Mr M) — was an emotionally safe place for them to be. In most cases
there seems to have been a balance between safety and danger; in one case
only, Mrs S, did the member feel secure most of the time. (It is perhaps worth
noting that the first session of all was directive.)

The directive groups
Mrs E, Mrs J, Mrs S and Mrs Y felt comfortable in the group's first session:

- *By the end of the session I felt we were becoming more comfortable with
  each other.* (Mrs E, Aug. 23)
- *The structured approach sat comfortably with me as a concept.* (Mrs J,
  Aug. 23)
- *I felt quite comfortable in the group as a whole. I felt quite safe.* (Mrs S,
  Aug. 23)

164

- *A mix of people I know well and others I do not know at all, so for me at first a formal setting was quite a good setting in which to discuss issues.* (Mrs Y, Aug. 23)
- *I felt more able to be engaged precisely because I knew what was expected of me.* (Mr M, Aug. 23)

Mrs Y was explicit about her feelings of insecurity and the need for safety:

- *It was quite important for me to look at the make-up of the group members a bit. I did not fully open up with my thoughts in the first meeting.* (Mrs Y, Aug. 23)

Several members recorded anxiety with regard to the expression of strong views about religion:

- *Our Biblical evangelical member gets quite 'preachy' at times . . . I can admire so much that she does which I could not do — it is the manner of it that puts me off.* (Mrs E, March 4)
- *One person seems to have fundamental tendencies, and there is potential conflict here.* (Miss H, Aug. 23)
- *I was right to hold back in sharing what God had done for me that week . . . When I converted to Christianity I shared my testimony with a vicar and a lay reader because I naively believed I was in a safe place. I was wrong . . .* (Mrs J, March 4)
- *Slight uncomfortable feelings when two people began discussing an issue intently.* (Mrs S, Jan. 28)

Mrs K, on the other hand, was disturbed by the lack of real congruence and honesty which she perceived in the group:

- *People were just trying to get things right. There was a sense of rigidity and restraint stereotyping.* (Mrs K, Nov. 30)

Mr L was discouraged by feelings of isolation:

- *The group was balanced in favour of the female gender which was at times slanted against male comment.*

The process groups
These sessions drew more comment from the group members than did the directive ones. Mrs A and Mr M echo Mrs K's misgivings with regard to the genuineness of people's sharing:

- *I felt the 'hard' challenges about sharing were avoided. Daring to share is risky . . . you can have the experiences without recognising the labels.* (Mrs A, Sept. 2, Nov. 12)

165

- *Because they were far less free than their prima facie format would suggest. [these sessions] caused me some disquiet. What I had to offer or contribute would not be accepted by the group . . . it was better to say very little.* (Mr M, Nov. 19)

The necessity to be careful what one might say was exposed by other group members, for various reasons involving safety:

- *Since people are sharing some personal situations and feelings (including Roger), perhaps the need for group privacy should be reminded; but I felt it was not a suitable time.*(Mrs E, Sept. 2)
- *I daren't raise the Lord's view for fear of what? What am I afraid of? Upsetting people? . . . I realised that God's power frightens some who I would have thought walking in it.* (Mrs J, Nov. 12, Feb. 11)

Others felt the Process Group to have been a positive experience:

- *It was interesting how open people felt able to be, and how words were often inadequate to express clearly what people were trying to say.* (Mrs E, Nov. 12)
- *(One person in the group) has a deep and mature-sounding faith. It makes me feel safer, less alone . . . I am less worried about appearing stand-offish and unco-operative . . . Tonight God reminded me that nothing is impossible for him.* (Mrs J, Nov. 12, Feb. 11)
- *I felt safe in the group . . . The whole experience tonight was very comfortable. R's leadership and control is democratic and somehow reassuring.* (Mrs S, Feb. 11, March 11)
- *I have found it very interesting that there have been no real conflicts in the group as to what matters to people both in their spiritual life in a church and their commitment to the Lord.* (Mrs Y, Sept. 12)

The art-based groups
The purpose of this kind of groupwork is to use indirect ways of contacting emotionally sensitive areas of experience. It involves forms of expression which group members may be unused to and associate with embarrassment (Mrs A; Mrs J; Mrs S; Mrs Y; Mr L).

- *Distressing scenarios crowded my mind . . . bothered about getting things wrong, being silly.* (Mrs A, Sept. 8)
- *I didn't want to share anything personal. Suddenly I didn't feel safe any more.* (Mrs J, Nov. 19)
- *It felt quite scary. The issues were deep-seated.* (Mrs S. Nov. 19)
- *I felt I had spoken out of turn on some of the ideas.* (Mr L. Sept. 8)

For Mrs K the element of danger added to the degree of self-disclosure as

- *The session made people take risks'* (Mrs K, Sept. 8).

Others found the use of imagination illuminating:

- *I chose a picture of lots of people in a boat at sea 'cos I don't like not having my feet on the ground, and the boat had no means of propulsion or steering.* (Mrs E, Nov. 19)

Describing a later art-based session, Mrs E explains,

- *When you do get into a scenario, things you never expected or realised can make themselves known, which can be exciting or scary.*

She adds,

- *I wonder if my unimaginative 'pair' subconsciously chose not to take the risk.* (Mrs E, Jan. 21)

To imagine something as a group and participate in giving it artistic form and presence, letting the result speak for itself, was a novel experience for two group members who preferred drawing conclusions — or having them drawn for them — to simply making connections for themselves:

- *A strong sense of awkwardness. Felt a bit was missing because there was no feedback to the discussion.* (Mrs A, Jan. 21)
- *The whole evening felt rather disjointed, and it would have been better for me if there had been more time for sharing comments and stories.* (Mrs E, Nov. 19)
- *As always, we didn't have time to draw threads together . . .* (Miss H, Jan. 21)

Mrs J saw the substitution of exploration for instruction characteristic of the art-based groups as a definite danger:

- *Creative approaches just interfere with my learning and become an end in themselves.* (Mrs J, Jan. 21)

She liked things to be spelled out clearly:

- *It didn't feel safe when [the member she didn't recognise as a Christian] was there.*
- *I don't mind being with non-Christians — I welcome it. But I need to know that is the situation. Then we can proceed in a way that aims to be acceptable to all without making assumptions about beliefs.* (Mrs J, March 18)

At the same time Mrs J valued the art-based format as a mitigation of the dangers involved in being too confrontational. Mrs A, however, regretted the absence of instruction:

- *In some ways it was a relief that the creative activities seemed to reduce the theological content — less chance for tensions and difficulties to arise.* (Mrs J, March 18)
- *I think, as always, I want straightforward and clear answers, a sure-fire method that will work in terms of sharing truth — how to give everyone the right answers.* (Mrs A, Jan. 28)

Their experience contrasts with the feeling of safety described by Mrs S in connection with the three art-based groups she attended:

- *I am feeling much more comfortable in the group.* (Mrs S, Sept. 8)
- *I enjoyed the fact that I could share with one other person some of my deepest and most traumatic hurts — plus it was safe to do so.* (Mrs S, Nov. 19)
- *I felt very comfortable, relaxed. One member of the group talked about difference, but not in any hostile or difficult sense.* (Mrs S, March 18)

(iii) Enrichment ↔ Impoverishment

This is the dimension referring to the members' comments regarding their own enjoyment or dissatisfaction with the sessions they attended. It is, of course, closely associated with both the preceding dimensions, as all four constructs overlap and refer to one another. Enrichment/impoverishment is perhaps the most variable factor, referring as it does to a slowly emerging judgement regarding the value of the enterprise taken as a whole, something which characteristically changes or is at least modified with new evidence, some of which may support an initial assessment, some modify it or contradict it altogether. Judgements vary with the information available; or, in practical terms, it takes time to make cognitive and emotional sense of the unknown — particularly when an experience runs counter to the way in which a person may be used to looking at life, and the unknown turns out to be otherwise than predicted.

The art-based groups

As we saw in the last section, some, if not all, of the group members came new to this kind of groupwork. Mrs S had considerable experience of creative approaches, but the others may well have been nervous about what to them was a novel way of doing groupwork and might well involve the use of talents which they considered they did not possess (Mrs J, Mr L). Some members (Mrs E, Mrs J, Mr L) found the format itself confusing or distracting, at least to begin with:

- *The wandering round at the start felt very unnatural.* (Mrs E, Sept. 8)
- *Some people like acting; I don't. What did God make of it/me/us?* (Mrs J, Sept. 8)
- *I have found it difficult to take in the complete content of each week's theme. I felt very much discomfort at times with the artistic evenings.* (Mr L, March 18)

Sometimes the feeling of impoverishment went deeper, so that the whole approach was kept at arms' length:

- *Some people seemed to find the drama more powerful than I did . . . I still don't feel comfortable enough with all the group to be able to share major events.* (Miss H, Sept. 8, Nov. 19)
- *I got the impression that one or two people had found the meeting deeply moving. But I don't know how or why. I certainly wouldn't attend a group like this through choice.* (Mrs J, Nov. 19, March 18)

Commenting on the third of the art-based groups (Jan. 21), Mrs J says,

- *I saw the creative point of the exercise, but I can't act and so couldn't engage with it. There was nothing spiritual in it for me.* (Mrs J, Jan. 21).

Mrs Y, on the other hand, felt impoverished by members' refusal to join in whole-heartedly:

- *One or two people did not want to participate, and I found this irritating. Sometimes we are not as forthcoming as we could be; we hold back.* (Mrs Y, Jan. 21)

Mrs Y speaks for others who found the art-based groupwork enriching:

- *High impact, as the issues were 'felt' in the body as well as the brain. Gave rise to a massive number of connections and reflections in a short space of time. Transformational and . . . practical . . . the heart is touched and this will translate into real action . . . Wonderful possibilities.* (Mrs A, Sept. 8, Jan. 21)

Mrs A found the lack of discussion impoverishing because there was '*more juice to be squeezed from these issues, more learning from sharing*'; all the same, the sessions themselves, as they stood, awakened a response which was more important to her than having time to discuss things:

- *It is beyond my comprehension, and that is joy and not burden to me. The way we respond comes out of the situation.* (Mrs A, March 18)

Mrs E found the art-based groupwork engaged her own interest in the dynamics of human relationship:

- *I felt (the different contributions) gave quite an insight into group members* (Mrs E, Sept. 8).

She goes on to point out that the session was also personal for her:

- *Someone spoke about how Jesus was an example of someone betrayed by friends, yet not only forgave but restored them. This resonated with a situation of my own, and I shared with them how helpful to me this observation had been.* (Mrs E, Sept. 8)

In spite of her comment about others being more affected by the drama than herself, Miss H admits that *'one person's contribution was very moving'* (Sept. 8). Later on she is more enthusiastic:

- *It was good to see everyone again. This was a creative session, very good . . . it was pretty obvious how the three exercises linked to the story.* (Miss H, Jan. 21)

The same process was at work with Mrs J:

- *I think I more or less made the connection at the end with some of the creative tasks.* (Mrs J, Nov. 19)
- *I liked the welcome tonight. It was honest. I liked [Miss H's] surprise that I could choose something very specific to delight her, and was very encouraged to hear her belief that God was directing her and really wanted her to enjoy the sense of excitement she expressed.* (Mrs J, March 18)

(On two other occasions, Nov. 19 and Jan. 21, Mrs J mentions making closer contact with individual group members during art-based sessions.)
Mrs S's reactions to the art-based groupwork also changed over sessions:

- *I found the group a little slow and felt a bit of irritation that they were being ponderous. One person was a little irritating tonight.* (Sept. 8)
- *Strong feelings arose when I reflected on my own story and the stories of others in the group — quite stressful. We seemed rushed at the end, with little time to process the material.* (Nov. 19)

Her final verdict on the occasion, however, was appreciative and positive:

- *The picture that I wrote a story about reminded me of finding peace. An honest and liberating session.* (Mrs S, Nov. 19)

Mrs Y's comments were, to her own surprise, consistently favourable:

- *I had not expected the Arts group to be like this. The whole experience was helpful and memorable. This is the groupwork which so far I have found the most moving.* (Sept. 8)
- *Everyone opened up and talked more about themselves, so it was a really good session, with everyone in the main being quite open on deep issues. This group worked better than I expected an art-based group to work.* (Nov. 19)

Mr L, despite his reservations about the approach, commented that,

- *The theme made me examine my own ethos — very thought-provoking* (Sept. 8).

Writing about his experience of the final art-based group he says how much he has valued the course as a whole in spite of feeling '*very much discomfort at times with the artistic evenings*':

- *Overall I found it very spiritually rewarding — which had its benefits. I was impressed by the deep commitment of some members in their knowledge of the faith plus the spirituality they brought to the group.* (Mr L, March 18)

Mrs K had no reservations:

- *I enjoy this kind of drama-based session . . . The session showed there is no obvious answer to life and we should avoid stereotyping.* (Mrs K, Sept. 8)

Mr M made no comments regarding his feelings about the art-based session except to say that he valued the fact that they, like the directive groupwork, provided the structure which the process sessions lacked.

The directive groups
This is the format aimed at providing opportunities for guided discussion of the kind whose absence was remarked on by some of those taking part in the art-based sessions (Mrs A, Miss H, Mrs S, Mr L). For the majority of the group it was the most familiar kind of groupwork, and they came to the group already accustomed to the procedures involved which they had found helpful or aversive. Some found the format limiting:

- *It was irritating to be moved on when the discussion was heading off at an interesting tangent. After the meeting I felt I hadn't really got far with the topic.* (Mrs E, March 4)

171

- *At first it seemed rather stilted, people rather reticent. It seemed as though it might be hard work . . . I didn't feel this session worked too well. As we were from different churches it was difficult to apply the questions.* (Miss H, Aug. 23, Feb. 11)

Mrs J, too, remarks that she found '*the content of the material not always especially helpful*' (Mrs J, Aug. 23). As the course went on, she became more explicit:

- *There seemed to be a reluctance to address in any deep way how we shared/didn't share our faith. No-one gave a living testimony . . . Roger cut [Mrs S] short when she was sharing a lovely testimony that filled her with such joy.* (Mrs J, Jan. 28, March 4)

Mrs S herself draws attention to the presence of a 'worry' which a group member was feeling which did not get addressed (Mrs S, Jan. 28). Mrs K also directs attention to the effects of being directed:

- *I felt that the sharing was only on the surface. Again, it was the confident ones who took charge.*

Others, however, were more appreciative of this approach:

- *I loved the connections you could make, mythical and symbolic connections — I get ideas and inspirations, 'a-ha' moments.* (Mrs A, Jan. 28)
- *The 'ice-breaker' worked well in giving more insight into one another — lovely variety of revelations . . . The material encouraged some sharing at depth — members of the group encouraged others to contribute or expand what they originally said.* (Mrs E, Nov. 30)
- *More in-depth sharing tonight — interesting divergences but many similarities . . . This was a much better session for me — structured! Began with experiences of school — very telling.* (Miss H, Nov. 30)
- *It's so encouraging to hear what God has done for others in their everyday lives. This was the most helpfully encouraging and edifying (session) to date for me. Tonight I have felt I was truly with Christians who have a living faith. I'd not felt this before in any of the other sessions.* (Mrs J, Nov. 30)
- *I enjoyed having the other members speak of their individual situations. I felt quite emotional when people shared their stuff . . . I found [R] reassuring. He tends to pick up on other people's feelings and then by becoming quite academic manages to affirm everyone . . . The poem at the beginning made me feel I very much enjoyed being part of this group — it was very focused and worked hard.* (Mrs S, Aug. 23, Jan. 28, March 4)
- *Quite a lot of the discussion reminded me of events or things in my*

172

church life and outside which have been happy. Very pleased that everyone in the group played a part in the discussions . . . There was plenty to talk about and most people had lots to say. Reduced numbers but people seemed very committed. (Mrs Y, Aug. 23, Nov. 30)

- *I felt at home with the evening's content and could relate to much of the topics discussed. Found the session spiritually uplifting. Didn't think I would — which just goes to show.* (Mr L, March 4)
- *It was clear.* (Mrs K, Nov. 30)

Mr M found both the directive and art-based sessions more acceptable than the process ones, because they seemed to work better. The structure of the group itself caused him concern:

- *There was a far from sufficient range of people present, the over-whelming majority coming from not dissimilar background and (myself included) getting on in years.*

The process groups

This kind of group in a church setting was also a novel experience for most members. Again, it represented a marked contrast with the kind of learning which some of them were used to in other groups they had attended. The most negative reaction was that of Mr M, who remained frustrated by the failure of an approach aimed at intellectual and emotional honesty to deal with how the group was actually interacting as a 'therapeutic setting' ought to have done:

- *What is important is how people behave in the group towards each other, rather than the pre-suppositions they bring — and since these for the most part are never challenged, there is an absence of 'truth.'* (Mr M, Feb. 11)

For Mrs J, truth was also being threatened by the group's reluctance to refer more consistently to its source:

- *I keep wanting us to look at the bible together and we don't. Sometimes it's easy to forget we are a group of Christians.* (Mrs J, Sept. 2)

Mrs E, Miss H, Mrs Y and Mrs S shared a feeling of incompleteness regarding this approach:

- *I think I'm relieved the next meeting will be the last. The group feels as if it is meandering now.* (Mrs E, March 11)
- *I feel very negative but for me the process sessions seem aimless. Many of us need the structure to feel comfortable.* (Miss H, March 11)
- *The group did not really spend enough time on gender issues. Time was a factor which did limit what one could say.* (Mrs Y, Sept. 12)

- *It felt much vaguer, and slightly frustrating.* (Mrs S, Feb. 11)
- *I thought we might be running out of time.* (Mr L, March 11)

The most considered judgement was that of Mrs K:

- *I don't think we really had time to do this kind of group properly. I got a sense of people having to do things they weren't ready for yet. I had a sense of missed opportunity.*(Mrs K, Feb. 11)

On the other hand, there were more positive things emerging from the experience:

- *I'm getting familiar with different people's style and approach which informs how I 'hear' and understand what they're saying . . . People were mostly willing to share experiences of talking to/being talked to in different situations and with very different outcomes . . . I shall miss interacting with [Mrs J] and [Mrs S] as they bring insights and energy I value.* (Mrs E, Nov. 12, Feb. 11, March 11)

Mrs J and others also mention the opportunities for making personal contact associated with this group format:

- *I have met a lovely person in the group. It's good being in the group with them . . . I enjoy one person's incisive way of putting their point across. It gives me hope. One person described how an exercise in artistic creativity was a deep spiritual experience. It was great.* (Mrs J, Sept. 2, Nov. 12)
- *Mrs E no longer looks dour to me, but very interesting and intelligent . . . it had been over a month since we last met, and I was not sure I would remember people's names. In fact I had no troubles at all, and this gave me a slight boost of confidence. When anger and depression were mentioned, I felt empathy.* (Mrs S, Sept. 2, Nov. 12)
- *I observed the discussion that took place was very relaxed.* (Mr L, March 11)

(iv) Validation ↔ Rejections

Because it concerns the way in which we feel about ourselves as human beings, validation is intrinsic to the process whereby we learn what is really important for our own happiness and the well-being of the world in which we live — and also the way these things are related to each other. Because of this fact, the dimension validating/rejecting may be considered the most important one of all. Learning about ourselves in this way is a healing process as well as an educational one. The significance of validation of personhood for an analysis of the Process Groups considered here stands out clearly.

The process groups

Some members were reassured about themselves and their attitudes to life:

- *The triumph of hope over experience. I have come away from groups in a state of confusion and unhappiness — listening to the other people's stories told very candidly made me feel relieved quite a few times — a positive experience.* (Mrs A, Nov. 11)
- *I spoke to [Mrs A] about how God had spoken into my life the previous night. She actually wanted to listen and was encouraged by it.* (Mrs J, Feb. 11)
- *I was very tired (but) very soon I was glad I was there, was a part of the group and accepted and affirmed. Practically everyone is reassuring, I could talk to everyone really closely. I was glad I said about the small, almost trivial way God influences my life.* (Mrs S, Sept. 2, Feb. 11)
- *Participation is the way I learn. The openness of the discussions brought to my memory things which were very positive. I have taken great encouragement from the people in the group . . . One or two people have been able to express their commitment in more detailed terms, and I have felt this quite helpful personally.* (Mrs Y, Sept. 2, Nov. 12, March 11)

Not everyone found the format liberating, however:

- *I'm not quite sure what I was meant to come away with. The session reinforced the feeling that this style doesn't really work for me.* (Miss H, Nov. 12, Feb. 11)

The absence of structural guidelines exposed Miss H and others to aversive influences within the group itself:

- *I am finding I have to try to understand viewpoints which are completely alien to me (and) are not my understanding of the Gospel.* (Miss H, Nov. 12)
- *I did feel quite strongly when one member said what a responsibility it would be to have received a conversion as St Paul did — it shook me because I have received a clear vision and have not broadcast it as much as perhaps I should have.* (Mrs S, Feb. 11)
- *People were saying how great it was, but I wasn't convinced and didn't feel able to participate properly. Was it just me? Was I trying to make it what it wasn't?* (Mrs K, Feb. 11)
- *Some members of the group suggested I was being 'sarcastic' when I was merely being facetious. I think there was a kind of recognition on the part of the group that I was not 'at home' in it, and the group leader said as much on several occasions to justify my inclusion in it.* (Mr M, comment Sept. 2, Nov. 9, Jan. 28)

175

The art-based groups

Some members found the approach invalidating because they believed themselves inartistic, or questioned the suitability of art for Christian learning:

- *The introductory exercise didn't seem to have much relevance to what came after.* (Mrs E, Nov. 19)
- *I simply cannot relate to what they describe happening within themselves ... It's not the medium that's a problem. I just don't use these things to learn about God and my faith ... Being rejected by Christians is especially hurtful.* (Mrs J, Sept. 8, Nov. 19, March 18)
- *This was a session I did not enjoy because I lack imagination ... Once again I felt out of my depth.* (Mr L, Sept. 8, Nov. 19)

Mrs Y found the sessions emotionally disturbing: '*Many times in this course I found myself remembering how unhappy I had been*', but cathartic in their effect:

- *I was feeling stressed and inadequate, but in a very short space of time I felt better. I was able to talk about some of my own issues.* (Mrs Y, Nov. 19)

Mrs Y said she had been reminded of her work with homeless people (Sept. 8). Others were similarly affected:

- *The Rejected Helper is a poignant theme in my own life. With God's help I am receiving some insights into this area ...* (Mrs A, Sept. 8)
- *Last week someone spoke about how Jesus was an example of someone who was betrayed by friends, but not only forgave them but restored them. This resonated with a situation of my own, and I shared with them ...* (Mrs E, Sept. 8)
- *My own description of a dramatic change was quite stressful but (the session) was really liberating.* (Mrs S, Nov. 19)

Relationships within the group were sometimes strengthened:

- *I felt that (the different contributions) gave quite an insight into group members ... I did my version of Jesus getting me to open the door to him. My 'pair' seemed apologetic that he had not had a Damascus Road experience, but I said the brief said 'life-changing' with no religious tag ... We had to choose a present to give to our partners. I offered 'confidence and self-assurance'. We both came up with times when we'd been given words and/or actions that really affirmed us as valued individuals. The giver had really seen us as ourselves and also offered an unexpected validation.* (Mrs E, Sept. 8, Nov. 19, Jan. 21)

- *I thought the written comments about my picture were fascinating. One person actually got the correct quotation.* (Miss H, Nov. 19)
- *We all need to feel the validity of our own approaches is respected by others . . . I found grace to join in the first exercise, though I really didn't feel comfortable with it.* (Mrs J, Jan. 21, March 18)
- *I found one member reassuring — because I had been honest, opened myself out and was accepted for who I am . . . I felt accepted and comfortable with who I am by not trying to be anything or anyone else. I'm glad I said I enjoy Rod Stewart, 'cos I do, and even though others may not approve it is a very important part of me. Everyone in the group seemed to affirm me today — even the dominant and 'bolshy' personalities.* (Mrs S, Sept. 8, Jan. 21)

The directive groups
Validating experiences:

- *I felt we were all being listened to with great attention, and this is very affirming. Aspects of hurt and distress were met with empathy. I felt the evening had been just right, rather than feeling rushed or foreshortened. I was struck by the intense 'vision' experiences and could have added my own.* (Mrs E, Nov. 30)
- *Hearing the testimony of others was wonderful. It was a revelation to hear stories of faith from people who are 'private' . . . I was pleased that [Mr L] found spiritual stimulation in the group. It is very grounding when people are willing to be real with you.* (Mrs J, Nov. 30, March 4)
- *For many years I would not talk openly about my dyslexia, so I was glad I had mentioned it to the group.* (Mrs Y, Aug. 23)
- *In all it turned out to be a very stimulating evening for me.* (Mr L, Aug. 23)
- *It was helpful to me to describe something.* (Mrs K, Nov. 30)

There were, however, occasions when people felt rejected:

- *Started badly, with hanging around outside because no-one had opened the front door. Very irritating, it made me feel unwelcomed and undervalued.* (Mrs E, Aug. 23)
- *Although this is my favourite format, it didn't really work for me. I find faith-sharing a difficult topic. I hate soap-box or door-knocking evangelism . . . The session reinforced the feeling that this style doesn't really work for me.* (Miss H, Jan. 28, Feb. 11)
- *Last week, Roger, you cut me short when I said that, rather than being intimidated by the powerful testimonies of some very ordinary Christians I chose to embrace the gospel and was converted. This shocked me . . . I have felt throughout the discussion sessions that there was a reluctance in some quarters to accept the testimony that I have.* (Mrs J, March 4)

- *Memories brought up (because) my church group not able to give me the support I needed.* (Mrs Y, Aug. 23)
- *The general feeling I got was that maybe I didn't know enough to present my opinions.* (Mrs S, Aug. 23)

Differential analysis according to groupwork structure

The final stage in the analytical process consists in interpreting the material in its synthesised form in order to identify differential effects of varying structures for groupwork in the experience of those taking part in the twelve sessions. Glancing at the results without attempting to analyse them statistically, it is apparent that, in terms of the evidence presented by group members, the art-based groups scored highest in two out of four thematic areas — enrichment/impoverishment and validation/rejection — and the process and directive groups in one area each — belonging/alienation and safety/danger. The process and art-based groups elicited three times as many positive comments as the directive groups with regard to 'belonging' and almost twice as many for 'validation.' The directive groupwork registered as slightly more dangerous than process, but much safer than art-based. These results stand out most clearly and I would consider them to be the most important ones.

This list represents the contributions of only eight out of the nine group

	Belonging	Alienation	Safety	Danger	Enrichment	Impoverishment	Validation	Rejection	Totals
Directive	4	6	7	8	14	8	6	5	58
Process	12	11	7	6	14	9	11	5	75
Art-based	12	4	6	11	19	15	13	6	86
	28	21	20	25	47	32	30	16	

Differential analysis of the distribution of the four constructs within the three kinds of group structure members; Mr M's input was not presented on a session-by-session basis. Some of the material returned by other group members took the form of a summary included at the end of the sessional record; this, too, is omitted from the above table (Mrs Y, Mr L, Mr M). In addition, it occasionally happened that an item stood out as ambiguous, and a choice had to be made as to which pole of the construct it referred. (A good example of this is Mrs K's statement that the arts-group session on August 23 *'made people take risks.'* This has been recorded under 'danger'; but Mrs K actually intends it as a positive reaction as she believes risk-taking to be necessary!)

From a statistical point of view, then, these results have to be taken as something of a 'straw poll.' There was no way of calibrating the intensity, and consequently the personal importance, of judgements made; a comment might be interpreted as very positive or negative or only marginally so. The main reason why Mr M's contribution has not been included here is because, although he states a definite preference for the directive and art-based approaches, in actual fact this judgement is more theoretical than experiential, as he was genuinely unhappy with the way in which, for him, any of the sessions had turned out.

Another consideration which is not obvious from the above table is the cumulative effect produced by repeated experiences of group membership — something intrinsic to any groupwork project, but only rarely mentioned in these submissions. The impression gained by the group leader (i.e. myself) was that the directive format became less popular over time while the art-based groupwork grew more popular. Mrs E's remarks that *'Later Process and Activity sessions were easier because we knew each other better and were literally easier with one another'* (March 11) may be contrasted with Miss H's verdict on the third directive session: *'Although this is my favourite format, it didn't really work for me this evening'* (Jan. 28). Perhaps the most striking evidence regarding a member's gradual change in attitude is provided by Mrs J who, like Mrs A, Miss H and Mr L, had expressed a preference for structure from the outset:

- *I just don't use these things to learn about God and my faith.* (Mrs J, Nov. 19)
- *Creative approaches just interfere with my learning.* (Mrs J, Jan. 21)
- *I liked the welcome tonight. It was honest. I liked [Miss H's] surprise that I could find something very specific to delight her . . . I really wanted her to enjoy the sense of excitement she expressed.* (Mrs J, March 18)

There is little doubt that the process orientated groupwork never achieved its full potential and that this is largely owing to the circumstances in which it took place — that is, subject to the expectations aroused by the leader's role as a figure of authority and the fact that it took place in the setting most closely associated with his authority. Also, it made use of a format generally understood to need more than four sessions to work to its best advantage. Mrs A,

179

who was used to this kind of groupwork and seems to have expected it to fall short of the ideals of freedom of expression which it officially espoused, was appreciative of the efforts made in this direction, however:

- *The triumph of hope over experience! I have come away from groups where this approach has been used in a state of confusion and unhappiness — listening to other people's stories told very candidly made me feel relieved quite a few times — a positive experience.* (Mrs A, Nov. 11)

As an authentic 'process-orientated' groupwork structure, this was compromised from the start by the factors mentioned above — leadership associated, if not identified, with authoritarianism and lack of an opportunity to 'develop its full potential.'

Nevertheless, the 'process' groups certainly captured group members' attention, as is demonstrated by the number of judgements to which they gave rise. So far as 'belonging/alienation'— and this dimension is certainly a vital one for congregational learning — the 'process' groups scored appreciably higher than the 'directive' ones, three times as highly in fact. The charge of 'group therapy' made by Mrs J is unjustified. Because learning about ourselves in this interactive, *inter-relational* way is both educational and psychologically healing, the process group format only really makes sense if its effect is emotionally liberating, but even then the contrast with directed learning can prove too much for some, in which case the effect can be neither therapeutic nor educational, but simply pointless:

- *I was conscious of having nothing to offer at this stage . . . Oh dear, I feel very negative, but for me the process sessions seem aimless. Many of us need the structure to feel comfortable, 'at home'.* (Miss H, Sept. 2, March 11)
- *I think I'm relieved the next meeting will be the last. The group feels as if it is meandering now.* (Mrs E, March 11)
- *It felt much vaguer, and slightly frustrating.* (Mrs S, Feb. 11)

Others, however, were relieved and given a sense of freedom:

- *On my journeying home as I thought about the evening . . . I felt blest.* (Mrs A, Nov. 12)
- *We started just sitting in silence. It seemed very comfortable doing this.* (Mrs E, Feb. 11)
- *This was for me the best session of the whole programme . . . There was a widely spread sense of a desire to share experiences of God.* (Mrs J, Feb. 11)
- *The openness of the discussions brought to my memory things that were very positive.* (Mrs Y, Sept. 2)

- *I was very tired (but) soon I was glad I was there, was a part of the group and accepted and affirmed.* (Mrs S, Sept. 2)

It was, however, a freedom which could be abused:

- *There was a danger of hi-jacking by individuals.* (Mrs A, Sept. 2)
- *One or two people could get a bit much.* (Mrs Y, Sept. 12)
- *I sensed that one person was out on a limb and wanted to include and affirm them — they seemed to be disregarded by the majority.* (Mrs S, Nov. 12)
- *Some very confident people who hogged it all at the expense of the shy ones.* (Mrs K, Sept. 2)

Obviously this kind of groupwork gave rise to a wider range of feelings than either of the other approaches, which has the effect of making the task of analysis more difficult. On the other hand a more nomothetic approach, one which concentrated on drawing precise conclusions regarding the attitudes expressed and the intensity and frequency of their occurrence, would almost certainly miss the important point about these groups — that they managed to combine belonging and alienation, which are opposed categories of experience in an almost equal degree, while giving rise to a high level of responsiveness. As with the art-based groups, opportunities to stand back and draw conclusions about the experience while it was actually going on were kept to a minimum during the session itself: members were intended to interpret after the event rather than during it. While it was going on, they were encouraged to become involved in the action. The comments regarding 'unfinishedness' reflect members' experience of directive groupwork.

Each of the three groupwork formats gave rise to mixed reactions from the group members within dimensions of evaluation which all three shared. What conclusions, then, may be drawn from these judgements?

Drawing a conclusion

Investigation of the reports submitted with regard to three different groupwork approaches shows that involvement in groups engages individuals in four inter-connected ways. When structures are varied, emphasis falls on different areas of personal experience, all of them belonging to the awareness of participating in an inter-personal focused way of learning about the self in its relationships with others.

No doubt more could be gained from an examination of the material at this stage of the analytical process. However, enough has been drawn from it to demonstrate the importance of the four experiential themes and their interdependence. All four must be present in order for a group to function as an effective mode of human shared learning. The different group structures represented give prominence to different aspects of the same core group experience of belonging-safety-enrichment-validation which may be said to be characteristic of groupwork itself. Interpreting the evidence emerging from the twelve sessions, each of the four dimensions may be seen as operating in harmony with its fellows in individuals' awareness of themselves and one another within a group guided by a shared concern for the well-being of persons. Each 'core theme' represents a dimension of awareness which, through the holistic action of personal relationships, makes the others more salient. Together they live out a relationship that is diverse yet focused, social yet personal.

It cannot be realistically claimed that this is anything like scientific analysis. Four 'core themes,' influenced by and proceeding from their association with other related ideas and experiences, found expression in the depositions of nine group members in the form of dimensions of evaluation of a shared experience. The evidence remains evidence. The conclusion being drawn — that this somehow 'explains' the groupwork phenomenon — ignores the fact that the investigation itself omitted to control for the presence of independent variables which might be held responsible for any conclusions drawn. For one thing, members of the groups already shared a world-view which would invariably affect the way in which they interacted within any group setting; also they were neither balanced not properly randomised with regard to age, gender, personality type, Christian tradition, etc.; the limitation of number of group sessions and group structures allowed for (four of three kinds) was bound to have a differential effect with regard to the type of group structure; the cumulative effect of having twelve sessions in succession was bound to distort any discernible effect produced regarding particular kinds of group, making any attempt at comparison between approaches that much harder.

Even more basic than what must appear as methodological high-handedness is the absence of a theory to be tested. How can anything be proved if there is nothing to prove? If the purpose of the exercise is not to demonstrate that something or other is the case and to do so by means of procedures which are available for precise measurement and also replicable by others using the same approach (Robson, 1973), then what use can it be? Four associated psychological constructs do not constitute a theory, as defined by the Concise Oxford Dictionary (Allen, 1990) as 'supposition explaining something, esp. one based on principles independent of the phenomenon to be explained.' However, it may be argued that it is precisely this independence which has repeatedly undermined attempts to understand the phenomena involved in human relationships. It may be necessary for predicting the way things are likely to work out, but not people.

When describing what it is that happens between, among and within people, the person who is in charge of the project is not capable of laying her or his own personhood aside without actually changing what he or she is trying to describe. In the study of personal relations, empathy and imagination may be more reliable instruments than the pretence of an unattainable objectivity. In order to understand another person we must, first of all, allow them to be themselves. What and who they are is something they themselves will show us — and our own ideas about what it is likely to be are no real substitute. Husserl (1960) calls this the acceptance of 'the things themselves;' he sees it as the basis of all human discovery, on the basis that we will never learn anything if we know it already.

This is one of the guiding principles of action research (Curtis et al., 1999), which is the exploration of what is actually going on rather than a systematic attempt to make the evidence fit what is already believed to be happening. This is obviously very relevant to any research involving people: a human phenomenon must be allowed to precede theories regarding its own nature. In any investigation explanations are bound to emerge within the investigator's own mind. Interpretative Phenomenological Analysis (Smith et al., 2009) requires them to stay there until those being investigated have explained the situation which they find themselves in.

Interpretative Phenomenological Analysis (IPA) has recently been described as 'both a phenomenological and a hermeneutic approach in qualitative psychology,' underpinned by the work of such phenomenological philosophers as Husserl, Heidegger, Merleau-Ponty and Sartre, and hermeneutic philosophers such as Dilthey and Gadamer and, of course, Schliermacher (Gee, 2011, 9).

As we saw earlier, tt directs our attention to the way we lay hold on what we actually know about the world by means of being ourselves alive within it. It includes us as participants in what we know, rather than entities capable of making detached, 'objective' judgements. Gee (2011, 8) points out that: 'Adventurous interpretation is encouraged [by IPA],' since genuinely inductive interpretation, facilitated by the disciplined use of consecutive stages, is the pathway to Smith and Osborn's (2008) 'double hermeneutic', or 'two-stage interpretative process', involving both participant and researcher.

There is no need, therefore, for any apologies to be made regarding the investigator's use of the same interpretative approach as the individual group member when she or he recalled a particular session and set about trying to make sense of what had been said or done in it in the light of his or her feelings and thoughts about it. The interpretative action is the tool we use in order to make sense of impressions we recognise as 'standing out' for us with regard to an experience or set of experiences. For the present investigator/interpreter, ideas and feelings regarding belonging, safety, impoverishment and personal validation emerged as characteristic of participants' experience of the groupwork sessions, through a process of systematic interpretation and re-interpretation of the phenomenological evidence.

What the investigation suggests, therefore, is that these particular reactions taking place in groupwork represent interpretative dimensions intrinsic to the experience of groupwork itself. The nine people who took part in the twelve sessions recorded experiences which highlight the importance of the four dimensions which the analytic process elicited by successive levels of interpretative refinement. All nine group members expressed thoughts and feelings on these four subjects, without reporting reactions which could reasonably be considered to be divorced from their scope. These were the things they considered worth mentioning about their experiences of the groupwork. Their protocols were as free and open as they themselves could allow them to be, in circumstances in which openness and freedom were actually stipulated as a requirement for taking part. Examination showed that the material of these protocols fell into the four subject areas identified, and that no expression of interest or concern falling outside their parameters was consistently included within the material submitted for analysis. All nine people, it emerged, had something to say regarding belonging, safety, enrichment and validation and the importance of these things to them.

All nine individuals produced evidence concerning the four master themes emerging from their protocols. According to the research model adopted, this shows these dimensions of experience to be the organising principles of the way in which the value of the groupwork was assessed by those taking part. The nature of the research model makes it impossible to state this as true of all groupwork, undertaken in any circumstances whatever. Certainly, it may be regarded as a theory open to further testing; however the logic of Interpretative Phenomenological Research (Smith et al., 2009) leads us to regard it as an important piece if evidence contributing to the eventual emergence of a theory concerning groupwork experience.

The evidence shows that in this case the action of taking part in three recognisably distinct forms of groupwork produced reactions which were seen to be form-specific, the art-based groupwork giving more salience to safety/danger, enrichment/impoverishment and validation/rejection, the process group to belonging/alienation, the directive group scoring least in all four areas. The highest levels were attained by the art-based groupwork for enrichment/impoverishment (an aggregate of 34) and the process groups for belonging/alienation (23) and enrichment/impoverishment (23); the lowest scores were recorded for the directive groupwork in belonging/alienation (10) and validation/rejection (11). (It should be remembered that these scores refer to the degree to which the four subject areas played a part in the group-members' submissions — they do not reveal the force with which ideas and feelings were expressed.)

Implications for church policy regarding groups

In chapter 4, the investigation was defined operationally as involving the exploration of material recorded by individual members of a small group of people involved in alternative groupwork approaches in order to see whether or not evidence existed regarding the presence of differential effects attributable to variation in group structures. In the words of the Research Question (see Introduction):

- What would a comparison between instructional ('directive'), process-orientated and art-based groups reveal about the differences in their overall effect upon group members?

To which the corollary adds:

- What model may be proposed regarding groupwork in the Church of England?

The language of the research proposal includes 'process-orientated' and 'art-based' within the category of experiential as opposed to directive, so that the 'central theoretical argument' throughout has been as follows:

> Directive and experiential groupwork has a differential effect upon group members and may be successful in the groupwork of the Church of England.

It is obvious, then, that we have reached an important stage in the course of our argument. The suggestion made at the beginning still stands — that different groupwork approaches would, if employed, meet the Church's needs in different ways. Now, however, we have some evidence drawn from this investigation, that this is likely to be so or rather, that three kinds of group-work were all different from one another in ways which the Christian Church has always considered vitally important, that is, in the dimensions of belonging, safety, enrichment and validation so far as these things are to be taken personally. Because they are structured in varying ways, the groups promote different values as salient, those suggested by the way the group responds to the format; consequently different groups have been seen to have different effects, make different impressions.

In the results included in the last section, all three approaches were shown to have had effects which were distinguishable from one another with regard to the influence exerted upon people's experience of being group members. Broadly speaking, directed groups drew least response in the way of written comment, and art-based groups most (58 as opposed to 86), with the process-orientated groupwork somewhat nearer to the art-based than to the directive (75). For spoken response, therefore, looseness of direction would seem to be more productive than tightness (always remembering, of course, that belonging to a group in itself suggests a structure for co-operation).

This is not to suggest that tightly constructed groupwork emerged as noticeably more effective for didactic purposes. Judging by members' depositions, cognitive learning came second to other things and did not play an important enough part in people's experience to be recognisable as an ongoing theme within any of the work. The 'enrichment' remarked on in this area had more to do with group interaction, the satisfaction in being together as a group and learning to know one another in the process, than it had with the knowledge that they had been given any definite information. As in the other two kinds of group, the things which came from the experience which those taking part chose mainly to record were feelings and intuitions, ideas emerging from life generated within the group itself.

Certainly neither in the directed group sessions nor the more experientially focused ones were the things learned necessarily concerned with the transmission of information at a cognitive level; as we saw earlier on in this book, this kind of teaching and learning is not feasible within a group framework where personal agendas must be acknowledged as an essential part of the learning process. In groupwork, feelings are more important than ideas simply because ideas are formulated through their agency. What was being learned here was all about being in a group — in this case a group of people with whom it sometimes felt safe to share quite intimate and personal thoughts and feelings. Consequently, the lesson was one about the safety in sharing.

Seeing this was a group of Christians, all of them (except Mrs S) members of the same denomination — or even the same actual congregation — the feeling of being complete strangers to one another was certainly not an intense one. The subject of a shared faith and heritage emerged frequently in these sessions, and even those members who were critical of the way some of their fellow group members believed (Mrs H, Mrs J, Mr M) were willing to try hard to accept them as fellow followers of Christ. Instead of the fear of strangers, the initial threat lay in not feeling secure with people identifiable as dangerous friends. Safe within the written guidelines of the directive approach, with someone in charge who had the authority to make certain these would be followed, members felt more protected, less exposed to the danger of saying more than they wanted to do — either about one another or about themselves.

Even so, the result shows a higher level of agreement within the three approaches regarding this dimension than it does for the others. All groupwork involves the risk of exclusion, frustration and the fear of being found wanting by others in the group. (The higher 'danger' score emerging from the art-based group almost certainly reflects people's nervousness regarding what they perceived as a lack of skill on their part compared with other members of the group — something likely to diminish as time went on as the level of validation reveals.) All groupwork offers the prospect of emotional wounding, even though this may often be recognised by the people concerned to have had a healing effect (Mrs E, Mrs Y, Mrs S); but it is also true that groups hold out a chance of a very positive kind of enrichment, the joy of being together, exploring life in the company of others with whom one begins to feel a special bond of fellowship. It is a risky thing, as Mrs K said, to expose your feelings, opinions, convictions and abilities to others at such short range, but the opportunities for *koinwnia* (mutual sharing) afforded for groupwork among Christians are, as Mrs A discovered, 'mind-blowing.'

Looking at the reactions expressed in the material produced by these nine people it would not be possible to say that the directive groupwork, carried out in accordance with the instructions included along with it, had more impact on the way in which things were learned within the group than the other two approaches. They were enjoyed slightly more than the process and art-based sessions, but do not appear to have had as much to say about the major themes of the exercise, its 'regnant constructs,' as they did. Obviously these themes are of great importance to the Church, whose concern with personal and group enrichment can never be separated from questions about belonging, safety and validation — belonging to One Body, safe within the revealed love of the Father, validated by the saving acts of Christ.

This is what the Church itself teaches. We should not be surprised to discover these themes claiming special significance for Christians who are engaged in learning to work through the difficulties involved in acting in close co-operation with others; particularly when the other group members are recognised as sharing not simply their common humanity, but also a common trust in Him who is able to overcome all the forces which can divide people against one another, and ourselves against ourselves. The evidence presented here and the arguments produced in support of it suggest that there is more to be learned from, and taught by, groupwork than may be understood and appreciated by contemporary Christian churches.

I have limited myself in this book to the present state of affairs in a number of Church of England dioceses in which directive groupwork is becoming well established as a means of congregational learning. I am not aware at the present time of any Church of England diocese within England itself which has established process-orientated or art-based groups on a regular basis for congregational involvement — or indeed any 'officially recognised' learning groups apart from directive ones. The present investigation suggests that for purposes of Christian learning, a policy of limiting groups to those in which an authoritarian presence and structure restricts the scope allowed for self-expression on the members' part is seriously to undervalue groups as human phenomena by under-rating their ability to contribute to the way human beings learn some of the most vital things about themselves, one another and God.

This, of course, means how we learn about the Church. There are, as we saw earlier in this book, many different approaches to groupwork. The ones explored in this investigation were only three of many. Enough has been done here to show a recognisable degree of variation between the effects produced by three different group structures, each of which appear to give special emphasis to a particular aspect of groups: their promise of guidance (directive), self-understanding (process) and symbolic journey (art-based). There are other ways, of course, for us to learn how to live the reality of Christian belonging through our experiences in groups. The ones explored in this book are only three examples from an entire range of adaptations of what, after all, is a fundamental way of being human. At present it appears that within the Church of England at least, groupwork remains largely unexplored territory. The scope of its usefulness within the overall work of the Kingdom makes it an opportunity which is being missed.

Running groups which do not have their ways of proceeding laid out firmly in advance may well seem a dangerous thing to do when the Church itself is so easily seen as being under threat. To encourage church congregations to be adventurous in what they say and do when acting together as a group may well seem foolhardy, particularly in a time of decreasing numbers. The history of the Church shows that it has frequently felt itself to be under threat. Jesus teaches us not to be anxious but to 'strive first for the Kingdom of God' (Mt 6:33). Those who close in on themselves strive only for their own security. This being so, there is certainly a case for suggesting that contemporary, twenty-first century Christianity should be adventurous in its willingness to 'take risks for Christ' by engaging the world in His name and the power of Holy Spirit without carrying a handbook provided — and edited — by the church authorities. In fact, experiential groups direct themselves to areas of Christian belonging which the official teaching of the churches has failed to reach, owing to the tendency to close in upon oneself rather than admit to what may be perceived as an unorthodox idea or interpretation and condemned as such. In both the process and art-based groups people who were normally loth to speak out, and others who were used to leaving leadership to others, found a new kind of courage (Mrs A, Mrs Y, Mrs K). This kind of non-directive, non-authoritarian decisiveness is what the Church of England should show itself to be confident enough to appreciate in its attitude to Christian learning. As St Paul reminds us, maturity involves being given adult responsibilities (1 Cor 13:11).

Last, but certainly not least in importance — if the church can tolerate such a 'do-it-yourself' approach to so serious a subject — there are the hermeneutic possibilities of approaches which, like the art-based one employed here, move from the sharing of personal experience to the exploration of its relevance to the Christian story, starting out from what has already been learned in and through life and opening out its symbolic resonance in the light of bible story and Christian teaching. This kind of approach applies life to faith instead of expounding the reality of faith and then applying it to situations arising in life. This gives rise to an open-ended hermeneutic as women and men are encouraged to move from wherever they feel themselves to be at present, as Holy Spirit leads them to discover previously unimagined ways of drawing closer to the truth which beckons them. This 'hermeneutics of the imagination' is the approach which I personally would commend to the Church of England.

In the last analysis, it appears to come down to the straightforward question: how far may group members be trusted to teach one another how to be Christians, and how much do they still need to be taught? How much can they lead one another and how much must they be led? Can they discover their own versions of a vision?

Perhaps these are the real 'research questions.'

Note

1   In the following, passages in italics are direct quotations.

7

Recommendations for a New Model in Church Groupwork

Summarising her experiences as a member of the group, Mrs Y wrote:

> The learning was positive and practical . . . the diverse approach was useful for a changing church situation.

Mrs Y's comment widens the debate to include other churches and congregations than Church of England ones. Interest in groupwork within Great Britain has tended during the last half century or so to be somewhat polarised, although not always in the same direction, of course. During the 1960s it was characterised by dependence upon psychoanalytic models and later on by ideas drawn from humanistic psychology and psychotherapy, remembered particularly in Britain for Clinical Theology (Lake, 1966) and the first Pastoral Studies Diploma at Birmingham University (Lambourne, 1983). The accent was upon process-orientated approaches to the exclusion of almost anything else.

This kind of groupwork no longer appears to arouse very much interest; at least, it does not do so in England. After an interval of two or three decades, the pendulum swung towards a different kind of group altogether as the Church adopted a more overtly pedagogic stance, using groupwork in order to promote new conversions while reinforcing loyalty among existing members (Alpha, 1993). The Church of England invested much energy in setting up courses whose main aim is the strengthening of the Christian commitment of members of church congregations. These have succeeded in taking over the position in Church thinking and diocesan strategies previously occupied by various kinds of process-orientated groupwork. They have a more direct impact on church life because they are addressed specifically to congregations, of course.

Each of these pre-occupations conveys a powerful impression of the tradition which gave rise to it, either the therapeutic group or the catechism class. The implication is that two kinds of knowledge, psychological (or psycho-sociological) and scriptural (or religious), exist separately from each other and

189

are to all intents and purposes mutually exclusive. Groupwork is useful because it addresses the way in which, on one hand, minds and, on the other, souls go, or have gone, wrong. The sixties were an adventurous, exploratory era in English church life, and psychology and spirituality were obviously connected; the last years of the century saw a Church which was diminished in numbers and moved to reassert its beliefs in a world which seemed to threaten its existence; for both generations, groupwork seemed an obvious way of working towards a safer future for the Church as an institution. It would not be reasonable to attribute the sixties' interest in psychopathology to a form of secularism; quite the opposite. Its major Anglican proponents certainly regarded it as the expansion and consolidation of Christian biblical understanding. As Lambourne wrote at the time:

> In accepting the experience and knowledge of the community of faith to which they belong, they (church members) have the function of being God's agents by themselves being the place of corporate and personal formation, so they may be a source of health and holiness as a congregation for others. (1972, 119)

Nor can the present preoccupation with 'process evangelism' be written off as merely defensive; the impulse which gave it birth is considerably more creative than that.

All the same, the Christian groupwork scene has been clearly divided into two identities, those of a teaching aid and a learning process. At present it appears to be firmly locked into the latter position, a fact which, considering its previous immobility, tends to suggest that groupwork itself is much less adaptable than it actually is. There is really no necessity to stay trapped between the psychiatric clinic and the schoolroom. The present investigation has made this clear, by presenting three different group formats concurrently and producing evidence that a Christian worldview prevailed in all three, and that individual freedom, far from being diminished by group discipline was, in varying degrees, enhanced by it.

In varying degrees, where more freedom of response was built into the structure, awareness of a Christian identity on the part of individuals and the group was increased. Members felt they were truly accepted when the format allowed them to find their own way towards saying what they really felt about things and they were not being clearly pointed in what they knew to be the intended direction. There was more confidence that problems were sources of creativity, rather than unfortunate failures to be dealt with by whomever was in charge of proceedings. As Mrs J discovered, Christian testimony is much more enriching when it comes unforced and from an unexpected direction (Feb. 11). Mrs A simply enjoyed the variety of approaches while commenting that none of them spoke to her in the way she had hoped they might be able to do; none of them, she said 'got to the heart of my problem' (March 18).

These approaches failed to give Mrs A the assurance for which she craves, although, like Mr L, she valued the degree of intimacy they did permit her. Other group structures may have given more to both these people. As it turned out, there were some group members who felt unhelped by each of the formats used here: Mrs K, for example, found the directive group restrictive, while Mrs J was at first genuinely confused by the art-based groups and Miss H by the process ones. Apart from Mr M, however, all members agreed that they had found the course of sessions stimulating and enriching as a whole. It seems, then, that eight out of nine people benefited from the group experience itself, individual members finding particular group structures either helpful or otherwise.

The experience is one possessing power to attract. Differing versions of it draw different kinds of people in situations which are always bound to be different. This is what would be expected; it hardly needs demonstrating. What needs to be stressed, however, is the scope of its relevance for human needs, both actual and potential. People have a somewhat narrow view of its usefulness, as the history of the Church of England's relationship to it demonstrates. As we saw in the first chapter of this book, there are already many different forms of groupwork. It would be safe to suggest that each one of them possesses a degree of relevance for some or other aspect of congregational learning. Many things can be said, many subjects broached, in the language of group experience.

Group membership is a mode of human experience, a way of being alive which is distinguishable from any other. To regard it solely as a technique for manipulating people in however well-meaning a way is to ignore its real nature, which is to be a way of exploring what it is to be oneself by harnessing the awareness of shared humanity which it generates within itself and reflects out into the world outside. The group is much more than one out of many approaches which an agency might apply; in itself it is a medium for living together. This means that for as long as it is in session it is a particular way of looking at things, one which leaves its imprint on life beyond itself, through possessing a power to alter an individual's assessment of his or her own worth as a person.

The three uses of the medium we have been investigating all bear witness to this. It was not something which the medium contrived, but something brought about by the individuals themselves, using the group medium as a way of giving it expression. The way in which the medium was embodied, the structures created in order to present it, appears to have had a discernible effect upon the freedom of the women and men concerned to use it in order to learn the messages communicated by it. In the light of this it seems reasonable to suggest that other structures would be likely to affect the reactions of group members, giving them material to build on or reject in the course of arriving at an assessment of their experiences within the group and their comments on its progress.

The suggestion being made is that there is room for more than one kind of group within the learning strategies of a church organisation, specifically that of the church which we have been considering here, the Church of England 'at home' in England itself. As a general rule, dioceses should start moving out of the narrow channel in which they are presently confined (as indeed they once were before) and find ways of making more creative use of groupwork as a medium having an entire range of uses. Because the human group is so crucial to Christian awareness, using it in any way in the service of the gospel can only be considered to be a useful strategy for learning and teaching within the Church. The group itself is as manifold in its ways of responding as is the individual human being who takes up membership of it, a fact which in itself makes work with groups, whatever form it takes, an indispensable tool for changing lives and building up churches.

This, however, is not really the most important point. We are mainly concerned here with what Christian groups *are*, not what they *do*. In the Old and New Testaments God communicates with individuals in and through their membership with others of their race, nation, brother- and sisterhood. The foundation of the Christian Church reveals the divine intention by its group setting — in this case a heterogeneous, ever-expanding body of individuals bound together by the gift of a new life revealed as personhood in-and-through membership. Before anything that a Christian group may do, and however it organises itself, this is what it *is*: 'Now you are the body of Christ and individually members of it' (1 Cor. 12:27). St Paul himself points out how many different things a body member may do as an individual (1 Cor. 12:27–31) and how this individuality depends on the action of God in Christ regarding an individual's membership of the Body as an organic whole (1 Cor. 12:12–27).

It is this revelation of human relationship as unity-in-separateness which is our argument in support of a more flexible and comprehensive attitude to church groupwork on the part of the church we have been considering. Groups of Christians are not only necessary for teaching about the Church and its beliefs, and for carrying out acts of worship in an organised way: they are, the bible informs us, actually the Church itself. Their structure corresponds to the way they are aware of being led to express their calling, to embody their being in the world. At this basic level their structure is their identity. In the case of the group we are describing in this book they are identified by their structuring as pupils, individuals gathered together, artists of one kind of another; but these are simply ways of arranging their association, different expressions of group-ness.

On the other hand, as the investigation showed, they were ways which had an effect on the experience of those taking part. The choice of structure reveals the intentions of the choosers. This is so whether the format has been decided beforehand or evolves *in situ* during a process of exploration carried out by the group itself; whether the group itself decides or willingly accepts someone else's decision and tries to go along with it. This latter was the case in the three examples of structuring investigated here. In other circumstances, free from academic necessity, groups might be expected to organise themselves in a freer way than this, expressing their Christian belonging together along lines which they themselves have chosen.

Basically then, Christian groups respond to the Christian message about belonging — that each of us is established as our self through being an indivisible part of an undivided whole, the 'mystical Body of Christ.' The quality of human experience reached out for in our groupwork is nothing less than an expression of the sharing which is ours in the fullness of our belonging here and a foretaste of heaven. If this is so we should not be surprised to find 'belonging' as the most important of the values emerging from the interpretative analysis carried out in the last chapter. In our investigation we saw that there were varieties of structure, but the same core group experience. The secure belonging which signifies acceptance and makes human life and what happens in it worthwhile was either experienced or its absence noted.

Perhaps the most surprising thing here was the fact that negative reactions were so clearly stated. This group of churchgoing Christians rose to the investigator's challenge to be frank about any thoughts and feelings they might have. The themes associated with being part of a group of fellow believers certainly came to the surface, but what was recorded was often far from a simple expression of Christian love and fellowship. Members had been told that the purpose of the investigation was to try to be as honest as possible about how the sessions actually came across to each of them personally — to say what they felt rather than what they might think was expected of them. The investigator made efforts during the induction stage of the experiment not to communicate to those taking part any impression of what sort of responses in the way of reactions to the sessions would be likely to meet with his approval. Specifically, those involved were never asked to say in advance what they themselves considered to be the most important thing about groups; there was never any mention of belonging, safety, enrichment or validation. Similarly, there were no questionnaires, boxes to be ticked, multiple choice questions or categories to choose from. Those taking part were left not only to decide what to say but what to say it about, so long as it had some bearing on their experience of the groups.

The investigator's conclusion, therefore, is that the dimensions of experience which the nine people revealed in their depositions were not simply the result of their all being confessing members of the Christian Church. What was recorded was not the result of wishing to conform to the expectations of their calling; rather it came from a determination to be true to what they themselves felt and thought as this came to the surface in a setting the nature and purpose of which is to open up in individuals the ability to relate to one another in an unique way. Deciding to join a group is in itself a gesture of willingness to share. No wonder then that it plays so crucial a part in the lives of Christians. Churches themselves abide within the four dimensions vouched for by these particular group members — belonging, safety, enrichment and validation. These may be seen as the parameters of group belonging, associated with the phenomenon itself and not simply imported into it from elsewhere. The group itself is a pledge of our willingness to receive what we need most.

The twelve sessions carried out in this investigation are characteristic of groupwork as a human enterprise; they are identifying conditions of an experience which we call *group belonging*, which is most salient when commitment to the group is strongest. A glance at the results of the investigation described in Chapters 4–6 shows that the highest level of commitment turns out to have been registered in the art-based groups, where *belonging* and *validation* clearly outweigh their opposites. The process-orientated scores show more ambivalence, while the directive groupwork gave rise to feelings of *alienation* and *danger* outbalancing the security they provided. The highest levels of all were reached for *enrichment* on the part of all three approaches. Here again, there was a considerable level of dissension. In fact, the results do not lend any support at all to the idea that a Christian group will always confine itself to thoughts and feelings which conform to its theological identity.

The high level of disagreement revealed in this exercise may in fact be the most important thing about it. This group found all three approaches satisfactory on the whole. All three kinds of group were enriching with reservations. Two approaches, the process and art-based groups, produced the most interest and provided the greatest opportunity for self-expression. Consequently these two groupwork structures revealed more genuine commitment than the directive groups were capable of doing. They allowed 'belonging' to be lived out, not merely asserted. Any new model of groupwork for the churches should aim to allow the group to work without spending so much effort instructing it how to do so. Groups need freedom to find their own way, even if this means altering it as they go along, adjusting it to fit the purpose which they are discovering in it; in this way they, the members, will keep it alive as an expression of the life they themselves are sharing.

A new groupwork model, then, should be an adjustable one, flexible enough to respond to an awareness which is still gradually growing among its members, firm enough to allow those involved to feel that they enjoy the blessing of the church for what they are setting out to do together. A new groupwork model must encourage those taking part to feel that they are a creative expression of church life capable of teaching the magisterium as well as merely learning from it. In order to do this it must balance structure with freedom in creative ways, allowing the latter to affect the former and not just the other way round . . .

In other words, it must be an expression of courage, rather than another way of keeping hold of things to stop them getting any further out of hand. It should be outspoken, argumentative, disruptive, and the Church must dare to let it be so, because it is out of freedom of expression that real belonging comes. We say what we feel and show who we are, and receive acceptance from others. There are many expressions of group belonging, many ways in which the life which is in a group may speak for itself. They should not be restricted to one safe, well-tried approach, so well established that everyone thinking of joining in knows exactly what to expect, safe because the format is specially contrived to make sure that only one conclusion can be reached. What our present groupwork actually teaches is not understanding but conformity. It manages to do this by being the only way in which such things are ever said in this privileged milieu for sharing. If the deadlock is to be broken, Church groupwork must expand and diversify in line with the need for a variety of approached to learning — as exemplified in advances to mentoring along lines suggested by Lotter:

> E-mentoring [is] a possible means of doing mentoring in a completely different manner. (2010, 12)

The scope of the present book requires that this judgement is directed primarily toward local dioceses of the Church of England. What is being said, however, has relevance to all those situations arising in any Christian church or denomination where groupwork moves in one way only, where congregational learning depends upon a particular well-tried formula which has the effect of maintaining a fixed relationship of teacher and learner, in which the authority of the latter is never really questioned. The investigation into members' reactions carried out here suggests that real personal involvement within the group process resists this kind of directed approach, at least so far as adult members of a congregation are concerned. Members may enjoy taking part and at the same time resist doing so. Compared with an experience of sharing in a more democratic groupwork, where roles are interchangeable and personal reactions and feelings form part of the work of the group rather than an unacknowledged and unacknowledgeable undercurrent of things consciously held at a distance, groups which are structures as a way of putting over a particular point of view are bound to have an inhibiting effect. When they are still being presented in the same way, they run the risk of losing their impact.

What is more to the point, however, is that they fail to use the unique power of a group to expand its own awareness and break new ground for those taking part. The creativity inherent in what we have identified here as group belonging is inalienably associated with what Paul Tillich called 'the courage to be as a part' (1962, chapter IV). Groups have to be encouraged to encourage one another — to take on an identity of their own, a shared way of being which gives each individual member a strength and confidence which she or he was not aware of before, and which belongs both to them and the group in which they first experienced it. The evidence of its reality is the courage which it gives to live and work as an adult Christian:

> I do not call you servants because the servant does not know what the master is doing: but I have called you friends. (Jn 15:15)

Not all groupwork should conform to the process group model, however, or indeed to any one model which may yet emerge. There will also be room for various directive approaches. The clarity and authority which these embody remain valuable tools for church growth and the maintenance of congregational involvement and sometimes, as happened more than once in the preceding investigation, their enthusiasm also. Some approaches benefit from the fact that they are free-flowing, some because they provide focus, and others in their ability to alternate precision with open-endedness. The argument being presented here is that the dimension of human experience which we have observed and recorded as emerging from the three contrasting approaches contained within the investigation carried out is one which is likely to characterise other kinds of groupwork also. This remains a matter open for further exploration, of course; but the ground-based, phenomenologically directed procedures carried out in the present investigation succeeded in mapping an area for further study within a sphere of human operations, the reality of which resists reductionist approaches. The four dimensions of group experience located are, of course, open to qualitative examination at a later stage.

Nevertheless the work done so far in the present study leads me to a conclusion to be recommended to those engaged in deciding on the groupwork strategy to be used with regard to the training of church congregations. What we learn from biblical accounts of transformative events involving groups, taken in conjunction with the testimonies which emerged from the nine churchgoers who were involved here, shows that the group may be regarded as God's chosen medium for the sharing of truth about Himself, and that this truth is not always delivered in the way in which we expect it to be. The life that lives in the group itself — the special quality of human awareness emerging from group-mediated experience — calls us to recognise Holy Spirit as wind which 'blows where it chooses' (Jn 3:9) and be willing and prepared to let this happen. Congregational groupwork for the future should take risks it has been wary of taking. We should see a new, more courageous attitude to Christian learning, as those involved pay attention to what actually happens in groupwork among Christians, and discover ways to give Spirit room.

Any really serious involvement with groupwork requires courage. The three approaches sampled here all turned out to be experienced as risky by those taking part. The art-based group was the most frightening of the three, and this was to be expected because of members' anxiety about taking part in activities which seemed to require skills, or a level of skill, which they did not possess; but the directive groupwork turned out to be dangerous, too, slightly more so in fact than the process-orientated — and for exactly the same reason. Because art allows feelings to be expressed indirectly these groups avoided the main source of danger, which was that of self-exposure. Both process groups and directive ones were more obviously intended to encourage members to speak freely and frankly about themselves; and in a small group setting this can be a frightening challenge and cause people to withdraw into an attitude of self-protectiveness.

Even if the intention is didactic, this kind of defensiveness has to be taken into account. To put your feelings, opinions, skills in other people's hands, and to have to do so in order to qualify as an acceptable member of the group, you have to feel you can trust not only their goodwill, but their ability to understand. To confide the most important things about who you are and what has happened to you during your life, even if you know you are amongst fellow Christians, can be a nerve-wracking experience. It is not only the seal of authority which may or may not be supportive, but the simple presence of other people which opens us up to feelings of vulnerability, whether this refers to the immediate situation or draws us back into a previous one, or as is so often the case it is really both these things, and is therefore all the more capable of undermining our defences. It is out of this vulnerability and the defensiveness associated with it that the real strength of the group arises; for as St Paul reminds us, 'Power is made perfect in weakness' (2 Cor 12:9).

In summary, the importance of the investigation described in this book lies in the comparison of different group structures and the effect that this has on the thoughts and feelings of those involved. Previous investigations into the nature and purpose of groupwork (such as those described in chapters 1 and 2) have not attempted to compare group structures in order to assess differential fitness for purpose. The results of the present investigation point to the existence of a basic group experience as something inherent in the fact of group membership itself, as each of the three approaches gave rise to similar emotional and cognitive reactions in the individuals taking part. The four dimensions of group experience identified were all present to varying degrees in each group structure, thus suggesting that church groupwork may usefully be employed in more than one form.

As a result of this investigation therefore, I would make the suggestion that those responsible for arranging groupwork in churches should provide a range of groupwork formats in order to emphasize varying aspects of congregational learning. This book proposes that within the Church of England at least, and elsewhere if appropriate, a more experimental approach than the one currently favoured might usefully be adopted. In addition, it recommends further research into the nature and purpose of congregational learning, with particular attention being paid to extending its scope and flexibility. A more imaginative use of the fundamental group experience, involving the experimental comparison of group structures would greatly enrich the Christian learning experience. The book is offered in the hope that more research along these lines may follow.

Appendix A

Church of England Dioceses Contacted

Table A.1 Groupwork provision in Church of England dioceses

Diocese	Name of course	Aim	Target population	Length
Bath and Wells www.bathandwells.org.uk	'Changing Lives, Changing Churches'	Training & development	Congregation members	Variable
Bristol www.bristol.anglican.org	'Equipping God's People'	To help students increase knowledge, Christian conviction and practical competence	Students	2 Years
Chichester www.chichester.anglican.org	'Developing Discipleship models'	To provide opportunities for sustained study of various aspects of Christian belief and practice	Adult congregation members	Short courses
Coventry www.coventry.anglican.org	'Bishop's certificate on Discipleship'	Further exploration of faith through study of Bible and Christian ministry/learning/training study	Interested lay people	2 years
Derby (in association with Southwold and Leicester) www.derby.anglican.org	'Certificate in Christian Discipleship'	'Exploring Discipleship, Mission, Leadership, Collaboration, Enterprise and Vision'	Experienced pioneers and emerging leaders (in congregations)	6 evenings 3 Saturdays 1 weekend
	'Fresh Expressions'	'To be equipped in planting and sustaining fresh expressions of Church'		

Gloucester www.glosdioc.org.uk	'What Christians Believe' (and some exploratory short course material) (Education for Discipleship)	Education/instruction 'in order to inform and help people discover what it means to be a disciple of Christ today'	Various age groups	Variable
Hereford www.hereford.anglican.org		Courses similar to *Emmaus*	Congregation members	Variable
Leicester www.leicester.anglican.org	'Certificate in Christian Discipleship'	See Derby		
Lincoln www.lincoln.anglican.org	'Exploring Our Faith'	'To deepen our understanding of the Christian faith and grow in discipleship'	Congregation members and others seeking instruction	Variable
Norwich www.norwich.anglican.org	'Everyone Learning'	Single sessions aimed at teaching specific skills connected with church work (plus introductory workshop)	'Various age-groups open to non-churchgoers'	Variable
Oxford www.oxford.anglican.org	'Sharing Life'	'Learning for Discipleship and Ministry' (Christian approaches to pastoral care family worship, preaching, Baptism, Eucharist, spirituality)	Those interested in lay ministry of various kinds	Variable
Portsmouth www.portsmouth.anglican.org	'When I was sick'	'To develop skills for visiting the sick or people with other pastoral needs'	Congregation members	12 weeks
Rochester www.rochester.anglican.org	'Explore your faith further'	'To understand God and the Bible better.' Instruction plus introductory workshop (experiential)	'Anyone who wants to engage in a process that enables them to grow in their Christian faith'	10 weeks
St Albans www.stalbans.anglican.org	'Learning Congregations'	'An opportunity for all ages to learn about their	Congregation members 'of	Ongoing Sunday

		faith and make connections between their faith and daily lives' — 'a tool in Education for Discipleship''	all ages.' ('Those present in church on Sunday')	Sessions
Salisbury www.salisbury.anglican.org	'Learning for Discipleship'	'Learn about your faith, meet other Christians, deeper discipleship'	Aimed at various groups within the life of the local church	A number of courses consisting of 10 two-hour sessions
Southwell and Nottingham www.southwell.anglican.org	'Certificate in Christian Discipleship' ('Education for Discipleship')	'Enables people to explore their own Christian life and faith in depth' (Bible and Christian doctrine and practice)	'All wanting to know more about Christian faith and how it connects with everyday life and work'	90 sessions available over 3 years
Wakefield (2006) www.wakefield.anglican.org	'Everyday God'	Christian discipleship, Bible themes concerned with church membership and the personal application of Bible narrative. A workshop approach involving the sharing of information and experience among group members	Church members, current and prospective	Sessions during Lent
Worcester www. cofe-worcester.org.uk	'Authorised Lay Ministry'	'To release gifts in new and exciting ways' involving 'the Bible, theology, spirituality', 'the building blocks of all Christian ministry''	Those interested in training as lay people for particular areas of church life	Short courses involving weekend sessions

York www.dioceseofyork.org.uk	'Education for Discipleship'	To lead people to 'commit their whole lives to learning how to be Christ-like, serving God and engaging in his mission in the world'; to encourage 'lifelong learning' by 'exploring Christian identity'; to provide instructional courses aimed at teaching skills 'focused in partnership with other agencies'	Congregation members who wish to learn 'skills of discipleship'	Short courses

Appendix B

Summary of Protocols

Table B.1 First analytical stage: identifying constructs emerging from the data

Emerging Constructs

acceptance/rejection	Belonging/not belonging
inclusion/exclusion	
unity/disunity	
congruence/discord	Sharing/not sharing
empathy/unawareness (of others' feelings)	
coherence/incoherence	Impact/ineffectiveness
focus/blurredness	
relevance/irrelevance	
open-mindedness/closed-mindedness	Openness/closedness
self-disclosure/self-concealment	
reassurance/discouragement	Validation/disempowerment
anxiety/confidence	Safety/danger
containment/exposure	
courage/cowardice	
commitment/uncommitedness	Depth/shallowness
self-discovery/lack of self-knowledge	
thoughtfulness/triviality	
serenity/annoyance	Comfort/discomfort
facilitation/frustration	
self-confidence/self-consciousness	
fun/boredom	Freedom/constraint
release/inhibition	

Table B.2 Examples of the process of thematic elicitation*

Mr L	
Original material	**Emergent themes**
Directive	
Now J has gone I'm the only male in the group. I felt at home with evening's topics; spiritually uplifting, surprisingly ...	Isolation, gender-loyalty, 'at home'-ness, spiritually uplifting (surprising).
Process	
Good discussion, challenging set attitudes, excellent ideas from some members – a very stimulating evening, though I felt I'd spoken out of turn	Need to think deeply and courageously, but am I safe?
Group has come together well, but I begin to feel out of my depth, through inadequate Christian commitment and knowledge; tried to make some contribution.	Need for unity, lack of confidence, need to contribute.
Disappointment with content, also structure. Are we running out of steam? Relaxed discussion however.	Relaxed but lacking in structure and content.
Art-based	
Group coming together as a unit; theme challenging – thought provoking – but didn't enjoy session because of my own lack of imagination, which led to my not contributing much.	Unity, sense of exclusion through personal inability to contribute.
Once again out of my depth. Sessions becoming more intellectual and I find it hard to keep up, art not being my favourite subject – lack of time for discussion of stories behind pictures.	Inadequacy, need to share through discussion, conned by structure.

* The process of identifying thematic material from data supplied by group members.

Over the 7 months I have found it difficult to take in the complete content of each week's theme due to my own lack of resources – but I did enjoy coming together as a group.	Lack of clarity, sense of inadequacy, enjoyment of fellowship.
Summary	
Thought course too long, so that it lost continuity.	Continuity, concentration.
Impressed by deep commitment of members and their knowledge of the faith, also the spirituality they brought to the group.	Commitment, knowledge of faith, spirituality.
(I felt very much discomfort at times with the artistic evenings – not my forte.	Discomfort with arts approach.)
Participants worked well as a group, which brought out their strengths and weaknesses as individuals, especially in my own case.	Groupwork exposing our individual strengths and weaknesses.
Group balanced in favour of the female gender, which at times was slanted against male comment.	Inhibiting effect of gender imbalance.
Course very rewarding "and I did enjoy myself to socialise".	Bringing people together to socialise.
Mrs S	
Original material	**Emergent themes**
Directive	
Aug. 23	
Enjoyed feeling comfortable in group; feeling affirmed by sharing emotion; valuing not being made to feel stupid.	Comfortable, affirmed by sharing
Jan. 21	
Not feeling threatened by others' behaviour in group; feeling protected by theoretical comments of leader.	Safe, protected from others

March 4	
Felt relieved from anxiety, being focused by group. I feel I belong in group.	Belonging, focused by group
Process	
'Sept. 2	
Now I see the group as people I felt I had disclosed something of myself; I'm feeling annoyed by 'closed minds' in the group.	Belonging, able to disclose, frustrated by some individuals
Nov. 12	
I'm aware of the effect of seating on group's focus; enjoying self-discovery; needing not to get angry with those I don't think are 'coming clean'.	Self-discovery through group; focus on overcoming frustration
Feb. 11	
I need clarity not vagueness; desire for sharing and closeness; finding I can empathise without upsetting myself; being able to share faith.	Needing to focus on others; empathy as answer to ***; unself- consciousness
March 11	
I need to feel safe because there's someone in charge. I also need to feel the group accepts me if I show myself to them.	Needing structure; needing not to feel exposed as unacceptable.
Art-based	
'Sept. 8	
I was secure enough to contemplate terrifying things; enjoying role-reversal as a release and stimulation; feeling safe enough to get involved with another's pain; putting myself at others' mercy.	Feeling safe to empathise within dramatic frame.

Nov. 19	
I was accepted when taking responsibility in group. Story is a good way of expressing feelings; feeling accepted after self-disclosure.	Using story as a way of dealing with own shyness.
Jan. 21	
No need to be anyone except myself; now enjoying 'meeting up', having your tastes and interests validated; not being dominated.	Feeling secure enough in group to have old pain reactivated; gratitude for validation.

Table B.3 Summary table of Analytical Stage III

Mrs A	Mrs E	Mrs H	Mrs J	Mrs Y
Directive				
Openness, reality, intensity of feeling	Initial exclusion: comfort from shared insight.	Atmosphere of need to protect oneself, to respect others' views	Anxiety about material and group members; joyful sharing but lack of depth; frustration with self and anxiety about opposition; others' defensiveness; marginalisation, betrayal	Acceptance of hurt by others in past; growth into unity
Need to make symbolic sense to achieve clarity	Sharing, congruence, comfort – but shallowness	Safety, in-depth sharing, commonalities		Aware of ability to share painful memories
	Constraint, judgementalism, lack of focus	Resistance to speak about my own faith, need for privacy		
		Irrelevant subject matter		
Process				
Avoidance, 'nice-ness', surface sharing	Relatedness, fear of relaxing constraints	Repetitiveness, alienation, feeling pressurised, made to play a role	Anxiety about group intentions --- alienation from group structure; need to find connectedness	Learning to admit own vulnerability
Need for personal revelation/challenge --- and reassurance	Open-mindedness, clarity	Confusion, alienation from attitudes expressed	Joy, connectedness --- resistance to transformation	Empathy expressing old woundedness
	Comfort in sharing faith without disengagement or dogmatism	Absence of conclusions, format unhelpful	Frustration about depth and relevance	Empathy bringing reassurance and validation
	Interaction giving energy and insight – need for focus	Lacking direction, sociable but shallow		

Art-based				
Intense involvement, insight, self-revelation	Purposiveness, focus, collaboration, insight into 'forgotten' wounds	Resistance to involvement overcome	Bafflement, exclusion, not seeing the point as others do; unsafe	Engagement, frustrated by lack of time
Stimulation, self-expression, giving and receiving, interchange	Clarity: story as safe expression, containment, freedom	Defensiveness, imaginative involvement	Making connections at a personal level	Memories healed, confidence gained by sharing
Spiritual enlightenment, joy of disciplined interaction	Safe to be oneself, congruence, focus, enjoyment through stimulation	Belonging, group identity	Art does not help	
	Need for clarity, sharing as affirmation, hope	In-depth sharing, through trust and intuition, relevance	Sharing, comfortableness	
			Disappointment because of theological blandness	
Summary				
Deep sharing as a gift, not just structure alone	Focus, presence, freedom of expression			Discovery of the relevance of diversity for future of church.
Mrs S	**Mr L**	**Mrs K**	**Mr M**	
Directive				
Comfortable sharing	Isolation, gender loyalty	Pressure to conform; aversive effect of others' over-confidence	Not belonging, so excluded and not taken seriously	
Safety from fear of others	Feeling 'at home' and spiritually uplifted – surprised	Avoidance of confrontation; rigidity	Uncomfortable, so feeling unwelcome, not 'at home'	

Focused belonging			Better than P groups as I knew what was expected of me
Process			
Belonging and ability to self-disclose; frustration by some in group	Need to think deeply and courageously – but am I safe?	Need to 'get it right', so confident people took control	Need for content plus structure to produce engagement
Self-discovery, group focus overcoming frustration	Need for unity, lack of confidence, need to contribute	Lack of congruence, unexpressed differences	Lack of congruence – a stereotyped apportioning of role as 'agent provocateur'; disempowerment
Empathy revealed as answer to self-consciousness; need for structures, else exposed as unacceptable	Relaxed, but need structure and content	Failure of group to develop through lack of time – so no really honest sharing possible; feeling of personal failure to become part of the group.	Religious solidarity preventing individual viewpoints
Art-based			
Dramatic frame allowing empathy	Group unity but personal exclusion through inability to contribute	Co-operation in risk-taking, sharing in the action, denying stereotypes	
Story as a way of dealing with shyness	Inadequacy, need shared discussion – feel conned!		
Friends' validation	Lacking in clarity, sense of own inadequacy, but enjoying fellowship		
Authoritative validation allows old pain to emerge			
Summary			
	Gender imbalance; need clarity and concentration.		

209

	There was great commitment, knowledge of faith.		
	Art evenings made me feel uncomfortable.		
	Group work exposed individual strengths and weaknesses – but it brought us together to socialise.		

Table B.4 Poles of constructs (X = positive, O = negative)

Directive										
Group members	A	E	H	I	Y	S	L	K	M	
Belonging (+cognates)	X	X	X	O	O	X	O	X	O	Not belonging (+ cognates)
Sharing (+ cognates)	X	X	X	X	O	X	O	O	O	Not sharing (+ cognates)
Impact (+ cognates)	X	O	O	O	X	X	X	O	O	Ineffectiveness (+ cognates)
Openness (+ cognates)	X	O	O	X	O	X	X	O	O	Closedness (+ cognates)
Validation (+ cognates)	X	X	X	O	O	X	X	O	O	Disempowerment (+ cognates)
Safety (+ cognates)	X	X	X	O	X	X	O	X	X	Danger (+ cognates)
Depth (+ cognates)	X	O	X	O	X	O	X	O	O	Shallowness (+ cognates)
Comfort (+ cognates)	X	X	O	O	O	X	O	O	X	Unease (+ cognates)
Freedom (+ cognates)	X	O	O	O	X	X	O	O	O	Constraint (+ cognates)
Process										
Group members	A	E	H	I	Y	S	L	K	M	
Belonging (+ cognates)	X	X	O	O	X	X	O	O	O	Not belonging (+ cognates
Sharing (+ cognates)	X	X	O	X	X	X	O	O	O	Not sharing (+ cognates)
Impact (+ cognates)	X	O	O	O	X	X	O	O	O	Ineffectiveness (+ cognates)
Openness (+ cognates)	X	X	O	O	X	X	O	O	O	Closedness (+ cognates)
Validation (+ cognates)	X	X	O	O	X	X	O	O	O	Disempowerment (+ cognates)
Safety (+ cognates)	O	X	O	O	X	X	X	O	O	Danger (+ cognates)
Depth (+ cognates)	X	X	X	O	X	O	X	X	O	Shallowness (+ cognates)
Comfort (+ cognates)	O	X	O	O	X	X	O	O	O	Unease (+ cognates)
Freedom (+ cognates)	X	X	O	O	X	X	O	O	O	Constraint (+cognates)
Art-based										
Group members	A	E	H	I	Y	S	L	K	M	
Belonging (+ cognates)	X	X	X	O	X	X	O	X	X	Not belonging (+ cognates
Sharing (+ cognates)	X	X	X	O	X	X	O	X	X	Not sharing (+cognates)
Impact (+ cognates)	X	X	X	O	X	X	X	X	X	Ineffectiveness(+ cognates)
Openness (+ cognates)	X	X	X	O	X	X	X	X	X	Closedness (+ cognates)
Validation (+ cognates)	X	X	X	O	X	X	O	X	O	Disempowerment (+ cognates)
Safety (+ cognates)	O	X	O	O	X	X	O	O	X	Danger (+ cognates)
Depth (+ cognates)	X	X	X	O	X	X	X	X	X	Shallowness (+ cognates)
Comfort (+ cognates)	O	O	O	O	O	O	O	O	X	Unease (+ cognates)
Freedom (+ cognates)	X	X	X	O	X	X	O	X	X	Constraint (+ cognates)

Errata: Column J is incorrectly labeled as column I.

211

Bibliography

Abrams, D., J. Marques, and M. A. Hogg (Eds.) (2004). *The social psychology of inclusion and exclusion*. Hove: Psychology Press.

Allen, D. (1993). In K. McLeish (Ed.), *Key ideas in human thought*. London: Bloomsbury.

Allen, R. E. (Ed.) (1990). *The Concise Oxford Dictionary of current English: first edited by H. W. Fowler and F. G. Fowler* (Eighth ed.). Oxford: Clarendon Press.

Alpha (1993). *An introduction to the Alpha course*. London: Holy Trinity Church, Brompton.

Andersen-Warren, M. and R. Grainger (2000). *Practical approaches to dramatherapy: the shield of Perseus*. London: Jessica Kingsley.

Archbishops' Council (2003). *Formation for ministry within a learning church: the structure and funding of ordination training*. London: Church House.

Archbishops' Council (2005). *Shaping the future: new patterns of training for lay and ordained, formation for ministry within a learning Church*. London: Church House.

Bailey, E. I. (Ed.) (2002). *The secular quest for meaning in life: Denton papers in implicit religion*. Lewiston, NY: Edward Mellen.

Bakhtin, M. M. (1981). *The dialogic imagination: four essays*. Austin, TX: University of Texas Press.

Bannister, D. and F. Fransella (1971). *Inquiring man: the theory of personal constructs*. Harmondsworth: Penguin.

Bannister, D. and F. Fransella (1986). *Inquiring man: the theory of personal constructs* (Third ed.). Beckenham: Croom Helm.

Bateson, G. (1973). *Steps to an ecology of mind: collected essays in anthropology, psychiatry, evolution, and epistemology*. St Albans: Paladin.

Bavelas, A. (1950). Communication patterns in task oriented groups. *Journal of the Acoustical Society of America* 22(6), 725–730. Reprinted in D. Cartwright and A. Zander (1968) *Group dynamics: research and theory* (Third edition). London: Tavistock, 505–511.

Becker, H. S. (1963). *Outsiders: studies in the sociology of deviance*. New York: Free Press of Glencoe.

Beebe, S. A. and J. T. Masterson (2003). *Communicating in small groups: principles and practices* (Seventh ed.). Boston: Allyn & Bacon.

Bieling, P. J., R. E. McCabe, and M. M. Antony (2006). *Cognitive-behavioral therapy in groups*. London: Guilford Press.

Bion, W. R. (1961). *Experiences in groups, and other papers*. London: Tavistock.

Bolton, G. M. (1979). *Towards a theory of drama in education*. London: Longman.

Booker, M. and M. Ireland (2005). *Evangelism — which way now?* (Second ed.). London: Church House.

Bouyer, L. (1963). *Rite and man: the sense of the sacral and Christian liturgy*. London: Burns & Oates. Translation by M. Joseph Costelloe of *Le rite et l'homme*.

Bowlby, E. J. M. (1980). *Attachment and loss: Vol. 3 Loss, sadness and depression.* London: Hogarth Press.

Boyd, R. D. (1991). *Personal transformations in small groups: a Jungian perspective.* London: Routledge.

Brodbeck, M. (1958). Methodological individualisms: definition and reduction. *Philosophy of Science* XXV(1), 1–22.

Brown, A. G. (1986). *Groupwork* (Second ed.). Aldershot: Gower.

Brown, A. G. (1992). *Groupwork* (Third ed.). Aldershot: Ashgate.

Brun, B., E. W. Pedersen, and M. Runberg (1993). *Symbols of the soul: therapy and guidance through fairy tales.* London: Jessica Kingsley.

Buber, M. (1961). *Between man and man.* London: Collins. Translated by Ronald Gregor Smith.

Burnett, P. S. (1972). The use of understanding of group behaviour in lay training. In C. L. Mitton (Ed.), *The social sciences and the churches,* Chapter 6, pp.9–80. Edinburgh: T & T Clark.

Burr, V. and T. Butt (1992). *Invitation to personal construct psychology.* London: Whurr.

Butcher, S. H. (1951). *Aristotle's theory of poetry and fine art: with a critical text and a translation of the Poetics* (Fourth ed.). New York: Dover.

Cartwright, D. and A. Zander (Eds.) (1968). *Group dynamics: research and theory* (Third ed.). London: Tavistock.

Catholic Faith Exploration (1996).CaFE: bringing faith alive. http://faithcafe.org/.

Cattenach, A. (1994).The developmental model in dramatherapy. In S. Jennings, A. Cattenach, S. Mitchell, A. Chesner, and B. Meldrum (Eds.), *The handbook of dramatherapy,* Chapter 2, pp. 8–40. London: Routledge.

Chesner, A. and H. Hahn (Eds.) (2002). *Creative advances in groupwork.* London: Jessica Kingsley.

Christianity Explored (2001). Christianity explored. One life. What's it all about? http://www.christianityexplored.org/.

Colaizzi, P. F. (1978). Psychological research as the phenomenologist views it. In R. S. Valle and M. King (Eds.), *Existential-phenomenological alternatives for psychology,* pp. 8–71. New York: Oxford University Press.

Coleridge, S. T. (1817). *Biographia literaria or biographical sketches of my literary life and opinions* (2 Vols). London: Rest Fenner.

Coleridge, S. T. (1827).*Table talk.* London: privately printed.

Cooper, A. (1997). *Sacred mountains: ancient wisdom and modern meanings.* Edinburgh: Floris.

Corey, G. (1991). *Theory and practice of counseling and psychotherapy* (Fourth ed.). Pacific Grove, CA: Brooks/Cole.

Corey, M. S. and G. Corey (1997). *Groups: process and practice* (Fifth ed.). Pacific Grove, CA: Brooks/Cole.

Corey, M. S., G. Corey, and C. Corey (2010). *Groups: process and practice* (Eighth ed.). Belmont, CA: Brooks/Cole.

Cottrell, S., S. Croft, J. Finney, F. Lawson, and R. Warren (1996). *Emmaus: the way of faith. Introduction: a vision for evangelism, nurture and growth in the local church.* London: National Society/Church House.

Curtis, S., H. Bryce, and C. Treloar (1999). Action research: changing the paradigm for health psychology researchers. In M. Murray and K. Chamberlain (Eds.), *Qualitative health psychology,* Chapter 13, pp. 2–217. London: SAGE.

Davie, G. (1994). *Religion in Britain since 1945: believing without belonging*. Oxford: Blackwell.

Dawes, S. (1985). The role of music therapy in caring in Huntington's Disease. In E. Chiu and B. Teltscher (Eds.), *Handbook for caring in Huntington's Disease*, pp. 6–114. Melbourne: Huntington's Disease Clinic.

Diocese of St Edmundsbury and Ipswich (2002).Way ahead. http://www.stedmundsbury.anglican.org/index.cfm?page=landf.content&cmid=300#Way_Ahead.

Diocese of Wakefield (2008). Transforming lives. http://old.wakefield.anglican.org/events/transforminglives/index.htm.

Douglas, A. (2008, June). Celebrating group psychotherapy: a theme for 2008–2009. *BPS Psychotherapy Section Review* 44, 8–11.

Douglas, M. M. (1966). *Purity and danger: an analysis of concepts of pollution and taboo*. London: Routledge & Kegan Paul.

Douglas, T. (1993). *A theory of groupwork practice*. Basingstoke: Macmillan.

Duggan, M. and R. Grainger (1997). *Imagination, identification and catharsis in theatre and therapy*. London: Jessica Kingsley.

Elam, K. (1980). *The semiotics of theatre and drama*. London: Methuen.

Eliade, M. (1958). *Patterns in comparative religion*. London: Sheed and Ward. Translation by Rosemary Sheed of (1949) *Traité d'histoire des religions*, Paris: Payot.

Epting, F. and A. W. Landfield (Eds.) (1985). *Anticipating personal construct psychology*. Lincoln, NB: University of Nebraska Press.

Erikson, E. H. (Ed.) (1985). *Life cycle completed: a review*. New York: W W Norton.

European Association Dance Movement Therapy (2010). What is dance movement therapy? http://www.eadmt.com/what-is-dance-movement-therapy.

Fordham, M. (Ed.) (1995). *Freud, Jung, Klein: the fenceless field: essays on psycho-analysis and analytical psychology*. London: Routledge.

Foulkes, S. H. and E. J. Anthony (Eds.) (1957). *Group psychotherapy: the psycho-analytic approach*. Harmondsworth: Penguin.

Fransella, F. (Ed.) (2005). *The essential practitioner's handbook of personal construct psychology*. Chichester: Wiley.

Free, M. L. (2007). *Cognitive therapy in groups: guidelines and resources for practice* (Second ed.). Chichester: Wiley.

Freud, S. (1940). *An outline of psycho-analysis: SE 23:144–207*. London: Hogarth Press. Translated by James Strachey.

Galbraith, V. E. and N. D. Galbraith (2008). Should we be doing more to reduce stigma? *Counselling Psychology Review* 23(4), 53–61.

Garfinkel, H. (1967). *Studies in ethnomethodology*. Englewood Cliffs, NJ: Pentice-Hall.

Gee, P. (2011, May).'Approach and sensibility': a personal reflection on analysis and writing using Interpretative Phenomenological Analysis. *BPS QMiP Bulletin* 11, 8–22.

Gergen, M. M. and K. J. Gergen (Eds.) (2003). *Social construction: a reader*. London: SAGE.

Gersie, A. (1992). *Storymaking in bereavement: dragons fight in the meadow*. London: Jessica Kingsley.

Gersie, A. and N. King (1990). *Storymaking in education and therapy*. London: Jessica Kingsley.

Gladen, S. M. (2011). *Small groups with purpose: how to create healthy communities*. Ada, MI: Baker Books.

Goffman, E. (1963). *Stigma: notes on the management of spoiled identity*. Englewood Cliffs, NJ: Prentice-Hall.

Gorman, C. (1972). *The book of ceremony* (Third ed.). Cambridge: Whole Earth Tools.

Grainger, R. (1987). *Staging posts: rites of passage for contemporary Christians*. Braunton: Merlin.

Grainger, R. (1988). *The message of the rite*. Cambridge: Lutterworth.

Grainger, R. (1990). *Drama and healing*. London: Jessica Kingsley.

Grainger, R. (1993). *Strangers in the pews: the pastoral care of psychiatric patients within the Christian congregation*. London: Epworth.

Grainger, R. (1995). *The glass of heaven: the faith of the dramatherapist*. London: Jessica Kingsley.

Grainger, R. (1998). *The social symbolism of grief and mourning*. London: Jessica Kingsley.

Grainger, R. (1999). *Researching the arts therapies: a dramatherapist's perspective*. London: Jessica Kingsley.

Grainger, R. (2002). *The beckoning Bible: a group work approach*. Peterborough: Foundery.

Grainger, R. (2003). *Group spirituality: a workshop approach*. Hove: Brunner-Routledge.

Grainger, R. (2007). Dramatherapy at Holy Rood House: telling a new story. In J. Baxter (Ed.), *Wounds that heal: theology, imagination and health*, pp. 51–261. London: SPCK.

Grainger, R. (2008). *Theatre and relationships in Shakespeare's later plays*. Bern: Peter Lang.

Grainger, R. (2009). *The drama of the rite: worship, liturgy and theatre performance*. Brighton, Portland, Toronto: Sussex Academic Press.

Grainger, R. (2010). *Suspending disbelief: theatre as context for sharing*. Brighton, Portland, Toronto: Sussex Academic Press.

Grainger, R. (2011). *Bridging the gap: the Christian sacraments and human belonging*. Brighton, Portland, Toronto: Sussex Academic Press.

Grainger, R. (2012). *Continuing congregational training: a comparison of group-work initiatives within the Church of England*. PhD, North-West University, Potchefstroom, South Africa.

Gregory, R. L. (1974). *Concepts and mechanisms of perception*. London: Duckworth.

Gunzburg, J. C. (1997). *Healing through meeting: Martin Buber's conversational approach to psychotherapy*. London: Jessica Kingsley.

Hare-Duke, M. G. (1967, October).Getting into groups. *Contact* 21, 2–7.

Hulsey, P. (2003). *Foundations of faith*. Sanford, FL: Harvesttime International Institute.

Husserl, E. (1960). *Cartesian meditations: an introduction to phenomenology*. The Hague: Martinus Nijhoff. Translation by Dorion Cairns of *Méditations cartésiennes: introduction à la phénoménologie*.

Jackson, B. (Ed.) (2002). *Hope for the church: contemporary strategies for growth*. London: Church House.

Jacobi, J. (1942). *The psychology of C. G. Jung: an introduction with illustrations*. London: Kegan Paul. Translated by K. W. Bash.

215

Jacobs, E. E., R. L. Masson, and R. L. Harvill (Eds.) (2002). *Group counseling: strategies and skills* (Fourth ed.). London: Brooks/Cole.

Jenkyns, M. (1996). *The play's the thing: exploring text in drama and therapy.* London: Routledge.

Jennings, S. (Ed.) (1987). *Dramatherapy: theory and practice 1.* London: Routledge.

Jennings, S. (1990). *Dramatherapy with families, groups and individuals: waiting in the wings.* London: Jessica Kingsley.

Jennings, S. (Ed.) (1992). *Dramatherapy: theory and practice 2.* London: Routledge.

Jennings, S., A. Cattenach, S. Mitchell, A. Chesner, and B. Meldrum (1994). *The handbook of dramatherapy.* London: Routledge.

Jennings, S. and Å. Minde (1993). *Art therapy and dramatherapy: masks of the soul.* London: Jessica Kingsley.

Johnson, G. (2010). Salvation in the Old Testament: They weren't saved by animal sacrifices . . . They weren't saved by works . . . http://gregscouch. homestead.com/files/otsalvation.htm.

Jones, P. (2004). *The arts therapies: a revolution in healthcare.* London: Hove.

Jones, P. (2007). *Drama as therapy: theory, practice and research* (Second ed.). London: Routledge.

Jung, C. G. (1972). *Four archetypes. mother, rebirth, spirit, trickster.* London: Routledge & Kegan Paul. Translated by R. F. C. Hull.

Jung, C. G. (1997). *Jung on active imagination: key readings selected and introduced by Joan Chodorow.* London: Routledge.

Kapur, R. (2009, March). Managing primitive emotions in organizations. *Group Analysis* 42(1), 31–46.

Kelly, G. A. (1991a). *The psychology of personal constructs: Vol. 1. A theory of personality.* London: Routledge.

Kelly, G. A. (1991b). *The psychology of personal constructs: Vol. 2. Clinical diagnosis and psychotherapy.* London: Routledge.

Kempe, A. B. (1889). On the relations between the logical theory of classes and the geometrical theory of points. *Proceedings of the London Mathematical Society* (1), 147–182.

Kolb, D. A. (1984). *Experiential learning: experience as the source of learning and development.* London: Prentice Hall.

Laing, R. D. (1965). *The divided self: an existential study in sanity and madness.* Harmondsworth: Penguin.

Laing, R. D. and A. Esterson (1970). *Sanity, madness and the family: families of schizophrenics* (Second ed.). Harmondsworth: Penguin.

Lake, F. (1966). *Clinical theology: a theological and psychiatric basis to clinical pastoral care.* London: Darton, Longman and Todd.

Lamb, C. and D. Cohn-Sherbok (Eds.) (1999). *The future of religion: postmodern perspectives.* London: Middlesex University Press.

Lambourne, R. A. (1972). Authority and acceptance in pastoral counselling. In C. L. Mitton (Ed.), *The social sciences and the churches*, Chapter 10, pp. 10–112. Edinburgh: T & T Clark.

Lambourne, R. A. (1983). *Explorations in health and salvation: a selection of papers by Bob Lambourne edited by Michael Wilson.* Birmingham: Institute for the Study of Worship and Religious Architecture.

Landfield, A. W. (1971). *Personal construct systems in psychotherapy.* Chicago: Rand McNally.

Lewin, K. (1948). *Resolving social conflicts: selected papers on group dynamics.* New York: Harper & Bros.

Liebmann, M. (2004). *Art therapy for groups: a handbook of themes and exercises* (Second ed.). Hove: Brunner-Routledge.

Lord, K. (2006). *Implicit religion: definition and application.* Implicit Religion 9(2), 205–219.

Lorenz, K. (1952). *King Solomon's Ring.* London: Methuen. Translation by Marjoie Kerr Wilson of *Er redete mit dem Vieh, den Vögeln und den Fischen.*

Lotter, G. A. (2010, September). E-mentoring as effective tutoring tool in higher education. In A. Koch and P. A. van Brakel (Eds.), *Proceedings of the 12th annual conference on World Wide Web applications,* Durban. www.zaw3.co.za: Cape Peninsula University of Technology. A conference held 21–23 September 2010, Durban, South Africa.

Luckmann, T. (Ed.) (1978).*Phenomenology and sociology: selected readings.* Harmondsworth: Penguin.

Lyotard, J.-F. (1984). *The postmodern condition: a report on knowledge.* Manchester: Manchester University Press. Translation of *La Condition postmoderne* by Geoff Bennington and Brian Massumi.

Mackewn, J. (1997). *Developing Gestalt counselling: a field theoretical and relational model of contemporary Gestalt counselling and psychotherapy.* London: SAGE.

Malphurs, A. (2009). *Strategic disciple making: a practical tool for successful ministry.* Grand Rapids, MI: Baker Books.

Marshall Cavendish Corporation (2010). *Sex and society: 3 Vols.* Tarrytown, NY: Marshall Cavendish.

Mathers, J. (1972). The use of understanding of group behaviour in pastoral care. In C. L. Mitton (Ed.), *The social sciences and the churches,* Chapter 9, pp. 9–109. Edinburgh: T & T Clark.

May, R. (1976). *The courage to create.* London: Collins.

McLuhan, M. and Q. Fiore (1967). *The medium is the massage.* Harmondsworth: Penguin.

McNiff, S. (1998). *Art-based research.* London: Jessica Kingsley.

Meadows, P. and J. Steinberg (1999). The Y Course. http://www.ycourse.com/.

Miettinen, R. (2000, January). The concept of experiential learning and John Dewey's theory of reflective thought and action. *International Journal of Lifelong Education* 19(1), 54–72.

Mitchell, S. (Ed.) (1996). *Dramatherapy: clinical studies.* London: Jessica Kingsley.

Murray, M. and K. Chamberlain (Eds.) (1999). *Qualitative health psychology.* London: SAGE.

Natanson, M. (1978). Phenomenology as a rigorous science. In T. Luckmann (Ed.), *Phenomenology and sociology: selected readings.* Harmondsworth: Penguin. Reprinted from (1967) *International Philosophical Quarterly* 7(1), 5–20.

Ottaway, A. K. C. (1966). *Learning through group experience.* London: Routledge & Kegan Paul.

Palmer, B. W. M. (1972). Work and fellowship in groups and organisations. In C. L. Mitton (Ed.), *The social sciences and the churches,* Chapter 1. Edinburgh: T & T Clark.

Pargament, K. I. (2007). *Spiritually integrated psychotherapy: understanding and addressing the sacred.* London: Guilford.

Park, P. (2010, 07 May). The three pillars of great leadership — group process, not being a manager and service. http://ezinearticles.com/?The-Three-Pillars-of-Great-Leadership—Group-Process,-Not-Being-a-Manager-and-Service&id=4242505.

Peirce, C. S. (1958). *Values in a universe of chance: selected writings of Charles S. Peirce.* New York: Dover. Edited with an introduction and notes by Philip P. Wiener.

Perls, F. S., R. F. Hefferline, and P. Goodman (1973). *Gestalt therapy.* Harmondsworth: Penguin.

Pfeiffer, R. H. (1961). *Religion in the Old Testament: the history of a spiritual triumph.* London: Adam & Charles Black.

Piaget, J. (1953). *The origin of intelligence in the child.* London: Routledge & Kegan Paul. Translated by Margaret Cook.

Pitruzzella, S. (2004). *Introduction to dramatherapy: person and threshold.* Hove: Brunner-Routledge.

Pitruzzella, S. (2009). *The mysterious guest: an enquiry on creativity from arts therapy's perspective.* Bloomington, IN: iUniverse.

Polanyi, M. (1969). *Personal knowledge: towards a post-critical philosophy* (Second ed.). London: Routledge & Kegan Paul.

Pope, A. (1734). *An Epistle from Mr Pope to Dr Arbuthnot.* London: L Gilliver.

Popper, K. R. (1972). *Objective knowledge: an evolutionary approach.* Oxford: Clarendon Press.

Priestley, P., J. McGuire, V. Hemsley, D. Flegg, and D. Welham (1978). *Social skills and personal problem solving: a handbook of methods.* London: Tavistock.

Reading, L. (1967, October). Group membership: its cost and potentialities. *Contact* 21, 21–26.

Reason, P. and H. Bradbury (Eds.) (2008). *The SAGE handbook of action research: participative inquiry and practice* (Second ed.). London: SAGE.

Reason, P. and J. Rowan (Eds.) (1981). *Human inquiry: a sourcebook of new paradigm research.* Chichester: Wiley.

Richards, M. C. (1995).Foreword. In P. B. Allen (Ed.), *Art is a way of knowing: a guide to self-knowledge and spiritual fulfillment through creativity*, pp. vii-viii. Boston, MA: Shambhala.

Robson, C. (1973). *Experiment, design and statistics in psychology.* Harmondsworth: Penguin.

Robson, C. (1993). *Real world research: a resource for social scientists and practitioner-researchers.* Oxford: Blackwell.

Rogers, C. R. (1969). *Freedom to learn (A view of what education might become).* Columbus, OH: Charles E. Merrill Publishing Co.

Rogers, C. R. (1970). *Carl Rogers on encounter groups.* New York: Harper & Row.

Rogers, C. R. (1973). Video training seminar with counselors. Illinois University.

Santrac, D. (2012). Sanctury cult in relation to religious piety in the Book of Psalms, unpublished PhD thesis, North Western University, South Africa.

Schattner, G. and R. Courtney (Eds.) (1981). *Drama in therapy: 2 Vols.* New York: Drama Book Specialists.

Scheff, T. J. (1979).*Catharsis in healing, ritual and drama.* London: University of California Press.

Schütz, A. (1966). Some structures of the life-world. In A. Schütz (Ed.), *Collected papers: Vol 3. Studies in phenomenological philosophy*, pp. 16–132. The Hague: Martinus Nijhoff. Edited by I. Schüz.

218

Scull, A. T. (1977). *Decarceration: community treatment and the deviant: a radical view*. Englewood Cliffs, NJ: Prentice Hall.

Shotter, J. (1986). A sense of place: Vico and the social production of social identities. *British Journal of Social Psychology* 25, 199–211.

Smith, J. A., P. Flowers, and M. Larkin (2009). *Interpretative phenomenological analysis: theory, method and research*. London: SAGE.

Smith, J. A., M. Jarman, and M. Osborn (1999). Doing interpretative phenomenological analysis. In M. Murray and K. Chamberlain (Eds.), *Qualitative health psychology*, Chapter 14, pp. 18–240. London: SAGE.

Smith, J. A. and M. Osborn (2008). Interpretative phenomenological analysis. In J. A. Smith (Ed.), *Qualitative psychology: a practical guide to research methods* (Second ed.), Chapter 4, pp. 3–80. London: SAGE.

Soanes, C. and A. Stevenson (Eds.) (2004). *The Concise Oxford English Dictionary* (Eleventh ed.). Oxford: Clarendon Press.

Stroup, G. W. (1981). *The promise of narrative theology: recovering the gospel in the church*. London: SCM Press.

Suenens, Cardinal. L. J. (1977). *A new Pentecost?* London: Fountain Books. Translation by Francis Martin of *Une nouvelle Pentecôte?*

Suttie, I. D. (1988). *The origins of love and hate*. London: Free Association.

Thornton, L. S. (1942). *The common life in the body of Christ: on the theological foundations of the Church as they appear in the New Testament*. London: Dacre Press.

Tillich, P. (1962). *The courage to be*. London: Collins.

Tinbergen, N. (1965). *Animal behaviour*. London: Time-Life International.

Tuckman, B. W. (1965, June). Developmental sequence in small groups. *Psychological Bulletin* 63(6), 384–389.

Van Gennep, A. (1960). *The rites of passage*. London: Routledge & Kegan Paul. Translation by Monika B. Vizedom and Gabrielle L. Caffee of (1908) *Les rites de passage*. Paris: Nourry.

Walton, H. (Ed.) (1971). *Small group psychotherapy*. Harmondsworth: Penguin.

Whitacker, D. S. and M. A. Lieberman (1964). *Psychotherapy through the group process*. New York: Atherton.

Wiggins, J. B. (Ed.) (1975). *Religion as story*. New York/London: Harper & Row.

Wilson, M. (1975). *Health is for people*. London: Darton, Longman and Todd.

Winnicott, D. W. (1971). *Playing and reality*. London: Tavistock.

Woodall, C. (2011). *Covenant: the basis of God's self-disclosure*. Eugene, OR: Wipf & Stock.

Wordsworth, W. (1800). Preface. In W. Wordsworth (Ed.), *Lyrical ballads and other poems Vol. 1* (Second ed.). London: T. N. Longman & O. Rees.

Yalom, I. D. (1995). *Theory and practice of group psychotherapy* (Fourth ed.). New York: Basic Books.

Yeats, W. B. (1950). *Collected poems* (Second ed.). London: Macmillan.

Index

A
acceptance, 18, 25, 28, 30, 37, 4042, 49, 59, 61, 78, 79, 183, 193, 195
Alpha, 50–58, 63, 65n

B
belonging/alienation, 3, 129, 130, 132, 133, 137, 138, 141, 142, 144, 147, 148, 151, 152, 154, 155, 157–164, 180, 181, 184, 185, 193, 194
Bible, 51–56, 83, 192
  New Testament, 40–43
  Old Testament, 36–41, 49

C
catharsis, 31, 32, 176
conflict, 39, 40, 70, 71, 78, 165
  emotional, 40, 46, 78
control, 2, 39, 60, 69, 77, 95, 166
  emotions, 24, 32
  variables, 7, 92, 182
covenant, 36, 41, 42, 49, 65

D
dance, 82, 84
disciples of Jesus, 9, 42–47, 49, 50, 65
drama, 3, 29–32, 81, 84, 171
dramatherapy, 3, 32, 82, 87

E
Education for Discipleship, 1, 62, 63, 74, 75
Emmaus, 50, 52–58, 61, 63, 65n
enrichment/impoverishment, 129, 130, 132, 135–137, 140, 141, 143, 144, 146, 147, 150, 151, 153, 154, 156–158, 168–174, 184, 185, 194

F
fear, 30–32, 43, 47, 160, 186
followers of Jesus, 41, 44–47, 186

G
God, the Father, 36–38, 40–42, 44–47, 49, 51, 60, 69, 104, 105, 108, 110, 112, 117, 119–122, 124, 161–163, 165, 166, 169, 170, 172, 175, 176, 179, 181, 187, 192, 196
group
  dynamics, 10, 16, 17, 44
  identity, 13–15, 22, 24, 25, 36, 39, 41, 46, 48, 58, 66, 71, 76, 77, 79, 84, 103, 192, 195
  leader, 11, 12, 17, 37–40, 45, 46, 49, 74, 77–79, 89, 179, 180
  process, 1, 15, 16, 32, 37, 46, 48, 65, 71, 76, 78
  self-help, 40, 47, 48
  therapeutic, 22–25
groupwork
  art-based, 3, 29–34, 70, 81–84, 87, 96, 97, 106–108, 110–113, 115–117, 124–126, 130, 162, 163, 166–171, 176–179, 184, 185, 191, 194, 196
  directive, 3, 8, 70, 72–74, 77, 79, 84, 85, 95, 96, 101–103, 113–115, 117, 118, 120–122, 130, 163–165, 171–173, 177–179, 185–188, 191, 194, 196
  process-orientated, 3, 23, 29, 30, 32, 34, 46, 60, 62, 70, 76–80, 83, 85–87, 96, 103–106, 108–110, 118, 120, 122–124, 130, 160–162, 165, 166, 173–176, 178–180, 185–188, 191, 194, 196
  psychoanalytic, 25–28, 79

H
Holy Spirit, 42, 44, 108, 110, 188, 196

I
isolation, 23, 27, 29, 30, 35n, 165